Technology and Business Strategy

Igor Stepnov
Editor

Technology and Business Strategy

Digital Uncertainty and Digital Solutions

palgrave
macmillan

Editor
Igor Stepnov
Moscow State Institute of International Relations (MGIMO University)
Moscow, Russia

Financial University under the Government of the Russian Federation
Moscow, Russia

ISBN 978-3-030-63973-0 ISBN 978-3-030-63974-7 (eBook)
https://doi.org/10.1007/978-3-030-63974-7

This Palgrave Macmillan imprint is published by the registered company Springer Nature Switzerland AG.
The registered company address is: Gewerbestrasse 11, 6330 Cham, Switzerland

Contents

List of Contributors

Nidjad Asadli Center for Analysis of Economic Reforms and Communication, Baku, Azerbaijan
Moscow Institute of International Relations (MGIMO University), Moscow, Russia

Leyla Berdnikova Togliatti State University, Tolyatti, Russia

Alexander Blokhin Moscow Institute of International Relations (MGIMO University), Moscow, Russia

Lyudmila Chernikova Financial University under the Government of the Russian Federation, Moscow, Russia

Liu Dun Beijing Jiaotong University, Beijing, China

Akhmed Esendirov Moscow State Institute of International Relations (MGIMO University), Moscow, Russia

Nina Goridko V. A. Trapeznikov Institute of Control Sciences RAS, Moscow, Russia
RUDN University, Moscow, Russia

Maxim Inozemtsev Moscow State Institute of International Relations (MGIMO University), Moscow, Russia

Sergey Kamolov Moscow State Institute of International Relations (MGIMO University), Moscow, Russia

Vladislav Klochkov V.A. Trapeznikov Institute of Control Sciences of Russian Academy of Sciences, Moscow, Russia

Anna Kolesnikova LTD "ChKalAvia", Moscow, Russia
Moscow State Institute of International Relations (MGIMO University), Moscow, Russia

Julia Kovalchuk Moscow State Institute of International Relations (MGIMO University), Moscow, Russia
Moscow Aviation Institute (National Research University), Moscow, Russia

Elena Krasina V. A. Trapeznikov Institute of Control Sciences RAS, Moscow, Russia

Tatyana Kreydenko Financial University under the Government of the Russian Federation, Moscow, Russia
RUDN University, Moscow, Russia

Artem Krivtsov Moscow Institute of International Relations (MGIMO University), Moscow, Russia

Irina Larionova Moscow State Institute of International Relations (MGIMO University), Moscow, Russia
Financial University under the Government of the Russian Federation, Moscow, Russia

Istvan Lengyel Banks' Association for Central and Eastern Europe (BACEE), Budapest, Hungary

Alexander Litvinenko Saint Petersburg University of MIA of Russia, St. Petersburg, Russia

Julia Lozina Saint Petersburg University of MIA of Russia, St. Petersburg, Russia

Yuan Lunqu Beijing Jiaotong University, Beijing, China

Alekxey Medkov Market Economy Institute of the Russian Academy of Sciences, Moscow, Russia

Vladimir Osipov Moscow State Institute of International Relations (MGIMO University), Moscow, Russia

Galina Panova Moscow State Institute of International Relations (MGIMO University), Moscow, Russia

Zhaklin Sarkisyan Moscow State Institute of International Relations (MGIMO University), Moscow, Russia

Irina Selezneva V.A. Trapeznikov Institute of Control Sciences of Russian Academy of Sciences, Moscow, Russia

Anna Shashkova Moscow State Institute of International Relations (MGIMO University), Moscow, Russia

Igor Stepnov Moscow State Institute of International Relations (MGIMO University), Moscow, Russia
Financial University under the Government of the Russian Federation, Moscow, Russia

Grigory Tarasov Institute of Smart Cities Comparative Studies, Moscow, Russia

Kirill Teteryatnikov ANO Research and Expert Analysis Institute of Vnesheconombank (The Bank for Development and Foreign Economic Affairs), Moscow, Russia

Maya Tikhonova Moscow State Institute of International Relations (MGIMO University), Moscow, Russia
SOGLASIE Insurance Co. Ltd, Moscow, Russia

Michel Verlaine ICN Business School, Metz Technopôle, France

Geng Yuan Capital University of Economics and Business, Beijing, China

Alexander Yukhno Civic Chamber of Russia, Moscow, Russia

Kobilzhon Zoidov Institute of Economics and Demography, Academy of Sciences of the Republic of Tajikistan, Dushanbe, Tajikistan
Market Economy Institute of the Russian Academy of Sciences, Moscow, Russia

List of Figures

List of Tables

CHAPTER 1

Introduction: The Limits of Digital Leadership: From "Agile" to "Great Leap"

Igor Stepnov

The modern world and the digital world have become synonymous. This did not happen immediately but the planet has begun submitting to digital expansion steps which continue today. In the economy the victory of "digital" was marked by the fact that businesses included digital solutions in their core business models. Of the top 5% of companies in all segments none has adopted their strategies without mentioning the opportunities or threats of digital reality (Deloitte 2018; McKinsey 2016; PwC 2020). Over the past two years 67% of leaders have undergone disruptive changes in their operations based on an integrated approach to digitalization which is built on the intersection of innovation business experience and technologies (PwC 2018).

Digital solutions are changing almost everything. Communication has become different and provides previously unthinkable scales of

I. Stepnov (✉)
Moscow State Institute of International Relations (MGIMO University), Moscow, Russia

Financial University under the Government of the Russian Federation, Moscow, Russia

I. Stepnov (ed.), *Technology and Business Strategy*,
https://doi.org/10.1007/978-3-030-63974-7_1

interaction. The products and services of companies that have taken the digital path have expanded their capabilities and delivered more value to consumers. The new generalized digital consumer experience has become available for business thanks to Big Data. Collaboration and communication between consumers and suppliers are not only shaping a new business model but also creating ecosystems that would already be unthinkable without digital technologies.

Organizational decisions have changed, and for many entrepreneurs digital platforms have become the basic toolkit. The environment (digital arena) has also changed, and digital solutions have begun to gain an advantage in infrastructure, education, healthcare, transport, law, and so on.

Society has also changed. There is a new generation of people who prefer digital communication. Communication between people has been radically transformed: smartphones have created a new communicative environment, so cooperation between people has changed. Thanks to social networks, society is able to influence many processes, including the success of business strategies.

It is no coincidence that most current leaders, whether they are high-tech companies or individuals in social networks, are popular thanks to the digital environment.

As a result, digital transformation is changing all aspects of business management—organizations, current or projected business models, business processes, ecosystems, services, and products (Schallmo and Rusnjak 2017).

However, the new growth driver has made the world dependent both on the perception of new technologies by society, and on the fact that centuries of experience are not in demand in the digital environment and society has to accumulate new experience, including learning, making mistakes, assuming, and investing.

The modern economy, like the whole world, is under significant pressure from digital transformations, forming a new heterogeneous structure to replace the previously existing harmonious system of relationships, both between individual participants and entire market segments (Pénard and Brousseau 2007).

This book aims to find answers to certain challenges faced by the modern economy. Today, there is a search for mechanisms to transform new ideas of the digital format into leading technologies and leading business models. It is important to accumulate facts about both the success and failure of digital solutions. The limit of digital solution growth is the key problem: we need to identify whether the growth is infinite, limited, or will be eventually replaced by something else. Finally, the accumulation of facts about changes in the external environment–the most important category in the classical strategic approach–becomes essential.

This accumulation of knowledge was based on technologies that made it possible to form digital superiority and provide global leadership based on platform solutions. Technology has become a harbinger of new changes, and the digital world is looking forward to new, previously unthinkable, innovations.

The studies presented in the monograph showed a huge variety of options for business development and the achievement of technological leadership. They all, nevertheless, have one thing in common: the success of technologies is determined by new business strategies that effectively take into account the realities of the external environment and are implemented in business models.

It is digital business models that have become the foremost tool for effective adaptation to the changes and achievement of business goals on a sustainable basis. Perhaps the term "Digital Darwinism" (Kreutzer 2017) makes sense as an evolutionary question of survival or extinction, depending on the ability of companies to adapt to the new digital environment.

Today the indisputable advantage of the digital (and the final destination) in many areas of human activity does not deal with the question of choosing between "digital" and "non-digital", but rather shifts to the stage of comparing one "digital" with another.

There are four possible scenarios for each company related to technological development: ignoring digital change, living in two worlds, ensuring the necessary agility, and a big leap that will radically change relationships in a particular field of activity. Among them, agility, alongside a big leap (breakthrough), has become the basis for a variety of forms of manifestation of the latest technological and information solutions used by both business and the state.

Accordingly, having chosen one of the scenarios, companies should consider approaches to the choice of digital solutions in order to maintain their long-term progressiveness. As such, models of duopolistic competition can be used as ends of a spectrum between "old" and "new"; agent modelling, including digital twins; diffusion models of digital innovations; cyclical development models, and so on.

Given that the use of digital technologies has (as of yet) been insufficiently experienced, the practical value of the models of diffusion and competition between the old and the new is not yet high enough; moreover, they do not have a direct connection with the business model. Therefore, without denying each of the four approaches, we offer the possibility of considering the relationship between technology and business strategies based on a cyclical model. This model is the foundation for our assumption that the limits of digital leadership can arise: a) when the limitations of the business model occur, and; b) with the appearance of radical technological innovations (this is discussed in Chap. 2, "The Uncertainty of Technological Future"). This approach demonstrates the limits of digital leadership associated with business life-cycles, that is, having a time-related assessment, not just a value one.

Despite the widespread belief that technological advances are driving the development of digitalization, we agree with G. C. Kane (Kane et al. 2015) that it is the *strategy*, not the *technology*, that is the driving force behind digital transformation, proving the hypothesis that digitization, digitalization, and digital transformation manifest themselves at three different levels (current activities, organizational process, and the ecosystem level).

However, the methodology for developing strategies for digital transformation is also being radically renewed, abandoning the resource view that has dominated the strategy sciences for more than half a century. Resource approach created by E. Penrose, which defined the strategies for several decades, considered the formation of profit through the extensive growth of the volume of material and non-material resources available to the company (Penrose 1995). A. D. Chandler developed the role of resourcing strategic decisions and the corresponding allocation of resources, which can limit the process of strategy formation and its content (Chandler 1962). The resource concept by R. M. Grant (1991), competency-based concept by K. Prahalad (Prahalad et al. 2002), and the concept of dynamic abilities (Teece 2010) have brought the strategy closer to modern understanding. As a result, corporate development strategies began to be based on the company's ability to modify resources and competencies when the external environment changes. The transitional element from resource strategies to business models was the value chains proposed by M. Porter (1996; Porter and Heppelmann 2015).

The basic view of a company's environment was also shaped back in the 1950s as part of a strategy based on the LCAG model (Learned et al.

1965), enabling navigation of a target environment consisting of suppliers, customers, and competitors. The importance of considering institutional aspects is reflected in the works of G. R. Carroll and Y. P. Huo (1986), as well as L. G. Zucker (1987).

A compromise between resource views and a new digital reality is provided by the choice of an adaptive, flexible approach using the Agile methodology (Ghezzi and Cavallo 2018; Güner et al. 2018). In the new competitive environment, companies must use their resources as accurately as possible to survive. Companies create a competitive advantage by responding to the changing demands of customers in different markets in the shortest time and at the right time. In the event of uncertainty, the supply chain must be flexible so that companies can maintain a competitive advantage (Güner et al. 2018).

B. Demil et al. (2018), J.B. Barney and W.S. Hesterly (2014), D. Fred and R.D. Forest (2017), T. Hill (2000), and P. Robinson (2011) have established several critical principles of strategic design: the process of strategy development begins with an analysis of the environment; the environment has an ontological reality; the effectiveness of the strategy depends significantly on the choice of industries; ensuring that the internal environment corresponds to the external environment is the key to the success of all activities.

The digital environment has changed these provisions, so it can be said that developing a strategy begins with an analysis of the business models' effectiveness (Stepnov and Kovalchuk 2018); the environment has acquired the properties of virtual reality; industries are being replaced by ecosystems that transcend traditional industry boundaries; the correspondence of the external environment to the internal environment is replaced by value chains implemented on the platforms.

Again, any technology becomes successful within business models (Stepnov 2018). Therefore, to understand the ongoing changes, it is essential to initially focus on business models.

There is not one single publication that does not claim that the business model is becoming the dominant solution for digital strategies today (Tomičić et al. 2020). With the wide spread of the simple definition that "a business model is the organization of a business that makes it profitable", many, such as P. Hague (2019), extend this concept to the tasks of specific research (from tools to applied solutions).

The transformation of corporate strategies into a business model is presented in the work of C. Cordon et al. (2016), whilst J. R. Bughin et al.

(2019) investigate the problem of updating strategies when introducing new technologies. They conclude that it is advisable to radically update the strategy, in accordance with the positions of M. M. Crossan and I. Berdrow (2003) and of R. Agarwal and C. E. Helfat (2009). In their opinion, there is a positive correlation between the degree of strategy change and the phase of implementation of advanced digital technologies. This vision confirms the close connection between the technological structure of an enterprise and its development strategy, regardless of the stage of technology implementation.

The classic business model of value creation is based on M. Porter's value chain theory, presented back in 1996 (Porter 2008). More modern approaches view the business model as a means of obtaining value from customers in the interpretation of L. Massa et al. (2017). Porter described the value chain as a sequential process in which raw materials are gradually transformed into a better value proposition. A. N. Chesbrough shaped the architecture for creating such a value proposition within the business model (2010).

Exploring and exploiting the opportunities and benefits of a business model can be seen as motivating interactions in terms of dynamic opportunities (Gomes et al. 2018). Creating, delivering, sharing, and capturing values are considered key elements of a functioning business model (Osterwalder and Pigneur 2010). Along with new and transformed business models, there is a need to reflect the crossing of boundaries between industries, as presented in P. Weill and S. Woerner (2019). They single out three players in the digital arena: traditional players, new digital players, and players crossing industry boundaries.

We agree with this approach, but we also believe that crossing industry boundaries will become a common, trivial phenomenon soon. Therefore, we consider the intersectoral nature of modern business to be a common feature of digital business models and their distinctive features. It is this property, first of all, that has had a dividing, landmark character (before and after) concerning Porter's competitive strategies focused on market segments.

Woerner and Weill also insist that a key feature of the business model is flexibility (readiness to change), which does not allow "someone else to stand between the consumer and the company", which confirms our hypothesis that a readiness to change is the basis for adaptation of the resource approaches to the strategy formation.

The above provisions outline the contours of various strategic decisions for the commercialization of technologies, which are further referred to in the chapters of the book.

The material presented in this book is determined by the scientific need for the empirical accumulation of data on digital transformations in society. This is consistent with the book's goal of building an understanding of the barriers to new technologies and the possible trajectories of their implementation by the business. The first part of the book, "Digital Breakthrough", explores the radical decisions related to digital modernization and leadership achievement. We define the pinnacle of digital development as the creation of conditions for the widespread introduction of artificial intelligence. In our opinion, the current stages of digitalization are simply a prelude to such. The achievement of efficiency by artificial intelligence will be the logical conclusion of the current transformations.

The digital breakthrough leads to significant changes in the business environment, which is reflected in the second part, "Spurt economic's systems". The second part examines issues related to the modernization of the system from various aspects: from the labour market to legal support, from smart cities to the risks of modernizing economic systems, from investment strategies to radical innovations to modernization of the entire financial system. We understand that it is impossible to cover all aspects of the modern world updates in one book, but we hope that the book will contribute to the study of the emerging digital reality.

Earlier, in the introduction, it was shown that the analysis of the usefulness and effectiveness of digital technology solutions is mandatory for digital business models. However, due to the lack of accumulated experience, such business models and their strategic components require a methodological rethinking due to the fundamental novelty of digital solutions. In subsequent chapters, certain methodological aspects of digital solutions will be considered, allowing the reader to better understand the features of the digital age.

The logical continuation of the Introduction is Chap. 2, "The Uncertainty of the Technological Future" (by I. Stepnov). It presents a new view of technology as consisting of digital (managing) and transforming components. This view made it possible to look differently at the competition between the "old" and the "new", and make a choice in favour of a cyclical model to reduce the uncertainty of the technological future. The presented original cyclical model makes it possible to build a business lifecycle both for an individual entrepreneurial initiative and for a group of homogeneous organizations. A key aspect of this decision was to replace the evolution of organizations with the evolution of business models.

Chapter 3, "A Future with Artificial Intelligence: Strategy for Success" (by N. Asadli), reveals the barriers that stand in the way of the development of artificial intelligence as the highest modern strategic transformation. A special place in the chapter is occupied by the discussion that the use of artificial intelligence (first of all, the "weak" form) requires its implementation at the strategic level of management and not at its technical support. This discussion was followed by discourse about the choice of the strategy type that is most applicable to the existing processes of commercializing digital products. This vision allowed the author to carry out a comparative analysis of the possibility of strategizing digital solutions based on a generalized vision of three strategies: growth strategy, low-cost strategy, and blue ocean strategy.

The next chapter, Chap. 4, "Technological Revolution in Financial Intermediation" (by I. Lengyel et al.), considers financial innovation to be new technologies that radically reduce the cost of transferring and processing information. Financial intermediaries are expanding the possibilities for monetizing the value created in business models, which allows for more effective profit control. The chapter reflects discussions on the theoretical understanding and analysis of financial intermediation based on organizational changes in financial markets, the use of digital currencies, and the use of blockchain technologies.

Chapter 5, "The Digital Vector of Ensuring Economic Security of the Company" (by A. Krivtsov et al.), reveals the concept of economic security in the digital economy and identifies its basic elements in the context of business digitalization. The chapter clarifies the atypical risks inherent in the digital economy. It also shows the possibilities of functional strategies that make it possible to implement functional strategies, taking into account the digital development of the business environment. This approach reduces the degree of uncertainty in the medium term.

In the next chapter, Chap. 6, "Modernization or New Engineering: Models of Leadership in the Global Civil Aviation Market" (by A. Kolesnikova and J. Kovalchuk), the impact digitalization has on the industry is considered; in particular, a systematization of the main trends in the development of the civil helicopter industry is carried out. It is shown that digitalization enhances the possibilities of modernization due to increased productivity and the implementation of new-generation technologies (for example, additives).

Digital transformation has led to the emergence of a new phenomenon called "digital twins", whose role in forming forecast estimates is constantly increasing. Accordingly, in Chap. 7, "Digital Twins Application in Managing the Scientific and Technological Development of High-Tech Industries" (by V. Klochkov et al.), their application is considered at all stages of the life cycle of high-tech products: when shaping a development strategy, managing the process of applied research and development, during R&D, and the operation of products. This includes a discussion of whether mathematical modelling and digital twins can replace the experience and competence of experienced and highly qualified leaders. The chapter concludes that reducing management to solve such problems leads to the degradation of both the high-tech industries themselves and the Russian economy as a whole. The chapter also presents the results of a study into the reasons for the low demand for digital twins in the Russian high-tech sector.

The development of digital relations does not eliminate the problem of bankruptcy, and, in many respects, the reasons for such bankruptcies are caused by both the imperfections of business models and the use of outdated technologies. The problems of crisis management in the digital environment are covered in Chap. 8, "Individualization of Approaches in Scenarios of Survival and Development for Companies in the Digital Environment" (by Z. Sarkisyan and M. Tikhonova). Classifying companies into different, appropriate brackets for the digital age (industrial companies that emerged in the previous era of social relations, companies that are completing their digital transformation, and new types of companies created in response to digital challenges) is the foremost conclusion this chapter reaches. This made it possible to prove the hypothesis that the diagnostics of the financial condition begin to give false results when comparatively examining these identified types of companies. The results make it possible to prioritize an individual approach to digital companies due to the lack of accumulated experience.

Chapter 9, "Artificial Intelligence in Public Governance" (by S. Kamolov et al.), continues the authors' research into a digitally volatile environment and explores the use of artificial intelligence to improve public policy and service delivery, addressing digital uncertainty. The authors believe that, in the context of a slowdown in the growth of the global economy, the development of digital solutions can play a significant role in increasing labour productivity, ensuring GDP growth, and developing common ground for new digital business strategies.

Chapter 10, “Global Navigation Satellite Systems as Digital Solutions for Smart Cities” (by S. Kamolov et al.), focuses on the role of new technologies in the development for the emerging area of society known as “smart cities”, understanding that the development of global satellite systems is becoming an important mediator for dealing with modern digital challenges. Revealing the phenomenon of a “smart city”, the authors managed to form a holistic view of value chains in smart cities, which can be used in many business models and strategies.

The development of communication requires an improvement of information and communication interaction, putting forward ever-higher requirements for the transport structure and the system of trade routes. Chapter 11, “The Digital Trade Route to an Economic Space in the Eurasian Economic Union: Institutions and Technology” (by K. Zoidov and A. Medkov), shows that when developing digital trade routes in the Eurasian Economic Union (EAEU), special attention should be paid to the organizational and institutional features of electronic navigation seals (“smart” seals) and electronic invoices, the digitalization and automation of customs and other control operations, and the use of unmanned vehicles. These research results are highly valuable for business models since, in the digital environment, the provision of services to the consumer is a priority.

Labour is most susceptible to change in a digital society. That is why Chap. 12, “Digitalization as Objective Factor of the Substitution of the Labor by the Capital” (by V. Osipov et al.), probes the issues of providing society with a sufficient number of jobs. Based on the fact that developed countries are less and less in need of human labour and thus are abandoning it in favour of capital, it has been proved that the labour factor plays an insignificant role in the formation of the EU GDP compared to the factor of capital. Further research into structural (technological) unemployment, labour market problems in the digital economy, digital uncertainty, business strategy, and technology can be based on this study.

The second section begins with a discussion on the efficiency of investments in technological renovation (including equipment) and the definition of parameters for influencing economic growth. Chapter 13, “Investment in the Modernization and Reconstruction of Industrial Equipment: an Evaluation of Multiplier Effects in Russia” (by N. Goridko and E. Krasina), demonstrates the presence of a multiplier effect from investments in technical re-equipment. Such solutions allow enterprises to make full use of their resources with the use of modern technologies, reducing costs while increasing profits.

Continuing the theme of economic modernization, Chap. 14, "Risks of Modernizing National Economies in the Conditions of the Technological Leap" (by Z. Sarkisyan), investigates the risks faced by national economies. The advantages and limitations of catching-up development in the context of globalization and the use of technological transfer and the import of equipment are shown for those countries that have chosen this path. The prospects for the large-scale implementation of digital technologies in those world leaders that are actively increasing the pace of innovation commercialization are assessed, as are similar prospects for developing countries where, in addition to social inequality, digital inequality is increasing as well. An important conclusion is that each country, as a result of economic modernization, must choose its own set of advanced technologies to provide competitive advantages in the global market. As for recommendations to reduce the arising of modernization risks, it is proposed to use mechanisms of interaction between the state and business for the implementation of investment projects using digital technologies.

Chapter 15, "Imperfect Mechanisms for the Use and Protection of Intellectual Property as an Organizational Barrier in the Movement to Global Technological Leadership" (by A. Litvinenko et al.), through focusing on the growth of competition for intellectual capital among world economic leaders, determines the sequence of overcoming organizational barriers in the use and protection of intellectual property. Compliance with the intellectual property management mechanism is an important component of achieving global technological leadership. Understanding that the business model of any organization is intellectual property adds value to the provisions of this chapter.

Smart cities, as noted above, have great potential for the development of digital technologies; therefore, in Chap. 16, "Smart Cities Hyper-Economy as the Reflection of Digital Governance Leadership" (by S. Kamolov et al.), the authors put forward and prove the hypothesis that data-driven governance leads to the creation of a new creative economic environment which uses public data and transforms it into marketable information. According to the authors, the technological superstructure of "smart cities" should be perceived as a new and emerging environment for innovative technologies and business strategies.

Chapter 17, "Smart Contracts and Corporate Governance: Prospects and Risks of Business Digitalization" (by A. Yukhno et al.), carries out a study on the benefits and risks of using the so-called smart contracts in the practice of business digitalization. Despite the obvious benefits of smart contracts, the potential risks must be considered. This led to practical recommendations for business organizations regarding the use of smart contracts, as well as to conclusion that the technology of smart contracts currently requires thorough testing.

Exploring further the topic of smart cities and transport systems, Chap. 18, "Urban Mobility: from Traditional to Intelligent Forms of Mobility" (by T. Kreydenko et al.), highlights aspects of modern cities' technological transformation. It is shown that there has been a radical change in the paradigm of urban transport planning, from ensuring demand to finding effective managing tools. The authors demonstrate the feasibility of integrating urban mobility services into the global value chain.

The role of finance is important in any activity, which is why Chap. 19, "Banking Business Strategies in the Paradigm of Digital Solutions and Sustainable Development Goals" (by G. Panova), explores the issues of aligning banking business strategies with digital solutions and sustainable development. The author identifies the problems that prevent the active implementation of new approaches in the Russian investment and lending practice; one noteworthy problem is that the system for stimulating the implementation of digital solutions by companies with low environmental, social, and corporate risks is shown to be underdeveloped.

Digital transformation is also changing the insurance industry. Chapter 20, "The Role of the Directors' and Officers' Insurance Contracts in Corporate Governance" (by A. Esendirov and M. Inozemtsev), establishes the role of an insurance contract as an advanced business strategy. The analysis is carried out concerning two models of corporate governance: an outsider or distributed equity system (UK, USA) and an insider or concentrated equity system (Russia). The authors argue that the more effective the company's corporate governance system is in the conditions of digital uncertainty, the higher the probability of obtaining the most optimal terms of the contract.

As a continuation of the digital transformation of banking and insurance technology, Chap. 21, "On the Constitutional Court's Position about Freedom and Privacy as Business Strategy in the Banking Sector" (by A. Shashkova and M. Verlaine), considers the issues of digital uncertainty in limiting the constitutional rights of citizens to the inviolability of professional and banking secrets in the implementation of control and monitoring activities.

Finally, the Conclusion/Chap. 22, "Advantages and Challenges of Digital Technology" (by I. Stepnov), systematizes the limitations of digital technology development, the overcoming of which should be incorporated into digital business models. Such a solution will ensure the effectiveness of technology leadership as a basic strategy for the digital age, realizing a winner-take-all model.

Overall, this book aims to provide a multifaceted overview of the challenges when transforming new technologies into strategic decisions. Combining the works of renowned scientists and specialists in various fields, this book systematizes the experience in digital transformations, which creates the basis for both scientific understanding and theoretical and methodological generalization of the digital economy.

We sincerely hope that this book will become not only a cognitive source of knowledge about digital leadership and will be useful to scientists, economists, sociologists, and politicians, but will also allow each reader to see the transformation trends of society as a whole.

References

Agarwal, R., & Helfat, C. E. (2009). Strategic Renewal of Organizations. *Organization Science, 20*(2), 281–293.

Barney, J. B., & Hesterly, W. S. (2014). *Strategic Management and Competitive Advantage: Concepts and Cases.* Harlow: Pearson.

Bughin, J. R., Kretschmer, T., & Van Zeebroeck, N. (2019, January). Experimentation, Learning and Stress: The Role of Digital Technologies in Strategy Change. *SSRN Electronic Journal.* https://doi.org/10.2139/ssrn.3328421. Retrieved from https://ssrn.com/abstract=3328421.

Carroll, G. R., & Huo, Y. P. (1986). Organizational Task and Institutional Environments in Ecological Perspective. *American Journal of Sociology, 91*(4), 838–873.

Chandler, A. D. (1962). *Strategy and Structure: Chapters in the History of American Enterprise.* Cambridge, MA: MIT Press.

Chesbrough, H. (2010). Business Model Innovation: Opportunities and Barriers. *Long Range Planning, 43*, 354–363. https://doi.org/10.1016/j.lrp.2009.07.010.

Cordon, C., et al. (2016). *Strategy Is Digital, Management for Professionals.* Cham: Springer International Publishing Switzerland. https://doi.org/10.1007/978-3-319-31132-6_2.

Crossan, M. M., & Berdrow, I. (2003). Organizational Learning and Strategic Renewal. *Strategic Management Journal, 24*(11), 1087–1105.

Deloitte. (2018). Digital Maturity Model. Achieving Digital Maturity to Drive Grow. Retrieved from https://www2.deloitte.com/content/dam/Deloitte/global/Documents/Technology-Media-Telecommunications/deloitte-digital-maturity-model.pdf.

Demil, B., Lecocq, X., & Warnier, V. (2018). Business Model Thinking, Business Ecosystems and Platforms: The New Perspective on the Environment of the Organization. *Management, 21*(4), 12–13.

Fred, D., & Forest, R. D. (2017). *Strategic Management: A Competitive Advantage Approach, Concepts and Cases.* Englewood Cliffs, NJ: Pearson–Prentice Hall.

Ghezzi, A., & Cavallo, A. (2018). Agile Business Model Innovation in Digital Entrepreneurship: Lean Startup Approaches. *Journal of Business Research.* https://doi.org/10.1016/j.jbusres.2018.06.013.

Gomes, J. F., Iivari, M., Pikkarainen, M., & Ahokangas, P. (2018). Business Models as Enablers of Ecosystemic Interaction: A Dynamic Capability Perspective. *International Journal of Social Ecology and Sustainable Development, 9*(3), 1–13.

Grant, R. M. (1991). The Resource-based Theory of Competitive Advantage: Implications for Strategy Formulation. *California Management Review, 33*(Spring), 114–135.

Güner, H. M., Çemberci, M., & Civelek, M. E. (2018). The Effect of Supply Chain Agility on Firm Performance. *Journal of International Trade, Logistics and Law, 4*(2), 25–34.

Hague, P. (2019). *Management Concepts and Business Models: A Complete Guide.* Moscow: Alpina Publisher. (in Russian).

Hill, T. (2000). *Manufacturing Strategy: The Strategic Management of the Manufacturing Function.* London: Palgrave. https://doi.org/10.1007/978-1-349-14018-3.

Kane, G. C., Palmer, D., Phillips, A. N., Kiron, D., & Buckley, N. (2015). Strategy, Not Technology, Drives Digital Transformation. *MIT Sloan Management Review and Deloitte University Press, 14*, 1–25.

Kreutzer, R. T. (2017). Treiber und hinterguende der digitalen transformation. In D. Schallmo et al. (Eds.), *Digitale Transformation von Geschaeftsmodellen* (pp. 33–58). Springer. https://doi.org/10.1007/978-3-658-12388-8_2.

Learned, E. P., Christensen, C. R., Andrews, K. R., & Guth, W. D. (1965). *Business Policy, Text and Cases.* Homewood, IL: Irwin.

Massa, L., Tucci, C., & Afuah, A. (2017). A Critical Assessment of Business Model Research. *Academy of Management Annuals, 11*(1), 73–104.

McKinsey. (2016). *The Economic Essentials of Digital Strategy.* Retrieved from https://www.mckinsey.com/business-functions/strategy-and-corporate-finance/our-insights/the-economic-essentials-of-digital-strategy.

Osterwalder, A., & Pigneur, Y. (2010). *Business Model Generation: A Handbook for Visionaries, Game Changers, and Challengers.* Hoboken, NJ: John Wiley & Sons.

Pénard, T., & Brousseau, E. (2007). *The Economics of Digital Business Models: A Framework for Analyzing the Economics of Platforms*. St. Louis: Federal Reserve Bank of St. Louis.

Penrose, E. T. (1995). Research on the Business Firms: Limits to Growth and Size of Firms. *American Economic Review, 45*(2), 531–543.

Porter, M. E. (1996, November–December). What Is a Strategy? *Harvard Business Review*, 61–78.

Porter, M. E. (2008). *Competitive Strategy: Techniques for Analyzing Industries and Competitors*. New York: Free Press.

Porter, M. E., & Heppelmann, J. E. (2015). How Smart, Connected Products Are Transforming Companies. *Harvard Business Review*, no. 4. https://doi.org/10.1017/CBO9781107415324.004.

Prahalad, K. K., Faei, L., & Randell, R. (2002). *Creating Key Competencies and Using Them. MBA Course in Strategic Management* (pp. 357–383). Moscow: Alpina Publisher. (in Russian).

PwC. (2018). *Digital Champions* (in Russian). Retrieved from https://www.pwc.ru/ru/publications/digital-champions.html.

PwC. (2020). *Global Research Digital IQ 2020 Investment Pays Off. Your Future Is in Your Hands* (in Russian). Retrieved from https://www.pwc.ru/ru/publications/digital-iq-2020/digital-iq-2020-ru.pdf.

Robinson, P. (2011). *Strategic Management: Formulation, Implementation & Control*. New York: Mcgraw Hill Higher Education.

Schallmo, D., & Rusnjak, A. (2017). Roadmap zur Digitalen Transformation von Geschaefts-modellen. In D. Schallmo et al. (Eds.), *Digitale Transformation von Geschaeftsmodellen* (pp. 1–31). Wiesbaden: Springer. https://doi.org/10.1007/978-3-658-12388-8_1.

Stepnov, I. M. (2018). Digital Strategic Management as a Key Factor in Scientific and Technological Breakthrough. *Economika i upravlenie v mashinostroenii*, no. 3, pp. 59–61 (in Russian).

Stepnov, I. M., & Kovalchuk, J. A. (2018). Value Chain Modeling in Digital Strategic Management. *Uchet. Analiz. Audit [Accounting. Analysis. Auditing]*, (5), 6–23 (in Russian). https://doi.org/10.26794/2408-9303-2018-5-5-6-23.

Teece, D. (2010). Business Models, Business Strategy and Innovation. *Long Range Planning, 43*(2–3), 172–194.

Tomičić, M., Tomičić-Pupek, K., & Pihir, I. (2020). Understanding Digital Transformation Initiatives: Case Studies Analysis. *Business Systems Research, 11*(1), 125–141. https://doi.org/10.2478/bsrj-2020-0009.

Weill, P., & Woerner, S. (2019). *Digital Business Transformation: Changing the Business Model for a New Generation of Organizations*. Moscow: Alpina Publisher. (in Russian).

Zucker, L. G. (1987). Institutional Theories of Organization. *Annual Review of Sociology, 13*, 443–464.

PART I

Digital Breakthrough

CHAPTER 2

The Uncertainty of the Technological Future

Igor Stepnov

Introduction

New technologies play one of the most important roles in modern society. They impact all aspects of existence and transform a human's entire way of life. Technological advancement as an effect of scientific and technological progress changes economic, social, and political relations in human society, as referenced in the works of R. R. Nelson and S. G. Winter (1982), and S. Berg, M. Wustmans, and S. Bröring (2019). Technology affects companies' profit margins and society's economic growth. However, commercializing a new piece of technology which utilized an imperfect process is not an easy task, with there being so many sources of uncertainty (Bonnín Roca et al. 2017). It is this fact that underlines the need for efficient technological management in the frameworks of uncertainty.

Research on the various aspects of technology—mainly its role in society—is reflected in the variety of approaches developed by many different

I. Stepnov (✉)
Moscow State Institute of International Relations (MGIMO University), Moscow, Russia

Financial University under the Government of the Russian Federation, Moscow, Russia

I. Stepnov (ed.), *Technology and Business Strategy*,
https://doi.org/10.1007/978-3-030-63974-7_2

authors. The subject matter of the research may be the evolution of the term “technology” (Mitcham and Schatzberg 2009), original ideas of technological parasitism and the search for a unified technological evolution theory (Coccia 2019a, b), analysis of companies’ reactions towards a single new technology (Burk 2013) in the oligopolistic model (Zhang 2020), or the search for an answer to the question of whether old technology is able to create value in the relevant time period (Beckmann et al. 2016).

Nowadays, scientific and technological progress mainly manifests itself in the area of digitalization. Digital technologies have been popularized in recent years, thanks to such buzzwords as Industry 4.0, Internet of Things, Smart Manufacturing and Cyber Physical Systems. Moreover, in relation to different technologies, digital trends may demonstrate both technological turbulence, uncertainty, and acceleration.

The digital transformation and globalization have fully solidified the role of technology, having, in many ways, become an integrator of the ongoing changes. However, in the era of breakthrough discoveries, the uncertainty of the future becomes even more evident. The degree of market stability is inversely proportional to its uncertainty, and these uncertainties increase the probability of failure. The danger of the most popular contemporary technologies to become obsolete does not decrease over time but, on the contrary, rises. Still, the chance that new technology will become the winner is also quite high. F. J. Milliken describes uncertainty as a person’s perceived inability to accurately predict something due to a lack of sufficient information, classifying uncertainty as an uncertainty of the state, effect, and reaction (Milliken 1987).

The uncertainty of the technological future is both frightening and alluring. It is technological uncertainty that is the main condition for economic systems staying dynamic, which underlines the role of entrepreneurial initiatives in realizing the potential of the scientific and technological progress. According to I. Meijer, uncertainty has a major impact on innovational solutions and an entrepreneurs’ actions (Meijer 2008). Understanding uncertainty, risk, and opportunity assessment are all necessary for start-ups support. Uncertainties are present at almost all the stages of the entrepreneurial process, with success and failure depending on how entrepreneurs deal with these uncertainties.

Uncertainty serves as a basis for most risky projects, leading some start-ups to success and others to failure. Moreover, acknowledging uncertainty leads different companies to different results. Start-ups (and investors funding them) stimulate active innovation integration, while large companies limit their investments when an uncertainty arises, giving their preference to projects that have already been developed.

There are at least four types of uncertainty in the modern digital achievement race: uncertainty of new digital technology solutions; market success uncertainty; strategy (business models) uncertainty; public acknowledgment uncertainty. This is why uncertainty serves as basis for many decisions and discussions.

In S. Luthfa's opinion, uncertainty arises in the innovation process within the cycle of a lack of resources, lack of activity, and a limited understanding of the subjects due to a lack of knowledge, unjustified optimism, and a rational basis for ignoring information (Luthfa 2019).

In business, the inability of decision makers to fully get rid of uncertainty limits the efficiency of decision-making and requires approaches that would either help to reduce uncertainty or to conquer it (Sniazhko 2019). Having identified three types of uncertainty, S. Sniazhko specifies—drawing attention to a firm's uncertainty being determined by, among other things, past experience and naming information collection—cooperation and network establishment among the ways of reducing uncertainty.

R. E. Hoskisson and L. W. Busenitz analyze uncertainty from two points of view: in terms of perceived market uncertainty and in terms of a company's opportunities (Hoskisson and Busenitz 2002).

With that said, it is imperative that businesses themselves evaluate their readiness for technological reforms (Hizam-Hanafiah et al. 2020); this can be done through, for example, the six dimension system (technology, personnel, strategy, leadership, process, and innovation). Others (Dissel et al. 2009) believe that many technology-assessment decisions are still being made based on experts' opinions. For instance, the 6G future technology changes contours forecast (Yrjölä et al. 2020) in which experts' judgments go towards predicting possible scenarios.

However, the coming digitalization has a glaring problem: the degree of the uncertainty of changes that is predicted on the basis of futurism and not scientific research is too high. This situation is further aggravated by the fact that a number of researchers have been seen (Kovalchuk and Stepnov 2019) to have shifted their research focus towards popularizing the scientific and technological process instead of generalizing the occurring changes (Barrat 2013; Franklin 2018; Gordon 2016; Leonghard 2018; Rushkoff 2013). Taking on the role of forecasters of the economic consequences of breakthrough technologies (both as optimists and as pessimists), they often forget that both economics and scientific philosophy have long since developed a constructive system approach to researching new phenomena.

The prevalence of futuristic views is, in many ways, linked to digital technologies having basically no methodological research basis for determining their impact on society. This is because not enough historical experience of their use has been accumulated, including even religious and anthropological aspects (Checketts 2017).

The modern approach to accumulating empirical data and the technological future forecast has been best implemented in the approach developed by the research and advisory company Gartner (Gartner 2018).

The five stages of the Gartner cycle make it possible to estimate the time lag before the start of commercialization for a particular technology. The first stage is the launch of the technology: its invention in a research lab. The second stage is the inflated expectations phase: conference and press debates. The third stage is the disillusionment: doubts as to its usefulness. The fourth stage is the business environment integration stage: investigating the possibility to create new value on the basis of the new technology. The fifth stage is production growth: constructing a new business model for the use of the new technology. The Gartner 2019 cycle places such technologies as biorobots, augmented reality cloud, decentralized network, adaptive machine learning, nano-sized 3D-printing, and 5G in the first phases. Gartner expects these technologies to enter production markets no sooner than 5–10 years from now. Therefore, we have also, in accordance with the Gartner cycle, analyzed technologies placed no lower than in stage 4, that is, from the possibility of creating new value based on the new technology.

The gap in research is reflected in the following issue: technology assessments are mainly based on predictions in the framework of various approaches. The aim of the chapter is to attempt to create an evolutionary cyclical model for reducing uncertainty in experts' opinions on the advantages of future digital technology.

Methodology

For the purposes of forming a scholarly opinion, the chapter analyzes the theoretical aspects of technological uncertainty; the chapter also contains a comparative analysis of the discussions taking place in scientific works concerning this topic.

System analysis, being multi-disciplinary and providing model-building opportunities, was used as a basic research methodology.

The analysis is based on the multi-faceted character of the ideas concerning the future of technology, taking into account that the majority of notions surrounding the future are expert opinions based on the accumulated experience of industrial-age technologies. If one looks at the digital technology selection stages, at first, they all contained a certain element of hype (speaking in Gartner terms). At the end of this stage, one can already infer that digital technologies differ from industrial ones.

With that in mind, we chose cyclical theory and methodology as the most reasonable forecasting tool, as it is based not on the development of a single particular technology but rather on implementing technology into society and society's reaction towards the diffusion of new technology. This is why constructive propositions are based on the cyclical character of economic phenomena, which thus makes more accurate predictions in relation to the future using business periodization techniques for separate technology classes.

The subjective element of system analysis allowed the identification of researchers' stances on the technological future; the techniques and methods of system analysis relative to the objective reality helped to establish both a unanimous opinion among researchers by collecting them in cyclical development as well as contradictions that provided a different point of view. With that said, the business model that actively substitutes the organization in creating value for consumers through technology has become the subject matter of the research.

The method utilized meant researchers' approaches to describing the technological future could be systemized, leaving room for modifying the proposed techniques in the framework of a single model.

Results

New digital technologies are mainly linked to Industry 4.0 and the Internet of Things. This is the next generation of technology, providing a consumer with a guaranteed foregoing degree of satisfaction, but with value presented digitally. M. Cano-Kollmanna, T. J. Hanniganb and R. Mudamb have identified three global megatrends which serve as the basis for a majority of changes in the global economy occurring digitally (Cano-Kollmanna et al. 2018). The first megatrend is the transition from trade in goods to trade in business activities arising from global value chains. These business activities often produce intermediary products (not complete goods or services). The second megatrend is the growth of science-driven intangible assets along with value migrating to intangible goods (from patents to service models). Such migration has greatly elevated the importance of innovations as well as decreased technologies' life cycle. The third megatrend is the growth of developing markets, through which the first two megatrends can be implemented with high efficiency.

We choose the following statement (which has already been mentioned in the book's introduction) as a basic prerequisite for achieving the aim of the chapter: in order to reduce uncertainty in selection decisions, it is important to assess not the development of technology itself (which is essential for R&D), but rather its implementation into society and the economy. The technology is embodied in every value-based activity, and everything that a firm does involves some sort of technology. This is why we have chosen such categories as "strategies" and "business models" as a basis for the model being developed, as these categories most accurately reflect technologies in a company's activity.

For the purposes of assessing technology implementation in society, the following can be applied: oligopolistic models of competition (Zhang 2020), digital twins (Shao and Helu 2020; Ladj et al. 2020), technology value assessment (Razgaitis 2009; Park and Park 2004), innovation diffusion models (Rogers 1995), and development cycles (Kitchin 1923). In order to achieve our goal, we choose cyclical models, taking into account the elements of technology price assessment therein as an expression of value for the consumer and innovation diffusion as the most formalized solution to combine technology development and commercialization. Taking into consideration the insufficiency of the accumulated experience with digital technologies, the practical value of the diffusion and competition models is not high enough; moreover, they have no direct links to the business model. Therefore, we have no doubts that in developing most business concepts there can be no simultaneous, accurate, and proper combination of technological concepts (Tomičić et al. 2020), which underlines the importance of solving the uncertainty problem even more. As modern research focus mainly on knowledge, in order to assess the technology's potential, eight key elements may be used: the aims of the technological system and business aims; a product's life cycle; the desired behavior model during the product's life cycle; the product's structure; its technological properties; any link between the product's properties and the desired behavior; the potential effects of technology linked to the product; financial indicator estimates linked to the product (Mämmelä et al. 2018). From this list, it is evident that, for instance, the first two or three key elements may be used for services subject to implementation in 8–10 years (Chiesa et al. 2005); it is also confirmed that value changes depend on expert predictions made with parameter assessments.

A similar situation is inherent to factor analysis, which utilizes either some sort of foresight or the individual manifestations of economic reality elevated to the rung of "material" for formulating factors. Moreover, factor constructions are based on known solutions and imply an evolutionary development of existing processes, while revolutionary bifurcations are left with less and less room. However, we choose the growth business model complexity as a factor for our cyclical model (from platforms to ecosystems and digital society).

Business model dynamics are best reflected in the form of a business periodization (evolution) which would allow the demonstration of any change in business solutions, both in the mid-term and long-term.

Such a business periodization may be constructed on the basis of the company development cycle model introduced by us earlier (Stepnov 2001), presented in Fig. 2.1.

The time parameters presented in this model (Fig. 2.1) are based on different cycles discovered over the course of economic studies, with the model's shape corresponding to the stages of the innovative product adoption (Rogers 1995). Empirical verification during different time periods (mid 1990s, beginning of the 2000s, beginning of the 2010s) showed the validity of interval assessments. It should be noted that this model, being evolutionary, is part of a particular organizational solution or a small number of indiscrete solutions.

In order to justify the application of the selected model, it is necessary to specify the constant terms which ensure the continuity of the industrial

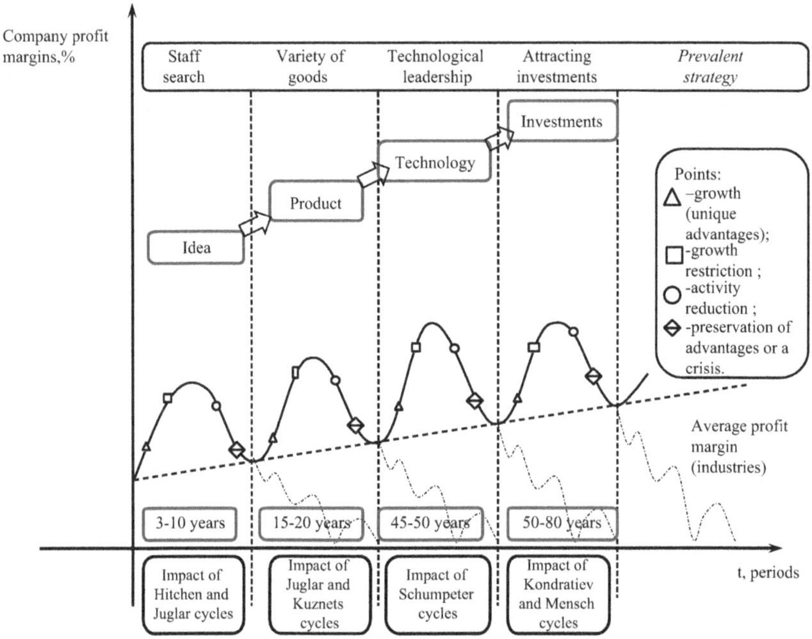

Fig. 2.1 A company's development cycle. (*Source*: *adapted and supplemented by the author based on*: Stepnov, I. M. (2001). *Innovation Management: Using Innovative Potential in the Industry*. Moscow: Fizmatlit (in Russian))

and digital eras, and the difference between industrialization and digitalization for its adaptation.

Basing our conclusions of the conducted studies, the following statements have been selected as constant terms:

- Scientific and technological progress is constantly proving itself as a sign of economic growth;
- Technology serves as the main source of change in the economy and society;
- Technology has the property to grow in complexity over the course of several stages of technological development, until the technological solutions currently in use have received a complete overhaul;
- Economic relations are cyclical, which take on the form of not one but several cyclical manifestations of different periods;

- The "creation boom" of new companies, their stages of evolution, and their maturity depend on technological development.

An updated version of the cyclical model is to be executed only after the role of digital technologies and management thereof has been established in digital business models (Stepnov and Kovalchuk 2020).

The digital breakthrough is characterized by the fact that radical changes occur simultaneously in almost all industries. Until now, society had never before witnessed such a phenomenon. All of the changes were of a fragmented, industrial character of consistent technological leaps with limited resources. The previous situation led to certain industries becoming prominent, having served as a sort of driving force behind progress.

Today, however, innovations—transcending or breaking down the boundaries between industries—are becoming a regular occurrence. A technology's universality does not always depend on an industrial character. The importance of this notion has led to the key aspect of the modern technological revolution being thoroughly understood: the pace of the spread of digital technologies does not depend on industrial barriers. As a result, the resources required for the specific industry are cut. One industry's solutions are adopted with minor tweaks in other industries. A decreasing need for special resources should be taken into account upon selecting technological research evolution areas.

During the industrial era, many different special resources were required for a technological breakthrough in each industry; modern technology, on the other hand, is aimed more at consumption of two resources—calculation capacity and data transfer speed—which greatly impacts the issue of resource competition and showcases the advantages of digital technologies. This has led to progress having stopped and being concentrated on a multitude of parameters that need resources. An opportunity has presented itself to concentrate on one or two parameters: computing capacity and data transfer speed (6G/NET-2030 and quantum computer for current goals).

The value of material technology is decreasing. Digitalization provides more growth for labor productivity as opposed to inventing new means of transforming materials. In this case it is possible to separate two types of technology: (a) general use technology, ensuring integration and being mostly digital and (b) digitally modified produ`ction and service provision technologies (i.e. the required data are received digitally).

In our opinion, such an approach leads to an erroneous conclusion and to the very hype (Hype Cycle) that Gartner warns against. Generally speaking, a change in general-purpose technology occurs faster than in transformative technology, which also makes it harder to accurately perceive trends, even though the theoretical model looks different (Fig. 2.2).

Besides, with two technologies and two trends in place, tracking is required for the four trends, which makes it more difficult to apply diffusion models, as in this case one should find out the degree to which society accepts not one but two technologies. A classic S-curve graph (technology diffusion) is, in this case, inaccurate, as there is no selection tool between two or more S-curves flowing at different rates (Fig. 2.2), which deprives this method of a unified solution. It is also possible to layer the third and fourth processes linked to trading the goods in for services and logistics, which distorts the general picture of changing technological paradigms. In

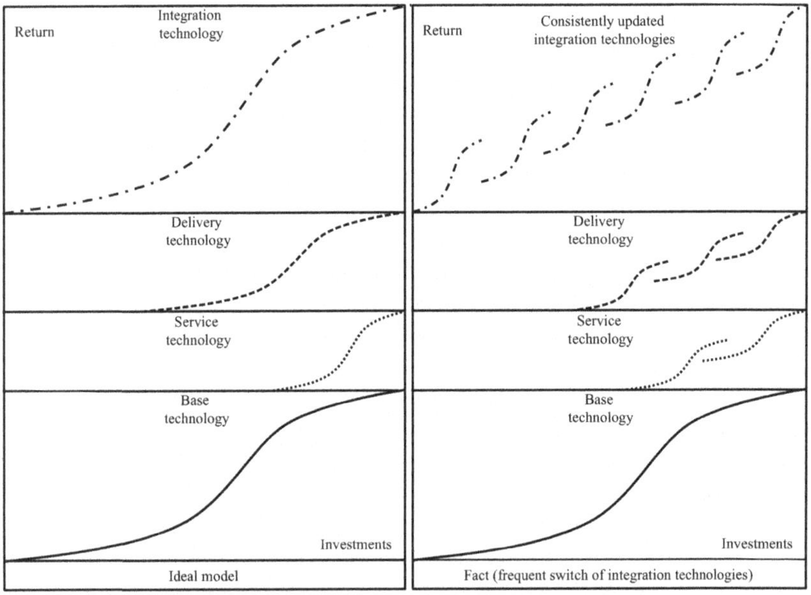

Fig. 2.2 Diffusion models, taking into account integrating technology, goods for services technology, and delivery technologies: (a) ideal model; (b) with the frequent change in integrating technologies taken into consideration. (*Source: developed by the author*)

this case the uncertainty of the future is not reduced, but rather it increases (due to the combinatory character of the interaction).

The solution singularity issue in a "three in one" situation, or rather in a "four in one" scenario uses the following pillars: integrational technology; service transition technology; logistics technology; material transformation technology that may often be solved by the Digital Twin technology (Shao and Helu 2020) but are rather limited at the level of operational solutions. Digital twins will not always provide accurate recommendations as they will be efficient in terms of the digital process and from the end consumer's point of view, which is still set to remain non-digital.

The logical conclusion would be presenting the new technology in a new format, considering the only available one which will move it closer to the possibility of it being used by artificial intelligence. This solution is based on specialization and universality principles.

The uniformity of understanding of, and ideas concerning, modern technology is ensured through identifying two or three components in one piece of technology. The first component is the material one (instrumental or transformational). The second for managing solutions is the creation of a technology data flow (e.g. for the Internet of Things), as well as the transfer of these data and management. The delivery technology (logistics) should, in this case, remain open and external. As such, a uniform idea of both the technology itself and the business models born from it will be sustained, which will reduce future uncertainty and corresponds to the goals of our study.

Thus, such an approach corresponds to specialization principles as well: the use of a specialized executive apparatus and the unlimited capabilities of the managing system. In this case one can discuss the technology inherent to ecosystems: an ecosystem technology, which is a complex reflection of the technological components being integrated into a single technology with actions being coordinated between components, that is, through protocols and standards.

The commercialization of new technologies creates risks that are dissimilar to industrial ones. An analysis of the value creation architecture in business models leads to the conclusion that supplier–consumer relations control is insufficient for the purposes of technological management. It is often misrepresented, suggesting that it is the technology that is the barrier defining the company's boundaries, which is why many studies are being conducted by consulting companies (Gartner, McKinsey amongst others) on technology issues. While these studies are focused on whether new technologies are "mature enough" to be used and integrated into different industries, it is important to understand that the integration of digital technologies is the key to success but not necessarily a leadership quality guarantee for companies. This is especially evident in the case of an unequal value distribution across the entire value chain. D. Teece's study dynamics should be noted (Teece 2018), as he turned back to the importance of new-age innovation profitability in digital models two decades after his well-known and acclaimed publications. According to D. Teece, network value creation and new transactional costs lead to irregular (and unequal) profits across the entire value chain. Such a notion leads us to the conclusion that business models may create another reason for uncertainty growth, namely the inequality of income distribution.

While we agree with this statement, let us note that inequality may already be present in the technological part of the business model, not merely in supplier–consumer relations. This is why we believe value creation control to belong mostly to technological solutions (including communications) and to the proprietary holders of these solutions, and not to the relations in the business model itself (often called market power).

We have already put forward the notion that digital investors bring in large profits, and we continue to regard this as relevant for the present day (Stepnov and Kovalchuk 2018), as the combination of business models and advanced technologies will strengthen the idea of super-profits even more, especially with the growing share of private ownership of information.

Based on the differences presented above in the model (Fig. 2.1), we propose making the following changes that will help reflect the technology selection recommendations (understanding their role and place) based on their input into the evolution of business models (Fig. 2.3).

Above all, let us focus on the fact that in Fig. 2.3 we analyze not "organizations" but rather "business models", demonstrating the fact that different organizational types begin to lose their purpose in the digital economy. In other words, the new business development spiral (digital business) is linked to the business model and to the business company types, including the strive to cut support costs.

The role of the formal association is somewhat diminished, as the many expenses of items inside the firm are starting to match external ones. Thus, it is possible to speak of switching from firms to business models in the future, although this distant goal will lead to the new cloud company or

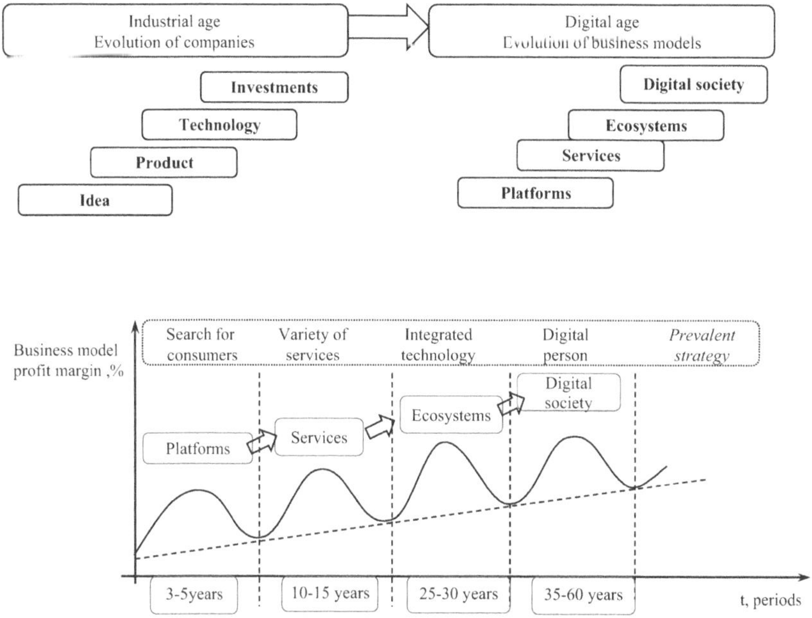

Fig. 2.3 Changes in the digital age cycle. (*Source: developed by the author*)

business model theory. A business model without a physical structure is edging closer and closer to the digital reality of the future.

Our approach is based on the notion that a consistent transition from general business model types, supported by various types of technology, is already happening and will be happening with a certain cyclicality (as has already happened in the industrial economy, and is yet to happen in digital economies).

In our opinion, the most accurate starting point for the widespread use of digital achievements should be the year the crisis comes to an end and the new economic growth starts. We believe such a time to have been 2010–2012. Digital technologies have led to organizations being unable to either create value or receive said value if they are incapable of solving internal problems by constructing internal platforms. As a result, a new wave of start-ups arose, aimed at platform solutions utilized in the outside environment. It is this factor that will determine further growth and it is this factor that should be focused on in analyzing this issue.

Therefore, with our classification (Fig. 2.1), the platform became an idea that has been implemented in numerous platform-based start-ups while barely having an impact on manufacturing, having left it with digitalization prospects.

As shown in Fig 2.3, we may speak of the platform period before integration begins, and now the “idea” (Fig. 2.1) can be switched to “platform”. The duration of this period came up from 3 to 5 years (for some firms from 1.5 to 10 years). During this interval or period, it was integratory technology that became the cutting-edge technology, as such technology was implemented mainly through communication. Rarely producing goods, such platforms had a significant impact on income distribution in the constructed value chain. It is obvious that, compared to the past decades, cash flow production was secured by a key resource: whereas once it was the number of executives (workers), for the modern model, on the other hand, the number of consumers (subscribers) plays the role of this resource.

It is also important to understand that it is in value chains that “light” digital victories of general-purpose technology have been achieved, having reduced transactional costs for a number of companies, thanks to which these companies received leadership. It should also, however, be noted that, with the large-scale spread and creation of an integral digital environment, such victories will be achieved more and more rarely and their profitability will be cut.

The end of the fast start-up growth period led either to bankruptcy, or to a transition to a new stage, or to acquisition by larger companies through the “sandbox” mechanism (cycle 2 in Fig. 2.3). Going off optimistic estimates, we believe the start of transition stage to have begun no later than 2015. However, a time shift is also possible due to financial barriers remaining the biggest problem with state funding programs, such as the Innovate UK or UK Research and Innovation in the UK has greatly reduced the number of small digital tech businesses going bankrupt (Masooda and Sonntaga 2020). Taking into account future technology selection solutions based on direct industrial needs and the necessary funding, the duration of the first stage is likely to be extended.

The estimates allow us to conclude that the duration of the second stage will continue up to 10–15 years and, therefore, on average the current stage will end by 2025–2030. Many researchers estimate 2030 to be the year 6G will become practically applicable, provided that no more radical innovations occur, especially those connected with quantum calculations. It is relevant to note that the second business model evolutionary stage is to have the following features: active replacement of goods by services and the development of the sharing economy. It is economically sound to use services in the digital economy upon assets becoming immaterial. Therefore, these are technologies that will ensure that possession becomes substituted for service consumption that will become key technologies, and it is this factor that should be taken into account upon selecting a technology.

The third stage will be determined by technologies for technologies and will be completely dedicated to creating digital ecosystems—it is then that our idea of a technology as a multi-component model will be in high demand. At this point, all the technological solutions will start to be fully implemented. It is completely obvious that the character of this stage will be of a global technological style, but its significance will be reflected through an ecosystem outlook. Modern leaders are undoubtedly already forming the first ecosystem approaches; however full-fledged development will occur only after the "service" stage. It should also be noted that the highest degree of digitalization possible will have been achieved by then, and digital advantages will turn into digital necessities. The frameworks of the third stage are yet unclear, but its qualitative significance is absolutely obvious.

For the fourth stage, as of right now, we may only speak of its duration and of the new society based on digital relations, the frameworks of which are only present in philosophical discourse. There is, however, another way. P. V. Coveneya and R. R. Highfield believe that, in analyzing the limits of the conceivable, digital computers (be they ordinary or quantum) are more limited in their capabilities than many realize. The power of computers gives them an aura of invincibility, but, upon transitioning to exoskeletons and quantum calculations, there will be a significant potential for going back to analogue calculations (Coveneya and Highfield 2020). Our model does not reject such a course of events, yet leaves room for discussion as to when this will happen: at the fourth stage of the cyclical model, or during the rise of the fourth quantum spiral (Fig. 2.4). The future will tell.

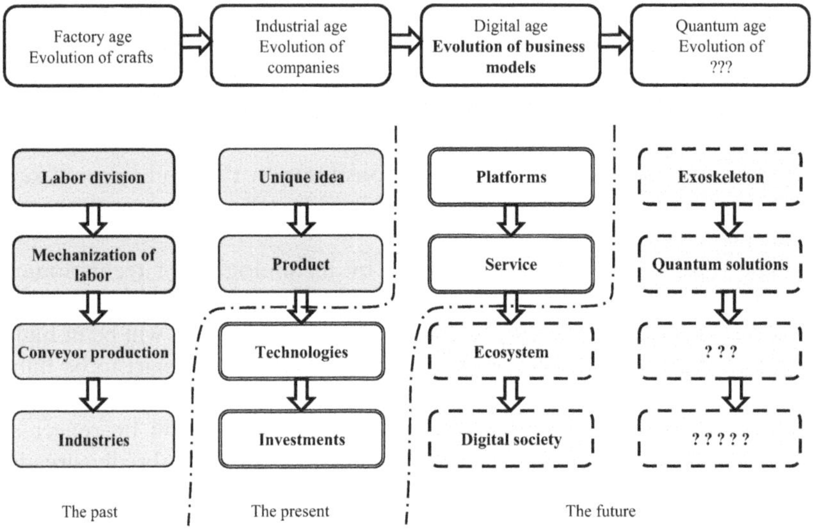

Fig. 2.4 Consolidated cyclicality model. (*Source: developed by the author*)

Conclusions/Recommendations

The digital future is becoming more and more real in its virtual aspect. The stage of easy income with the help of digital solutions is coming to an end; however, this provides a new opportunity for a technological breakthrough.

The chapter shows that, based on studying coincidences and contradictions of the industrial and digital ages, there appears to be a possibility for reducing the technological uncertainty of the evolutionary stages of the cyclical model. Based on the modified model, we have managed to accurately place technology into every development stage.

Each company should secure its own choice and determine its path based on the presented facts and other business chronologies in order to understand the future prospects. We should undoubtedly tread with caution concerning the resource planning model while understanding the change in relations in a digital environment.

The thesis of the possibility to construct a cloud company based on business models without organizational and legal solutions is quite important as it allows a great cost reduction and flexibility increase.

The acquired quality model, along with the proposed business periodization, ensures the understanding of technological development and lessening of uncertainty, which is imperative for the development of the economy as a whole and of its individual stakeholders.

References

Barrat, J. (2013). *Our Final Invention: Artificial Intelligence and the End of the Human Era*. New York: Thomas Dunne Books and St. Martin's Press.

Beckmann, O. C., Royer, S., & Schiavone, F. (2016). Old but Sexy: Value Creation of Old Technology-Based Businesses Models. *Journal of Business Models, 4*(2), 1–21.

Berg, S., Wustmans, M., & Bröring, S. (2019). Identifying First Signals of Emerging Dominance in a Technological Innovation System: A Novel Approach Based on Patents. *Technological Forecasting and Social Change, 146*, 706–722. https://doi.org/10.1016/j.techfore.2018.07.046.

Bonnín Roca, J., Vaishnav, P., Morgan, M. G., Mendonça, J., & Fuchs, E. (2017). When Risks Cannot be Seen: Regulating Uncertainty in Emerging Technologies. *Research Policy, 46*, 1215–1233. https://doi.org/10.1016/j.respol.2017.05.010.

Burk, R. C. (2013). *Technology Upgrading in Imperfectly Competitive Markets*. The University of North Carolina at Chapel Hill. Order No. 3606650.

Cano-Kollmanna, M., Hanniganb, T. J., & Mudamb, R. (2018). Global Innovation Networks—Organizations and People. *Journal of International Management, 24*, 87–92. https://doi.org/10.1016/j.intman.2017.09.008.

Checketts, L. (2017). New Technologies—Old Anthropologies? *Religions, 8*(4), 52.

Chiesa, V., Gilardoni, E., & Manzini, R. (2005). The Valuation of Technology in Buy-Cooperate-Sell Decisions. *European Journal of Innovation Management, 8*, 157–181. https://doi.org/10.1108/14601060510594710.

Coccia, M. (2019a). Theories of the Evolution of Technology Based on Processes of Competitive Substitution and Multi-Mode Interaction between Technologies. *Journal of Economics Bibliography, 6*(2), 99–109. https://doi.org/10.1453/jeb.v6i2.1889.

Coccia, M. (2019b). What is Technology and Technology Change? A New Conception with Systemic-Purposeful Perspective for Technology Analysis. *Journal of Social and Administrative Sciences, 6*(3), 145–169. https://doi.org/10.1453/jsas.v6i3.1957.

Coveneya, P. V., & Highfield, R. R. (2020). From Digital Hype to Analogue Reality: Universal Simulation beyond the Quantum and Exascale Eras. *Journal of Computational Science*, 101093. https://doi.org/10.1016/j.jocs.2020.101093.

Dissel, M. C., Phaal, R., Farrukh, C. J., & Probert, D. R. (2009). Value Roadmapping. *Research Technology Management, 52*(6), 45–53. https://doi.org/10.1080/08956308.2009.11657599.

Franklin, D. (2018). *Megatech. Technology and Society: 2050 in the Forecasts of Scientists and Writers*. Moscow: Bombora (in Russian).

Gartner. (2018). *Gartner Hype Cycle*. Retrieved from https://www.gartner.com/en/research/methodologies/gartner-hype-cycle.

Gartner. (2019). *Hype Cycle for Emerging Technologies, 2019*. Retrieved from https://www.gartner.com/en/documents/3956015/hype-cycle-for-emerging-technologies-2019.

Gordon, R. (2016). *The Rise and Fall of American Growth. The U.S. Standard of Living since the Civil War*. Princeton: Princeton University Press.

Hizam-Hanafiah, M., Soomro, A. M., & Abdullah, N. L. (2020). Industry 4.0 Readiness Models: A Systematic Literature Review of Model Dimensions. *Information, 11*(7), 364. https://doi.org/10.3390/info11070364.

Hoskisson, R. E., & Busenitz, L. W. (2002). Market Uncertainty and Learning Distance in Corporate Entrepreneurship Entry Mode Choice. In M. A. Hitt, R. D. Ireland, S. M. Camp, & D. K. Sexton (Eds.), *Strategic Entrepreneurship: Creating a New Mindset* (pp. 151–172). Oxford: Blackwell.

Kitchin, J. (1923). Cycles and Trends in Economic Factors. *The Review of Economics and Statistics, 5*(1), 10–16.

Kovalchuk, J., & Stepnov, I. (2019). Research of the Technological Future's Uncertainty. *MGIMO Review of International Relations, 12*(6), 214–224. https://doi.org/10.24833/2071-8160-2019-6-69-214-224.

Ladj, A., et al. (2020). A Knowledge-Based Digital Shadow for Machining Industry in a Digital Twin Perspective. *Journal of Manufacturing Systems*. https://doi.org/10.1016/j.jmsy.2020.07.018.

Leonghard, G. (2018). *Technology vs. Humanity: The Coming Clash between Man and Machine*. Moscow: Publishing house AST (in Russian).

Luthfa, S. (2019). A Study of How Uncertainty Emerges in the Uncertainty-Embedded Innovation Process. *Journal of Innovation Management, 7*(1), 46–79.

Mämmelä, J., Juuti, T., Korhonen, T., Julkunen, P., Lehtonen, T., Pakkanen, J., & Vanhatalo, M. (2018). Evaluating the Value and Costs of Technology in the Manufacturing Industry. In *Proceedings of the NordDesign 2018*, Linköping, Sweden.

Masooda, T., & Sonntaga, P. (2020). Industry 4.0: Adoption Challenges and Benefits for SMEs. *Computers in Industry, 121*, 103261. https://doi.org/10.1016/j.compind.2020.103261.

Meijer, I. (2008). *Uncertainty and Entrepreneurial Action. The Role of Uncertainty in the Development of Emerging Energy Technologies*. Utrecht: Utrecht University.

Milliken, F. J. (1987). Three Types of Perceived Uncertainty About the Environment: State, Effect, and Response Uncertainty. *The Academy of Management Review, 12*, 133–143.

Mitcham, C., & Schatzberg, E. (2009). Defining Technology and the Technological Sciences. In A. Meijers (Ed.), *Philosophy of Technology and Engineering Sciences*. Amsterdam: Elsevier B.V.

Nelson, R. R., & Winter, S. G. (1982). *An Evolutionary Theory of Economic Change*. Cambridge: MAL Belknap Press of Harvard University Press.

Park, Y., & Park, G. (2004). A New Method for Technology Valuation in Monetary Value: Procedure and Application. *Technovation, 24*, 387–394.

Razgaitis, R. (2009). *Valuation and Dealmaking of Technology-Based Intellectual Property: Principles, Methods, and Tools*. Hoboken, NJ: John Wiley.

Rogers, E. M. (1995). *Diffusion of Innovations*. New York: Free Press.

Rushkoff, D. (2013). *Present Shock: When Everything Happens Now*. New York: Penguin.

Shao, G., & Helu, M. (2020). Framework for a Digital Twin in Manufacturing: Scope and Requirements. *Manufacturing Letters, 24*, 105–107. https://doi.org/10.1016/j.mfglet.2020.04.004.

Sniazhko, S. (2019). Uncertainty in Decision-Making: A Review of the International Business Literature. *Cogent Business & Management, 6*, 1–32. https://doi.org/10.1080/23311975.2019.1650692.

Stepnov, I. M. (2001). *Innovation Management: Using Innovative Potential in the Industry*. Moscow: Fizmatlit (in Russian).

Stepnov, I. M., & Kovalchuk, J. A. (2018). Platform Capitalism as the Source of Digital Rentier's Superprofit. *MGIMO Review of International Relations, 4*(61), 107–124 (in Russian). https://doi.org/10.24833/2071-8160-2018-4-61-107-124.

Stepnov, I., & Kovalchuk, J. (2020). Digital Business Model: Technology Management and Profit Control. *Innovations in Management, 3*(25), 68–79 (in Russian).

Teece, D. J. (2018). Profiting from Innovation in the Digital Economy: Enabling Technologies, Standards, and Licensing Models in the Wireless World. *Research Policy, 47*(8), 1367–1387. https://doi.org/10.1016/j.respol.2017.01.015.

Tomičić, M., Tomičić-Pupek, K., & Pihir, I. (2020). Understanding Digital Transformation Initiatives: Case Studies Analysis. *Business Systems Research, 11*(1), 125–141. https://doi.org/10.2478/bsrj-2020-0009.

Yrjölä, S., Ahokangas, P., & Matinmikko-Blue, M. (2020). *White Paper on Business of 6G*. University of Oulu, 6G Research Visions, no. 3. Retrieved from http://urn.fi/urn:isbn:9789526226767.

Zhang, Y. (2020). When Should Firms Choose a Risky New Technology? An Oligopolistic Analysis. *Economic Modelling, 91*, 687–693. https://doi.org/10.1016/j.econmod.2019.12.011.

CHAPTER 3

A Future with Artificial Intelligence: Strategy for Success

Nidjad Asadli

Introduction

The massive increase in the number of digital solutions used in business is becoming a significant difference in modern economic activity. For example, according to the Accenture consulting company (World Economic Forum 2018), the global costs of **digital transformation** technologies will grow by 16.8% annually and the use of digital technologies may add 1.36 trillion dollars (2.3%) to the GDP of the leading global economies (including 1.8% to the GDP of developed countries) and 3.4% to the GDP of developing countries in 2020.: According to the Russian Ministry (TASS 2019), the number of enterprises using digital technologies in Russia will increase fourfold over the next 5 years, and their profits will double. It should be noted that a sharp increase in the popularity of digital

N. Asadli (✉)
Center for Analysis of Economic Reforms and Communication, Baku, Azerbaijan

Moscow Institute of International Relations (MGIMO University), Moscow, Russia
e-mail: nijat.asadli@ereforms.gov.az

I. Stepnov (ed.), *Technology and Business Strategy*,
https://doi.org/10.1007/978-3-030-63974-7_3

tools is accompanied by significant business errors that have strategic consequences and lead to losses (Bughin et al. 2018)—for example, Uber losses increased six-fold in 2019 (Habr 2019) and amounted to 5.2 billion dollars (Uber Investor 2019); in 2018, the company which provides shared workspaces and related services for WeWork startups had a total loss of $ 1.9 billion against total revenue of $ 1.8 billion (RIA Advisors 2019); the Wag! startup, created in 2015, whose activities are related to dog walking (the so-called "Uber dog"), attracted $ 300 million of investments, but in 2019 it reduced its staff due to the emergence of the Rover company, a competitor which provides services not only for dog walking but for cats too (CNN Business 2019). Assessment of WeWork's financial results is quite indicative (Fig. 3.1), since this company chose technological startups' activity as the source of its income, which makes its effectiveness an indirect indicator of the success of startups and unicorns; the loss-making Wag!, on the other hand, shows that copying a business model is also fraught with negative financial consequences. It was the negative results that unexpectedly (but quite justifiably on the part of company management) led to the strategic level of management expressing

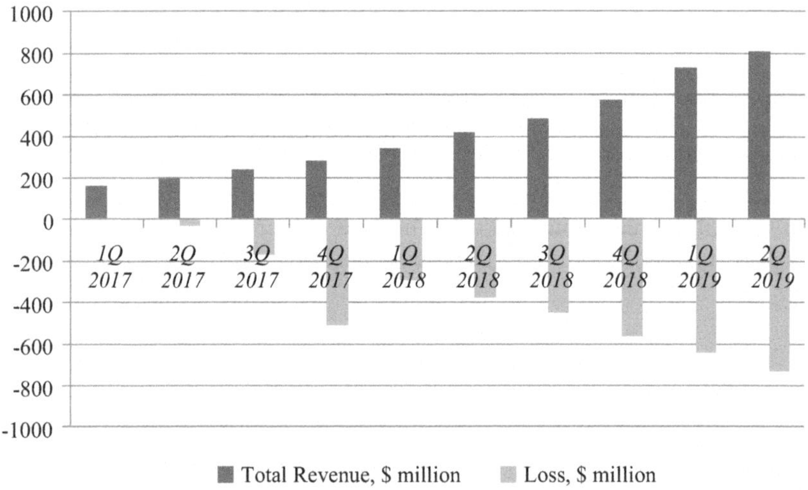

Fig. 3.1 WeWork financial performance. (Source: Compiled by the author using the following data: Craft.co (2019). *WeWork Stock price, funding rounds, valuation and financials*. Retrieved from https://craft.co/wework/metrics)

their interest in implementing digitalization technology programs, including those related to artificial intelligence.

It is quite obvious that this interest in strategizing arose not from scratch but in connection with the disappointing results of several startups focused on digitalization, the consequences of digitalization, its widespread use, and so on. The reason for this failure may be that there are currently no "strong" artificial intelligence systems that can completely replace a human being (Agrawal et al. 2019), and larger systems (or even some elements) of "weak" artificial intelligence are becoming more widely used to solve particular problems.

The relevance of the strategic implementation of the digital management format is confirmed by the following provisions:

Firstly, it turned out that the proposed—and widely developed—digital tools, despite their wide support and popularization, turn out to be quite expensive solutions which require not only significant initial costs but additional current ones too, especially when developing the concept of augmented management. The degree to which such costs are based, alongside attempts to predict them, are not entirely reliable, due to their experimental nature.

Secondly, as practice shows, obsession with pilot projects (like one of the features of the project office functioning, most often used in the development programs of the digital economy) is not a guaranteed commitment to further scaling. As it turned out, scaling has not become an integral attribute of a digital project, but instead required additional costs and primary solutions to be correspondingly adapted.

Thirdly, digital solutions and, especially, artificial intelligence have turned out to be dependent on the type of strategy the company uses. It is clear that many well-known strategies (including growth strategies, cost-reduction strategies, or blue ocean strategies) are, on the one hand, immune to digitalization in a particular industry, and, on the other hand, their choice requires additional justification.

Fourthly, a major role is played by the functionality of the leader in charge of digitalization. Despite the wide popularity of "digital officers", strategic management professionals should deal with the issues around introducing artificial intelligence, especially in industries that are experiencing not the first wave (such as medicine and education) but the second or the third wave of digitalization—aircraft construction, chip design, and so on.

Fifthly, passion for private tools, including those for digital marketing, is not currently leading to unequivocal proof of the effectiveness of the digital analysis. Artificial intelligence has not yet been able to turn the speed of computing and the amount of data used into quality, not yet offering a truly unique solution.

Sixthly, the issue of subordination arises—most managers are not going to be subordinate to artificial intelligence, although surveys of specialists and employees show that they are ready to work under the guidance of artificial intelligence. There are enthusiastic reviews on this in popular literature, but no professional research has been done in this area.

Seventhly, the interaction of Artificial Intelligence will affect work. Different types of artificial intelligence, made by various companies, are not yet demonstrating any meaningful cooperation; if this were possible, it may have not only a competitive advantage but also provoke the leakage of commercial information. However, the existing view of evaluating digital solutions has not yet shown any meaningful assessment of this provision.

These provisions not only confirmed the relevance of the study but also served as the basis for the proposed solutions.

Methodology

The combination of the provisions specified in the introduction has created a very important issue from the point of view of management: how is it possible to integrate digital technology, such as artificial intelligence, into management to achieve leadership? For this study, the task is limited by the author's hypothesis that management efficiency at present can only be achieved through the strategic use of digital and artificial intelligence technologies. Hence, an additional subtask arises: whether any strategy is yet suitable for application, or whether it is necessary to select the strategies that are most susceptible to artificial intelligence, and which strategies are susceptible to technological updating in the field of data processing.

Given the insufficient formalization of the tasks, in this study, we used such techniques as expert opinions, and surveys of business representatives, which are traditionally used to confirm the choice of strategy justification and special techniques for building strategies. We needed to confirm the data or to refute the research hypothesis, which is why we evaluated the results of surveys and identified the trends conducted by the largest consulting agencies (PWC, KPMG, Deloitte, EE&Y, McKinsey).

The research methods used include techniques and methods for processing the results of a sociological survey, processing the available empirical data (based on statistical approaches), preparing bibliographic reviews, and the results of the author's approach to comparing the potential of strategic decisions based on the matrix model.

Results and Discussion

To create a new digital value for increasing company efficiency, the only methods completely insufficient for implementing new technological programs are technological methods. Many companies implement pilot projects (not only after testing or approbation but also after practical use), but so far the potential of digital solutions has still not been established in business forecasts for additional income. This makes companies consider the digital part of business strategies as a technology, not as a source of additional income. Embedding digital tools and artificial intelligence is not a process that has been fully developed (Gans et al. 2019); initially, doing this should begin by choosing the intelligent solutions that are already known or whose consequences are also already identified with a high degree of probability. The strategic capabilities of artificial intelligence pose significant threats; incorrect actions can lead to irreversible consequences for the entire business.

Although modern intelligent solutions have several properties that, from the point of view of introducing innovations based on system analysis, are not unique, technical developers have only discovered these properties suddenly and unexpectedly. The most important of these is the understanding of the fact that modern intellectual solutions, like technical solutions in the past, do not have the built-in ability to generate cash flow and require appropriate organizational and management design. Most researchers take the position of either utopian solutions (with pessimistic forecasts) or are optimistic about the effectiveness of these decisions in the future, as digitalization and artificial intelligence increases.

The key issue is obtaining a competitive position in existing and emerging markets (for example, when replacing a product with a service), designing of which is just beginning. The issue of how regulation in such markets will take place is under debate, as is how equilibrium will be achieved, but the possibility of achieving equilibrium in digital markets should be taken into account when choosing strategies. To simplify the research task, we assumed that achieving (or not achieving) equilibrium happens after introducing digital technologies.

Summarizing well-known assessments of consulting companies and industry reviews ("Global Trends and Retail Opportunities in the Digital Transformation Era" by PwC (2018); "Digital Technologies in Russian Companies" by KPMG (2019); "New Rules of the Game in the Digital Era, Deloitte Research 'International Trends in Human Resource Management' for 2017" by Deloitte (2017); "Technology Industry" by E&Y (2019); "The economic essentials of digital strategy" by McKinsey (2016); "Trending Topics" by Gartner (2019)), we were able to provide the manifestations of the digital revolution in the modern society:

- robotics and automation of professions. As professions are automated, replacing employees with machines and algorithms is possible, but employees should be retained after automation to ensure that they are employed. These processes are also accompanied by job growth in the field of information technology and artificial intelligence (Frank et al. 2019), due to the growing need for new algorithms and data. It should be noted that the widely used indicator of the number of robots per one thousand jobs does not reflect the implementation of software (or algorithmic) robots, the number of which is increasing but is not reflected in statistics, as they are usually included into software;
- creating a new reality, both virtual and augmented, which particularly allows the creation of new spaces for trade and cooperation. The high complexity of virtual reality so far gives an advantage to the augmented reality, especially when organizing trading platforms or platforms for joint activities;
- the development of artificial intelligence tools in decision making. The concept of augmented management has already arisen, which is characterised not only by the use of various numerical models, but also by their actualization using practical activity data;
- the development of management tools. This is based on the concept of the Internet of Things, which leads to a significant advantage for such management compared to a traditional one;
- the development of infrastructure for digital activities. First of all, this includes the creation of 5G networks;
- increased crop yields. This is the comprehensive result of introducing software solutions, prognostic capabilities of artificial intelligence, infrastructure, and so on;

- biohacking. Biohacking helps to form and design the future markets based on an understanding of how needs are formed and how the interaction of artificial intelligence and humans will be organized;
- financial technologies. These not only provide resources with new innovative solutions, but also create new segments of financing.

These manifestations are provided in Table 3.1, where the author assessed the impact of digital innovations on basic strategies using results of 17 enterprises experts opinions. To conduct a comparative analysis of those strategies that make it possible to integrate with digital solutions, including artificial intelligence, three basic strategies were selected out of the number of business strategies: they include growth strategies (Ansoff 1988), cost-reduction strategies (Porter 1996; Collins and Hansen 2011; Thompson et al. 2013), and blue ocean strategies (Kim and Mauborgne 2005). These strategies were initially declared as having equal opportunities; initially, many companies chose a cost-cutting strategy for digitalization, but this proved to be viable only on a large scale, which meant that fast-growing companies achieved the greatest success either due to their growth strategy (which is more common) or due to the blue ocean strategy (which is much less common). However, it turns out that the influence individual digitalization factors have on the entire set of strategies is heterogeneous; the reason for this lies in the distinguishability of the factors influencing value creation and various processes.

An essential factor in the effectiveness of implementing digital solutions was the speed of updating new solutions—when a new effective solution seemed much faster than the previous one—reached its payback; this means that with digitalization (more precisely, with increased rates of digitalization and intellectualization), it turned out that readiness for change reduces efficiency (Ansoff 1984). Therefore, when assessing the impact of automation on strategies, this fact was also taken into account.

Considering the choice of strategies, two different solutions can be formed: either the creation of a matrix of factors and typical strategies or the creation of a lattice of models in which a separate model (which will be included in the integral model) is made for each factor. In our opinion, program-targeted methods are more applicable in terms of the first approach, whereas in terms of the second method the coordination of models is closer to the concept of portfolio formation. Considering that, under the same factor impact, artificial intelligence and digital solutions in general (as one of the manifestations of the digital economy) can affect

Table 3.1 Matrix for evaluating the feasibility of digital solutions or their consequences in typical strategies

Digital solutions and their consequences	*Growth strategy*	*Cost-reduction strategy*	*Blue ocean strategy*
Digital resources			
• databases	Yes	No	No
• data processing algorithms	Yes	No	No
• 5G network	Yes	No	Yes
• internet of things	Yes	Yes	Yes
Digital costs			
• replacing workplaces with machines	No	Yes	No
• replacing workplaces with algorithms	No	Yes	Yes
• retraining after automation	No	Yes	No
• retraining after release	No	Yes	Yes
• new jobs (IT and AI)	Yes	No	Yes
Digital finance			
• cryptocurrency	Yes	No	No
• digital payments (FINTECH)	Yes	Yes	No
• involving money in the economy when implementing a technological trend	Yes	No	Yes
Digital consumption			
• pricing based on artificial intelligence	No	Yes	No
• needs assessment	Yes	No	No
• creating a need	Yes	No	Yes
• the transition of trade into virtual reality	Yes	No	Yes
• transition of trade into augmented reality	Yes	No	No
Digital decision making			
• artificial intelligence	Yes	No	No
• augmented artificial intelligence	Yes	No	Yes
• virtual reality	No	No	Yes
• augmented reality	Yes	No	Yes
• increasing crop yields	Yes	No	No

Source: Developed by the author

business performance differently; it is now more appropriate to use matrix models, while data accumulation will provide more advantages to the portfolio models.

First of all, it should generally be concluded that it is the growth strategy involving the company's intensive development that receives the greatest advantage in Table 3.1. High costs for implementing digital solutions have a negative impact on the choice of a cost-cutting strategy

(Stepnov et al. 2018), since the volume of scaling should be substantial, but this is not yet achievable for many types of businesses.

The question of whether the development of artificial intelligence technologies demands a separate line of research, or should be integrated into the company's strategies (together with other technical solutions) has not yet been answered. Examples, however, of successful projects aimed at increasing yield answers it: it is clear that the complexity of the solution takes precedence. The analysis shows that the more successful strategies are the ones for increasing revenue (sales) based on digital solutions. Moreover, it is impossible not only to confirm but also to theoretically substantiate, the fact that, after introducing artificial intelligence, the one single initial cost reduction will then continue to reduce costs (except for making settlements and using the Internet of Things).

Conclusions

Technical methods for implementing these new technological programs, including algorithmization and data availability, may not be enough to create a new digital value to increase the efficiency of companies.

Enthusiasm alone from field experts for solving technical problems, leaving economic efficiency beyond their competence, cannot make artificial intelligence tools commercially successful. Therefore, commercializing digital solutions must be based on their integration with common strategies, not on creating independent solutions.

Creating a new digital value is only possible when a specific strategy is selected, which is then integrated into either growth strategies, cost-reduction strategies, or blue ocean strategies. In our opinion, it is the growth strategy that is most suitable for artificial intelligence, since the more widely advertised cost-cutting strategy has not yet proven indisputably successful when considering the influence of digitalization factors on the strategy's feasibility. At the same time, the responsibility for introducing artificial intelligence and technologies, in general, should be shared by all company leaders who implement the strategic vision, otherwise there can be not only indifference but also resistance to innovations, as was well known before new digital solutions were introduced.

It is also very important, in our opinion, to provide strategic support for scaling these projects rapidly. Figuratively speaking, artificial intelligence should not become a prize but a working tool available to most divisions of companies responsible for sales growth.

Further development of strategic research will be aimed at assessing the competitiveness of artificial intelligence in individual market segments.

References

Agrawal, A., Gans, J., & Goldfarb, A. (2019). Economic Policy for Artificial Intelligence. *Innovation Policy and the Economy, 19*, 139–159.

Ansoff, I. (1984). Modes of Strategic Behaviour. In I. Ansoff, D. Kipley, A. O. Lewis, & R. Helm-Stevens (Eds.), *Strategic Management Implanting* (pp. 311–336). Cham: Palgrave Macmillan.

Ansoff, I. (1988). *The New Corporate Strategy*. Somerset, NJ: John Wiley.

Bughin, J., Catlin, T., Hirt, M., & Willmott, P. (2018). Why Digital Strategies Fail. *McKinsey Quarterly*, no. 1, pp. 61–75.

CNN Business. (2019). *Dog-Walking Startup Wag Raised $ 300 Million to Unleash Growth. Then Things Got Messy*. Retrieved from https://edition.cnn.com/2019/09/27/tech/wag-dog-walking-softbank/index.html.

Collins, J., & Hansen, M. T. (2011). *Great by Choice: Uncertainty, Chaos, and Luck—Why Some the Thrive Despite Them the All (Good to Great)*. New York: HarperBusiness.

Deloitte. (2017). *New Rules of the Game in the Digital Age Deloitte's Study 'International Trends in Personnel Management' for 2017* (in Russian). Retrieved from https://www2.deloitte.com/content/dam/Deloitte/ru/Documents/human-capital/russian/hc-2017-global-human-capital-trends-gx-ru.pdf.

E&Y. (2019). *Technology Industry*. Retrieved from https://www.ey.com/ru/ru/industries/technology.

Frank, M. R., Autor, D., Bessen, J. E., Brynjolfsson, E., Cebrian, M., Deming, D. J., Feldman, M., Groh, M., Lobo, J., Moro, E., Wang, D., Youn, H., & Rahwan, I. (2019). Toward Understanding the Impact of Artificial Intelligence on Labor. *Proceedings of the National Academy of Sciences of the United States of America, 116*(14), 6531–6539.

Gans, J. S., Stern, S., & Wu, J. (2019). Foundations of Entrepreneurial Strategy. *Journal Management Strategic, 40*(1), 736–756.

Gartner. (2019). *Trending Topics*. Retrieved from https://www.gartner.com/en/information-technology/insights/trending-topics.

Habr. (2019). *Uber Had a Record Loss due to the IPO and the High Level of Competition* (in Russian). Retrieved from https://habr.com/en/news/t/463131/.

Kim, W. C., & Mauborgne, R. (2005). *Blue Ocean Strategy: How to Create Uncontested Market Space and Make the Competition Irrelevant*. Boston, MA: Harvard Business School Press.

KPMG. (2019). *Digital Technologies in Russian Companies* (in Russian). Retrieved from https://assets.kpmg/content/dam/kpmg/ru/pdf/2019/01/ru-ru-digital-technologies-in-russian-companies.pdf.

McKinsey. (2016). *The Economic Essentials of Digital Strategy.* Retrieved from https://www.mckinsey.com/business-functions/strategy-and-corporate-finance/our-insights/the-economic-essentials-of-digital-strategy.

Porter, M. E. (1996). What Is a Strategy? *Harvard Business Review, 74*(6), 61–78.

PwC. (2018). *Global Trends and Opportunities for Retail in the Era of Digital Transformations* (in Russian). Retrieved from https://www.pwc.ru/en/retail-consumer/publications/assets/pwc-retail-trends-final.pdf.

RIA Advisors. (2019). *WeWork's $ 1.9 Billion Loss Is A Typical Tech Bubble 2.0 Story.* Retrieved from https://realinvestmentadvice.com/weworks-1-9-billion-loss-is-a-typical-tech-bubble-2-0-story/.

Stepnov, I. M., Kovalchuk, J. A., Gorchakova, E. A., & Lukmanova, I. G. (2018). High Technology as a Driver of Changes in Industry (For Example Textile Industry). *Izvestiya Vysshikh Uchebnykh Zavedenii, Seriya Teknologiya Tekstil'noi Promyshlennosti*, no. 3, pp. 268–272.

TASS. (2019). *Industry: The Number of Enterprises Using Digital Technology Will Increase by Four Times in 5 Years* (in Russian). Retrieved from https://tass.ru/nacionalnye-proekty/6579888.

Thompson, A., Strickland, A. J., & Gamble, J. (2013). *Crafting and Executing Strategy: Readings and Concepts.* New York: McGraw-Hill Education.

Uber Investor. (2019). *Uber Reports Second Quarter 2019 Results.* Retrieved from https://investor.uber.com/news-events/news/press-release-details/2019/Uber-Reports-Second-Quarter-2019-Results/default.aspx.

World Economic Forum. (2018). *Digital Transformation Initiative In Collaboration with Accenture.* Retrieved from http://reports.weforum.org/digital-transformation/wp-content/blogs.dir/94/mp/files/pages/files/dti-executive-summary-20180510.pdf.

CHAPTER 4

Technological Revolution in Financial Intermediation

Galina Panova, Irina Larionova, and Istvan Lengyel

Introduction

The world has entered a new phase of development known as the "digital revolution"—the mass introduction of Big Data and computer technologies. The observed changes across the world are defined as "digital society", "digital civilization", and "digital economy". The latter is a response

G. Panova (✉)
Moscow State Institute of International Relations (MGIMO University), Moscow, Russia

I. Larionova
Moscow State Institute of International Relations (MGIMO University), Moscow, Russia

Financial University under the Government of the Russian Federation, Moscow, Russia

I. Lengyel
Banks' Association for Central and Eastern Europe (BACEE), Budapest, Hungary
e-mail: istvan.lengyel@bacee.hu

I. Stepnov (ed.), *Technology and Business Strategy*, https://doi.org/10.1007/978-3-030-63974-7_4

to the global challenges of the Fourth Industrial and Technological Revolution. "Digital economy" was presented at the World Economic Forum in Davos and the G20 Summit in Hangzhou as a driver of economic growth.

Global trends in the development of financial markets (structural changes in the world economy, the high volatility of national currencies in emerging markets; financial globalization; increased competition in financial markets; the development of information technology, financial innovation and financial engineering; the accumulation of risks and tightening regulation after the crisis) influence the domestic economy greatly.

Dynamic changes under the influence of technological revolutions in financial intermediation are seen in the banking sphere: (1) the automation of management and accounting; (2) electronic money transfer records on magnetic and optical media; (3) all payment transactions being carried out on the basis of information and computer technologies (ICT).

Promising ICT utilization in banks is to develop remote customer service channels (including automated electronic offices with customers using robots, biometric data, and identification by (amongst other individual characteristics) voice, the retinas, or the shape of lips). Private customers use plastic cards, mobile phones, computers, or internet banking in order to work speedily, reduce the cost of providing services, and improve the safety performance of operations for banks and their customers.

The digital revolution rapidly burst into the conservative sphere of the world of money. Truly revolutionary development was the emergence of the new alternative forms of money, called "electronic", "cyber", "digital", and "virtual". The emergence of private digital currency is associated with the development of the internet industry, cost optimization, e-commerce companies (Aliexpress, Ebay, etc.), and the emergence of the major international payment systems (ApplePay, SamsungPay, LGPay, AliPay, etc.). However, some experts consider private digital currencies (bitcoin, etherium, litcoin, etc.) as a tool of the internet industry on the one hand, yet, on the other, as an instrument which optimizes tax deductions and develops the shadow economy, drug-trafficking, and traditional currencies (US dollar, Euro, Pound sterling, Japanese Yen etc.) losing their influence in the market.

However, it is important to emphasize that digital currency is only one element of modern payment and settlement systems. The emergence of new digital currencies involves the development of norms and rules regulating their use; information infrastructure; definitions of information security issues; regulation of cyber-risks; training and education in the field of information technology; improving financial literacy; the formation of research competences. It also requires thinking in terms of opportunities and risks for humans and society in general, as well as the practical use of mechanisms and establishment of digital platforms.

The emergence of digital currencies involves (amongst other things) the development of a particular regulation; creating an information infrastructure; information security; regulating digital risks; and retraining and improving the financial literacy of the population. In this context, a number of central banks have started developing their own (national) digital currencies (Bank of China, for example). The Parliament of Japan adopted a law in 2017 under which digital currencies received the status of legitimate money; now bitcoins are used for payments in cashless form through the electronic settlements system. Regulators believe that the digital currency use will improve security, reduce the cost of cash emission, improve transparency of calculations, and so on. The likelihood of this, and the impact of the digital economy on the scope of traditional money, are still debatable.

Criminals managed to steal amounts in cash equivalent to 49 million dollars from the British Central Bank (2006), 69 million dollars from Brazil's Central Bank (2005), and 17.2 million dollars from the Bank of France (2009). Since then there is no evidence of large robberies of central banks or private commercial banks in the form of cash. However, information and computer innovations have resulted in the rapid rise of an era of electronic theft. The objects of theft have become non-cash money and customer information (personal data, information about transactions, credit, etc.). In the era of the "digital civilization", information becomes a commodity that has its price and consumers. In 2016, hackers attacked SWIFT and stole 81 million dollars from the Central Bank of Bangladesh. Recently, a number of countries have enacted laws on personal data protection. However, the number of victims is now millions of people worldwide. Hacker attacks on banks are no longer limited to the theft of money and information. Now this digital threat may be destroying or weakening a bank's competitive position (e.g., bank systems after infection by viruses, etc.).

Most modern people, especially representatives of the younger generation, are reliant upon their smartphone, electronic device, or a bank card. Data security on these devices, the regulatory framework for the protection of personal data, and how secure savings are raises many questions.

Prospects of the digital economy are unthinkable without productive cooperation between business and state; the conditions of such interaction are transparency, credibility, and innovation relationship.

Methodology

The study uses comparative methods, benchmarking to market practices, and international consultancy recommendations. Among these are the results of research projects conducted by Allen, Santomero, Merton and other theoretical and empirical researches. Merton, for example, was an early contributor to the theoretical understanding and analysis of financial intermediation; speaking about the so-called functional perspective, he pointed out that any financial system should ensure the implementation of a complex of basic functions and structures for regulating the financial sector's institutions, which are much less stable and may transform within country jurisdictions (Merton 1995).

The new approach sparked debate in economic literature and attempts were made to find an explanation of the organizational changes in financial markets. Confirmation of these changes has been the rapid development of the so-called shadow (unregulated) banking system. The participants of that system perform intermediary and credit functions for households and companies faster and at less expense than traditional banks. However, innovations supported financial and credit institutions growing in their efficiency and functioning, yet at the same time led to a significant increase in systemic risks that materialized during the global financial crisis (2008–2009).

The foundations for the analysis were the reports and other materials of the World Bank (2020), Bank for International Settlements (2001), PwC, Deloitte Center for Financial Services, Bloomberg, Citibank, La Caixa Bank (Spain), Banking Association for Central and Eastern Europe (BACEE, Hungary), Association of Russian Banks (ARB), Sberbank and Tinkoff Bank (Russia), and other such institutions.

The main objectives of the chapter are to reveal the modern problems of the change in the finance industry, how it impacts traditional banks, and the method for its further development.

Results

Fintech Companies and Traditional Banks: Constructive Engagement and/or Destructive Competition

The key to increased productivity in banks is the automatization of their services. New advertising technology is founded on the principle of "to every client—an individual approach and separate product" ("one to one"). It allows the bank employee to instantly receive data on the socio-demographic, professional, or property status of the client, as well as on the structure of their income and expenditure. All this information allows the banker to take the necessary and most effective solutions in the shortest possible time.

Resistance databases for storing customers' personal information are also an important parameter when considering this issue. Data security is a critical indicator of the banking business' efficiency. Privacy access implies the differentiation of levels of access to databases for employees of the bank. Innovative services increase the quality of the bank customer service, and ensure a high level of reliability of the payment system, whilst simultaneously releasing employees to work on more promising areas.

The introduction of new technologies require the banking sector development to look into the following: (1) modular design; (2) openness to new technologies and systems; (3) flexible banking modules and their adaptability to the needs of a specific bank; (4) scalability, expansion, and increasing complexity of functional systems with the development of the structure of commercial bank; (5) wide access to online databases with the preservation of differentiable access levels; (6) modeling of the banks' business processes; (7) the development and improvement of the system through the reengineering of business processes.

For example, "Sberbank" employees provide their customers automated banking services, introducing new remote service channels. Sberbank has implemented: Sberbank-Online (more than 30 million users); mobile application Sberbank-Online for smart phones (more than 18 million users); SMS-service "mobile banking" (more than 30 million users); the largest network of ATMs and self-service terminals (more than 90 thousand devices). These processes are due to lead to a twofold reduction in staff by 2025.

Tinkoff Bank is a Russian online bank that has no ATMs and offices. Instead, Tinkoff uses voice identification for fraud protection and accelerates the work of its call center, as well as using large data processing technology, including data from social networks to predict credit risk.

Financial technology is a prime example of how the technological revolution has affected quite a conservative financial sector, which is still using traditional services (deposits, lending, etc.). After all, the large retail banks are no longer the sole players in the financial market. Fintech is betting on high availability, speed, and comfort; it is currently gaining the trust of customers.

Modern Problems of Banks: Background Change in the Industry

The Problem of Millennials

Sociologists created the so-called Millennial Disruption Index to assess potential changes in the global economy that may arise from the growing involvement of younger people (millennials). According to it, the institutes most at risk are banks. It notes record low fidelity to banks: 53% of respondents believe that their bank does not offer anything special compared to others, 33% are ready to change bank in the next 90 days, and 33% see no point in banks. Most importantly, 73% more likely wish to use new financial services from major technology companies like Google and Facebook than have to deal with traditional banks. The needs of the new generation are an affront to the entire banking system.

The Problem of the "Under-Banked"

According to the World Bank, 2.5 billion adults (about half of the working population) are formally isolated from the global financial system. In many regions of the world, there are almost no banks; other populations (for a variety of reasons) simply do not trust their savings to banks. Nearly 60% of the adult population of Mexico has never opened a deposit in the official financial institution, yet 97% of the population lives in an area with a minimum of one point of access to the formal financial system. The proposed statistics of the Bank for International Settlements (2015) means serious weaknesses in the banking system of Mexico—otherwise one of the most stable in the world.

The Problem of the Consequences of the Crisis

After the crisis of 2008–2010, confidence in banks fell sharply. The crisis entailed serious new restrictions for banks: they increased lending rates (due to new capital and liquidity adequacy standards imposed by the Basel Committee on banking regulation) and grew commissions for payments and transfers (because banks have been looking for new ways to develop a new financial ecosystem). In addition, lending to small and medium-sized businesses significantly reduced.

Fintech Is an Attempt to Solve Problems

In light of falling reputation of banks, new opportunities for the development of fintech-companies and the fintech-industry appeared.

In the past, buying shares and investments was a habit of the rich. Today, the situation has changed. The creation of crowd-funding platforms (Kickstarter, Crowdcube, etc.) has provided everyone with opportunities to invest in different projects without any charges and minimal expenses.

One serious competitor for banking services is the P2P lending system, which is regarded as an equitable system of lending. The market of loans granted through the P2P system is constantly growing, and now provides clients the opportunity to open a deposit under more advantageous interest than in a bank. In the conservative financial industry, the demand has spawned the proposed creation of a new technology industry—FINTECH—serving three main directions: payments and transfers, equitable lending, and investing.

Payments and Transfers

About 23% of investments in Fintech in recent years have focused on the development of the system of payments and transfers. People around the globe submit $3 trillion to each other annually, so many entrepreneurs see in this area a lot of room for development. One of the most successful projects in this field recognizes the service of the international transfers system, Transferwise, which competes with the largest banks and such giants as Western Union.

The world's first mobile payment system M-Pesa was launched in 2007 by the Vodafone subsidiary and the largest cellular operator Safaricom. Now it provides access to basic financial services to the population of Kenya. User friendliness (the service was integrated into the SIM card) led to almost 85% of the adult population of the country enjoying mobile wallets to pay for cellular operators and small remittances.

Investing
Until recently, buying shares and investing in general were only for the rich. Today the situation has changed dramatically. Many crowd-funding sites (Kickstarter, Indiegogo, Crowdcube, etc.), where anyone can visit the site, download the app, and invest in one of many projects (from a rock band to a drone service center; or in projects for millennials, such as application Robinhood, where stocks can be traded for American companies and simple operations on the Exchange can be performed without any charges and minimum contributions), are undermining this traditional hierarchy.

Lending
The proportion of investments in financial technology as loans accounted for more than 46%. The P2P lending system is among the other serious competitors of banking services. Equitable lending first emerged in the UK in 2005, when the system Zopa was founded.[1] Today, the total volume of loans via the P2P system amounts to $2.6 billion. This figure is thus far incompatible with traffic in large banks, but the market is growing. Moreover, in addition, P2P loans provide the ability to open a deposit under more advantageous interest than banks offer. People can also open a deposit in the small electronic banks.

Competition or Cooperation?

Traditional banks are worried that their business may be at risk due to the development of the segment of financial technologies. Fintech companies expect to receive 33% of the traditional banking business. Citibank forecasts that the growth in the influence of financial technologies could lead to the loss of work for 30% of banks by 2025 (Citibank Report 2016); in early 2015, the Director General of the Spanish bank BBVA predicted that half of the world's banks will disappear under the onslaught of Digital industry and Fintech waves.

Banks need cooperation with Fintech-companies. Big banks can open up enormous opportunities for Fintech-companies and give them access to global payment systems. Many banks have already realized that cooperation is the key to survival and prosperity in the midst of a technological revolution, and cooperation is the more sensible solution than

[1] https://www.zopa.com/.

competition. For banks and startups, Fintech profitably joins forces to resist the onslaught of technology giants such as Apple, Google, and Facebook, which are gradually coming into the financial services market.

In addition, if the banks need to cooperate (mainly for survival) in a new environment, Fintech firms provide tremendous opportunities. Logging on to financial markets was always a complicated hurdle, as were other regulatory standards. Some services that seek to provide their own Fintech-company can be provided only to those who have a banking license. Moreover, the big banks can offer Fintech companies their broad customer base and access to global payment systems. As a result, cooperation with banks for Fintech companies is profitable, because it lowers the barriers of entry to the financial markets and invites a higher level of trust.

A good example of cooperation can be seen in the experience of leading Spanish bank La Caixa and its competent customer segmentation. To increase proximity to customers and increase their confidence in financial services, this leading Spanish bank found an innovative solution—it joined with Fintech teams to develop products targeted at different consumer groups. Some examples are:

- imaginBank—banking services within the Group of "La Caixa", existing only in the form of a mobile application focused on the 18–35 year-old segment of customers;
- Hola Bank—a service for expats to provide them banking services as "at home";
- Family-Bank is aimed towards Spanish families and offers various discount programs, preferential loans, and other services.

Due to the innovative approach, La Caixa bank expanded its market share for 6 years from 10.2% to 16.1% and became the largest retail bank in Spain, with 13.8 million customers.[2]

JP Morgan Chase uses cooperation with a Fintech start-up to credit 4 million small and medium business customers (Son 2015). It entered into partnership with OnDeck— one of the largest online platforms for lending to SMEs. This decision allowed a small self-funded startup to significantly reduce spending, which attracts borrowers and capital (loans are granted at the expense of JP Morgan). Also, the bank used the competitive advantages of startups such as flexibility and speedy decision-making.

[2] https://www.caixabank.es/particular/holabank/particulares_en.html#.

Thus, it has become obvious that the most natural option for banks will be building cooperation with small teams of experts in the field of financial technologies, to confront technological giants, maintain a client base, and reduce costs.

Financial Innovation, Risks, and Institutional Stability of Banks

The global monetary system now is "drifting away" from a system which unites the national monetary systems, based on national currency turnover, to a multi-currency system, based on the broad application of advanced information technologies.

Digital currencies are actively used very differently across the world; they are prohibited in some countries, while in others, on the contrary, they are very actively used. The most active users of bitcoins are clients from Spain, Sweden, Germany, and Argentina. South Korea plans to adopt a law on the legalization of digital currencies. Japan is the only country in the world where state control on digital currencies transactions has been implemented. At present, there is a high probability of public digital currencies coming into play.

On the contrary, Chinese authorities banned the production of bitcoins. The Central Bank of Russia continues to examine the treatment of digital currencies and use of technologies, taking into account the associated risks. CBR, as mega-regulator of financial markets, is highly concerned about the possibility of losing control of money supplies, as this is fraught with grave economic and political consequences. In the future, digital currencies will find their rightful place in the global payment system, provided effective adoption of new digital technology is used whilst keeping control of financial markets at the national and international levels.

Digital Currencies Market: Security Aspects

In general, cryptocurrency is a new phenomenon—an element of a fundamentally new monetary system. While one single solution for digital future monetary strategies does not exist yet, it seems essential that the competitive development of payment systems with a large number of electronic money issuers should be subject to mandatory control regulators in financial markets.

The main advantage of digital currency as a means of payment is its high level of security (Inozemtsev 2021). The Blockchain system determines the basis for its sustainability. The absence of an intermediary institution—not only for funds transfer, but also to confirm their occurrence in a hashed (encrypted) form—increases the level of confidence in the reliability and security of funds. The reliability of the system is based on the superiority of total power devices by market players over potential attackers. However, problems still appear while moving, for example, to new versions of the software, or the ingress of harmful software from the network, so teething issues are still ongoing.

Initially, the high growth rates of digital currencies explain the simplicity of their "production" and the need to provide major rewards for the first participants taking the risks and participating at an early stage of the system. Then, with the growth in demand for digital currency and rising costs on the single unit of cryptocurrency, emission rates decreases sharply.

Special keys provide transparency and anonymity of transactions. Any user is able to trace the path of circulation of each currency unit. The digital signature can be specified by email and the nickname of the person who conducted the transaction. However, the data is not directly associated with the person, who could remain anonymous. In addition, access to compromised electronic purses can only be accessed through this proof of identity to a digital signature, which verifies the owner of a purse from an attacker.

Adding timestamps in the course of transactions registers the chronology of their creation, which largely prevents fraud and demonstrates a way of handling of each currency unit. In addition, the validity of transactions can be easily verified by the system participants. Thus, Blockchain sets the sequence of transactions, improves cryptographic strength, and eliminates many kinds of fraud.

Financial Sector Technological Revolution. The Russian Case

According to the last data, Russia ranks among the top 10 internet using countries in Europe, being second after Germany. The results of a recent ESET company study demonstrated the commitment of Russians who actively use digital currencies.

Bills on digital assets, issuance, and digital currency circulations are currently under debate. Interaction amongst mega-projects is being developed with financial market participants engaged in digital currency transactions. The Central Bank of Russia (CBR) has gradually introduced new rules on the use of digital platforms. For example, a digital platform for remote client identification was introduced in 2018; this can increase the level of competition in the banking sector, while simplifying the interface and enhancing protection of customers' biometric data. At the same time, the CBR is working on digital platforms for fast payments systems (payments by email or phone number), as well as the development of plastic card payments systems. However, while a single decision on a further development strategy in this area has not been accepted, it can be assumed that digital technology can be used for upgrading or developing innovative public payment systems, which will reduce costs of treatment and increase the speed and security of payment transactions. Because the new payment system, operating on the basis of digital technology, will have the status of a state payment system; such institutions will receive the necessary support and the confidence of those economic agents that eliminate systemic problems in existing private payment systems.

On February 2, 2018, CBR opened the first Russian competence center on combating illegal activities in the financial market. The basic directions of its work are: identifying market players, working without licenses and entering them into a database; maintaining resistance to "financial pyramids", "black creditors", illegal insurance, and Forex dealers; collecting information on organizers of the fraudulent schemes; initiating inspections; and applying interventions to offenders.

The use of money surrogates is prohibited in Russia. However, there is fertile ground for the issuance of decentralized cryptocurrencies.

The Russian Ministry of Finance published the Bill "On Digital Assets" to identify the status of digital technologies used in the financial sphere and their basic notions, including cryptocurrency. According to the document, tokens, and other digital assets, can be exchanged for rubles, foreign currency, or other property, but only through the operation of digital financial assets exchange. The Bill also limits the amount by which non-qualified investors can buy tokens in one ICO (placing tokens to obtain financing) to no more than 50 thousand rubles.

According to Moiseev, the Russian Deputy Minister of Finance, cryptocurrency exchange for rubles and other assets can be permitted in some territories of the Russian Federation. In particular, the Ministry is currently considering the possibility of implementing organized trades on the Russian Island and the October Island, where a special regime can be entered. He stressed that the exchange of cryptocurrencies on the territory of Russia could solve the task of whitewashing the market. However, the Ministry of Finance and the Bank of Russia have not yet agreed on the exchange of cryptocurrency in rubles or other assets. According to the Central Bank of Russia, such transactions should be allowed only in respect of tokens. The Ministry of Finance in turn emphasizes that it does not involve the use of cryptocurrencies as legal means of payment in Russia. Currently, the Ministry of Finance is finalizing a draft law, which will define the concept of "cash surrogates" and establish responsibility for their use as a means of payment. This is necessary to protect the ruble as the sole legitimate settlement fund in Russia.

Ex Premier Dmitry Medvedev proposed legal regulation of digital money in international conventions at the forum "Digital Agenda in the Age of Globalization" in Almaty on February 2, 2018. In his view, Blockchain technology has a tremendous future. Given the evidence and the possibility of its application in Russia, this is a positive approach.

In September 2015, Russian mass media disseminated information about the possible issue of the first Russian virtual currency—Bitruble. The Qiwi payment system stated that it is ready to launch this cryptocurrency, provided that there was agreement with the Central Bank of Russia on this issue. The Company "Yandex.Money" is also interested in participating in transactions with cryptocurrency, if it is allowed by the Bank of Russia.

At the same time, regulators have repeatedly reiterated their misgivings about this payment tool. For example, on September 17, 2015, at the forum of innovative financial technologies "Finnopolis", chair of the Bank of Russia Elvira Nabiullina said that the Russian mega-regulator of financial markets will continue to examine the question of the treatment of digital money and the use of crypto-technology in the view of accompanying risks:

- The possibility of carrying out suspicious transactions. Using cryptocurrencies, which can be redeemed for real money, carries risks in the field of combating money-laundering;
- Russians in general are not well informed about the details of working with digital money. People do not always realize that accumulating bitcoins may lead them to lose their money, because they are not insured by a deposit insurance agency;
- CBR, as mega-regulator of financial markets, could lose control of the money supply, which is fraught with grave economic and political consequences.

Deputy Finance Minister Moiseyev reported that the Russian Government is going to discuss the draft law (on cryptocurrencies), but given that no global standards for the treatment and management of cryptocurrencies exist yet, in these circumstances, pre-emptive regulations in this field have meaning only after a "stable world practice" is worked out. The Finance Ministry believes that the Russian authorities should be wary of the emergence of cryptocurrencies in Russia, because they run the risk of money laundering.

French legal experts, and employees of one of their largest banks, Dominique Burrine and Ethier More demonstrate a similar approach. Because currently the international legal status of bitcoins is not defined, it is not possible to include this type of tool in any financial categories. Bitcoin is not currency. It does not have an exchange rate. It is not a means of payment and not even technically electronic money, according to legislation in many states. However, such uncertainty does not prevent some market players using cryptocurrency as a product amidst this risky financial instrument. The absence of cryptocurrency regulation does not give their owners any guarantees regarding prices and liquidity. Moreover, users are not protected from even bitcoins' simple technical failure. In this regard, their proposal to develop an international legal framework that would regulate the treatment of bitcoins and other cryptocurrencies, which was published in the specialist magazine "Les Echos", deserves attention and support.

However, digital money is located at the intersection of two technologies—financial and information. Recently it became known that the IBM Corporation, one of the largest technology companies, opened a Blockchain laboratory. The company plans to use large computing power to determine possible potential of cybercurrency. It is assumed that the lab will simulate cyber-currency practical cases, ranging from payment applications to the possibility of money laundering. The creators of the laboratory are intent on developing open standards for the use of Blockchain technology in the field of financial services; it will be a breakthrough for introducing crypto-technology into the payment systems mass market.

Deloitte Consulting firm has analyzed the factors that will have an impact on global financial markets in the coming years, and along with demographic, consumer, and similar factors, referred to the digital factors such as the development of artificial intelligence, neural networks, and Blockchain and cryptocurrencies. Deloitte Center for Financial Services qualifies Blockchain as "perhaps the most important innovation of all", considering that the technology has the potential to change the payments market, which is estimated at $26 trillion (Deloitte, 2015). Changes that can allow for Blockchain are speeding up transactions, reducing transaction costs, and eliminating intermediaries. Deloitte predicts that private Blockchain will also spread, particularly through banks.

Blockchain payment systems should significantly increase their volume of transactions in 2020, while the proliferation of other systems on the basis of this same technology will become a reality closer to 2025. Deloitte assumes that "probably Bitcoin and other digital currencies will dominate". However, their widespread adoption lacks two factors: the incompatibility between Blockchains and compliance with global regulatory standards.

Nonetheless, while one single decision on a further development strategy in this area is not yet accepted, experts have suggested that existing differences may eventually lead to the emergence of new digital currencies and have even started talking about a possible collapse of Bitcoin, because the transactions are anonymous, and their turnover until recently was not regulated in any way.

Crypto-technologies can be used for upgrading or developing innovative public payment systems, which will reduce the costs of treatment and increase the speed and security of payment transactions. Because the new payment system, operating on the basis of crypto-technologies, will have the status of a state, they will receive the necessary support and the confidence of economic agents that eliminate systemic problems ongoing in private payment systems based on digital currencies.

Given that payment systems are usually intended to achieve specific operating and economic performances, it is important to highlight some fundamental elements that require special attention: a formal agreement between members of the system; agreed and accepted technical standards; methods of payment orders and circulation between participants; concerted clearing procedures for participant claims and resolving liquidity problems; general procedures and work rules, including timetable, criteria for participation, commission rate, and so on.

In countries with advanced economies, stable monetary systems, and traditional banking, cryptocurrencies will occupy a niche in which their use is most effective. In developing countries with young and sometimes unsustainable monetary systems, the need to maintain tight control during their implementation is of great importance. For example, the huge territory of Russia, with (among other factors) relatively cheap electricity and a high level of education, allows experts to consider the question of Russia becoming an International Financial Centre of Cyber Currencies.

Progress has placed new demands on the economy and the existing payment systems. Distribution of payment systems on the basis of cyber currencies is a reality now. Financial regulators around the world are currently working on mechanisms for their implementation in a traditional payment system, which would enhance efficiency and competitiveness. However, cybercurrencies obviously will find their rightful place in the global payment system only if there is the effective adoption of new digital technologies (including Blockchain), while retaining control of financial markets at the national and international levels.

Conclusions/Recommendations

Digital transformation in financial intermediation shows finance–credit institutions still have the possibility to "survive", but this requires being receptive to technological innovation, maintaining financial stability, and focusing on the client. In other words, the business model of these financial intermediaries will become competitive.

However, major Russian credit organizations, which belong to a cluster of systemically important banks, favorably differ, and are not being slow on adapting their equipment and advancing in their use of technology and information from western institutions. At the same time, a large number of small-scale banks do not have sufficient resources for technological innovation. This does not mean that banks will not be able to overcome the challenges of the digital revolution. The future effectiveness of customer-oriented banks' business models will be determined by modern channels of financial products delivery, their selection in accordance with customer needs, and their responsiveness to price dynamics.

Taking into account the results of sociological surveys, an analysis of current practice and the prospects of development in the financial sphere shows that the innovative business model of modern credit institutions, in the context of the digitalization of the economy, is one of the promising future research directions.

Analysis of factors and development trends of both the global and the Russian economy is the basis for the scientific understanding of the situation and prompts proposals for specific steps to bring the Russian economy in line with new industrialization, ensuring its optimal stable growth and development. To achieve this, it is necessary not only to conduct scenario analysis, but also to develop a specific plan of action in the light of (at least): elaboration of a theoretical framework; methodologies for solving tasks; determining the necessary tools to ensure organizational and administrative, managerial, and institutional solutions. Scientists and practitioners need to build a strategy for socio-economic development in Russia on a qualitatively new level, taking into account the lessons of the global financial and economic crisis, as well as the latest trends of international development.

The competitiveness of the banking system—and the economy as a whole—depend on the ability of the system to provide high-quality and appropriate financial intermediation services for all Russian economic agents, whether of large- and medium-sized businesses, or small businesses and individuals.

Despite all the advantages of rapid technological innovations for banks, Fintech companies, and their customers, there are still many unresolved issues that should be discussed. The business model of the modern credit institution, in the context of the digitalization of the economy, is one of these problems. The authors do not share the views of those experts, scientists, and businessmen who predict that banks, in the context of this digitalization, will lose their market share as a result of Fintech company competition. Firstly, the significant risks remain; the majority of these risks are not defined yet and, consequently, possible loss is underestimated. Secondly, the majority of customers, especially in developing economies, are sticking to conservative behavior and prefer to work with monetary institutions. Thirdly, most countries do not have sufficient financial resources; moreover, there is evidence of debt pressure growing. Fourthly, the problem of security for cryptocurrency transactions and operations will be paramount; it is no coincidence that national regulators in different jurisdictions, in accordance with new standards, have expanded the list of operational risk to include cyber risks. Methodological and technological maintenance in this area, alongside the evaluation of risk impact, is only in its infancy. However, banking practices of distance work with their customers commits considerable losses. In this regard, the early recognition of this situation, from our point of view, will slow down the rapid use of financial technologies, which will create conditions for reformatting the business model of banks, which will in turn become more secure and familiar to the customers.

References

Bank for International Settlements. (2001). *A Glossary of Terms Used in Payments and Settlements Systems*. Retrieved from http://www.bis.org.

Bank for International Settlements. (2015). Press Release of the Bank for International Settlements on Implementing the Standards 'Basel 3' in Mexico. Retrieved from http://www.bis.org/press/p150316.htm.

Citibank Report. (2016). *Digital Disruption: How FinTech Is Forcing Banking to a Tipping Point*. Retrieved from https://www.citivelocity.com/citigps/ReportSeries.action?recordId=51.

Inozemtsev, M. I. (2021). Taxonomy and Typology of Crypto-Assets: Approaches of International Organizations. *Lecture Notes in Networks and Systems, 139*, 122–133. https://doi.org/10.1007/978-3-030-53277-2_14.

Merton, R. C. (1995). Functional Perspective of Financial Intermediation. *Financial Management, 24*(2), 23–41.

Son, H. (2015). JP Morgan Working With On Deck to Speed Small-Business Loans. *Bloomberg*. Retrieved from http://www.bloomberg.com/news/articles/2015-12-01/jpmorgan-working-with-on-deck-capital-for-small-business-loans.

World Bank. (2020). Retrieved from http://datatopics.worldbank.org/financialinclusion/country/mexico.

CHAPTER 5

The Digital Vector of Ensuring Economic Security of the Company

Artem Krivtsov and Leyla Berdnikova

Introduction

Economic security can be viewed as a qualitative characteristic of the economic system that ensures the stable functioning of business structures. In turn, the stability of the modern economic system of the state depends on the stable functioning of individual economic entities that represent its structural unit. Thus, there is a close interconnection of economic security at the macro and micro levels. A significant contribution to the study of theoretical, methodological and practical issues of sustainable development of an organization and its safety was made by scientists such as: M. A. Basuony (2014), S. Biazzo and P. Garengo (2012), A. A. Malgwi and H. Dahiru (2014), Y. Gong (2013), G. Lawrie and I. Cobbold (2015), H. Rampersad and S. Hussain (2014). However, digital

A. Krivtsov (✉)
Moscow Institute of International Relations (MGIMO University), Moscow, Russia

L. Berdnikova
Togliatti State University, Togliatti, Russia

I. Stepnov (ed.), *Technology and Business Strategy*,
https://doi.org/10.1007/978-3-030-63974-7_5

transformation processes significantly affect the activities of business units and require a detailed study of indicators that make it possible to timely diagnose the risks of reducing economic security. The lack of developments in this area entails the need for additional research and improvement of the elements of economic security and the algorithm for its management in the context of business digitalization, which confirms the relevance of the research topic.

The main goal of this chapter is to improve the theoretical and methodological apparatus aimed at ensuring the economic security of companies in the digital economy.

Methodology

In the process of executing this study, materials from scientific literature, periodicals devoted to the topic of research were used. In the course of writing the chapter, general scientific methods of cognition were used: analysis, synthesis, comparison, grouping, dialectical and complex approaches that allow to form reasonable conclusions.

Results

Currently, in scientific research there are various approaches to the concept of "economic security". On the one hand, the economic security of an organization is understood as a state of an economic entity that provides a high degree of protection of the key components of its structure and financial and economic activities from negative changes, and in which potential dangers are not allowed with a certain probability. On the other hand, the economic security of an enterprise is determined by the protection of its vital interests from the influence of external and internal factors.

Modern conditions of digitalization dictate new conditions for ensuring the economic security of organizations, protecting its interests and all types of corporate resources.

Digital transformation is characterized by the introduction of advanced technologies into the business processes of business entities. This transformation involves not only the acquisition and use of technological equipment, modern software products, but also changes in approaches to the perception of business processes, management methods, communication relationships with partners. Digitalization technologies provide new business opportunities. Digital communication channels, robotization, artificial intelligence, chat bots are becoming common elements of everyday life. It is digitalization that makes it possible to increase the productivity of personnel and the profitability of the enterprise, reduce the time for carrying out certain operations, and optimize the functionality of personnel. However, despite many positive aspects of digitalization processes, it carries atypical types of risks and requires special approaches to ensuring the economic security of organizations.

We believe that economic security in the context of digital transformation is determined by the protection of all areas of activity and business processes of the organization from the adverse impact of risks, building reliable protection of assets and corporate resources, using effective information and communication channels that contribute to the accumulation, broadcasting and storage of data, as well as the formation of conditions necessary for its successful development.

The economic security of an enterprise is a complex multifaceted structure that accumulates a system of interrelated elements. In Fig. 5.1, we present the main elements of ensuring the economic security of an organization in the context of business digitalization. In our opinion, these include:

- personnel and intellectual resources;
- financial resources;
- informational resources;
- progressive technology;
- IT technologies;
- communication links and technologies;
- material resources;
- innovation and intangible assets.

In modern conditions, these elements are involved in the digital transformation process and can affect the economic security of an organization.

The digital vector of economic development in general and business in particular contributes to the emergence of atypical types of risks that can lead to insolvency of the organization, loss of business activity, loss of market position and decrease in economic security. The reasons for such risks can be the influence of both external and internal factors. Internal factors that reduce the economic security of an enterprise in the context of digitalization include:

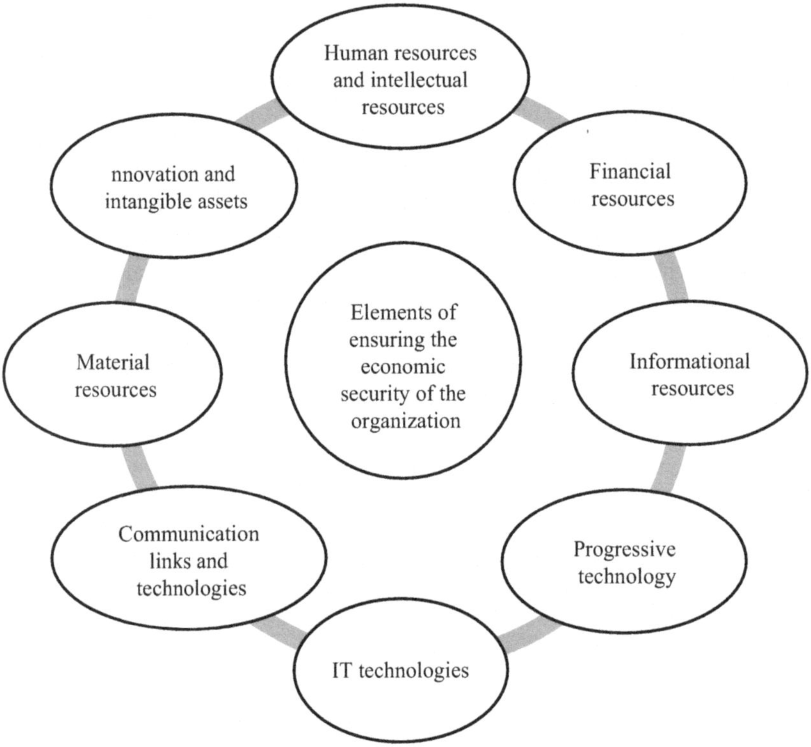

Fig. 5.1 The main elements of ensuring the economic security of an organization in the context of business digitalization. (*Source*: *developed by the authors*)

- shortcomings in strategic planning and determination of the company's development strategy;
- errors in tactical actions and untimely response to challenges from the external environment;
- ineffective resource management;
- lack of financial resources;
- lack of control over the business processes and financial flows of the organization;
- low protection of communication links;
- violations of technological processes;
- unfavorable climate within the team;

- dissatisfaction of personnel with working conditions and wages;
- low qualification of personnel;
- unjustified savings on the means of protecting assets and information.

External factors that threaten the economic security of an organization in the context of digital transformation include:

- instability of the external environment;
- financial crises;
- increased competition;
- changes in legislation that may directly affect the company's activities;
- decrease in consumer demand;
- growth of inflation;
- force majeure of a global scale (for example, a pandemic, earthquake, flood, etc.).

Based on the study, we will clarify the atypical types of risks of reducing the economic security of an organization that are characteristic of the digital economy. In our opinion, these include:

- the risk of cyber attacks associated with digital transformation;
- risks of external information technology impacts on the company's business processes;
- risks of data loss due to technical errors and software viruses;
- risks of leakage of databases and confidential information;
- risks of cyber fraud in the company's financial transactions;
- risks of protecting innovations and intellectual property due to imperfect legislation regulating and ensuring digital transformation processes;
- risks of information attacks;
- risks of spreading malicious content,
- risks of spreading false information compromising the business reputation of the enterprise.

The digital vector of ensuring economic security is based on an effective strategy. Its key types include: the strategy of preventive measures and the strategy of operational measures.

The strategy of preventive measures is aimed at proactively identifying potential risks and preventing or minimizing them. Preventive measures of this strategy include:

- preliminary assessment of counterparties' activities;
- analysis of planned transactions;
- market analysis;
- prevention of external and internal risks;
- regular control over the activities of the organization and others.

The strategy of operational measures can be used to ensure the economic security of the organization in order to prevent losses or compensate for losses from the implementation of economic security risks. The operational measures of such a strategy include:

- expansion of subdivisions for ensuring economic security;
- conducting official investigations into violations of economic security;
- expansion of the legal service of the organization and others.

However, ensuring the economic security of an enterprise in the context of digitalization is possible by combining various preventive and operational measures and applying effective functional strategies (Fig. 5.2).

The economic security of an organization is ensured by the efficient use of resources in order to eliminate threats and create guaranteed conditions for the stable functioning of an economic entity in the digital economy. In this regard, we propose an algorithm for managing the economic security of a company based on digitalization conditions (Fig. 5.3).

The proposed algorithm for managing economic security takes into account the requirements of business digitalization, provides for the influence of external and internal risks and allows achieving the strategic goals of the organization.

Conclusions

The economic security of the organization is ensured by the efficient use of resources in order to eliminate risks and create guaranteed conditions for the stable functioning of an economic entity in the context of business digitalization. The lack of unified approaches to regulating digital

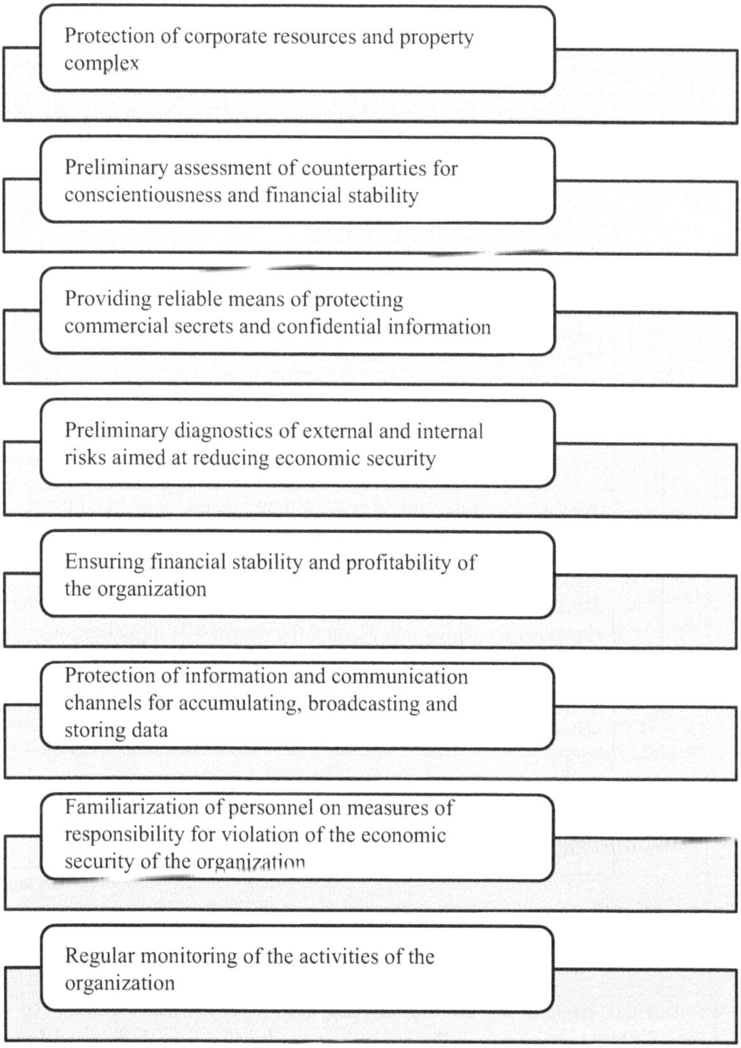

Fig. 5.2 Key functional strategies for ensuring economic security in the context of business digitalization. (*Source: developed by the authors*)

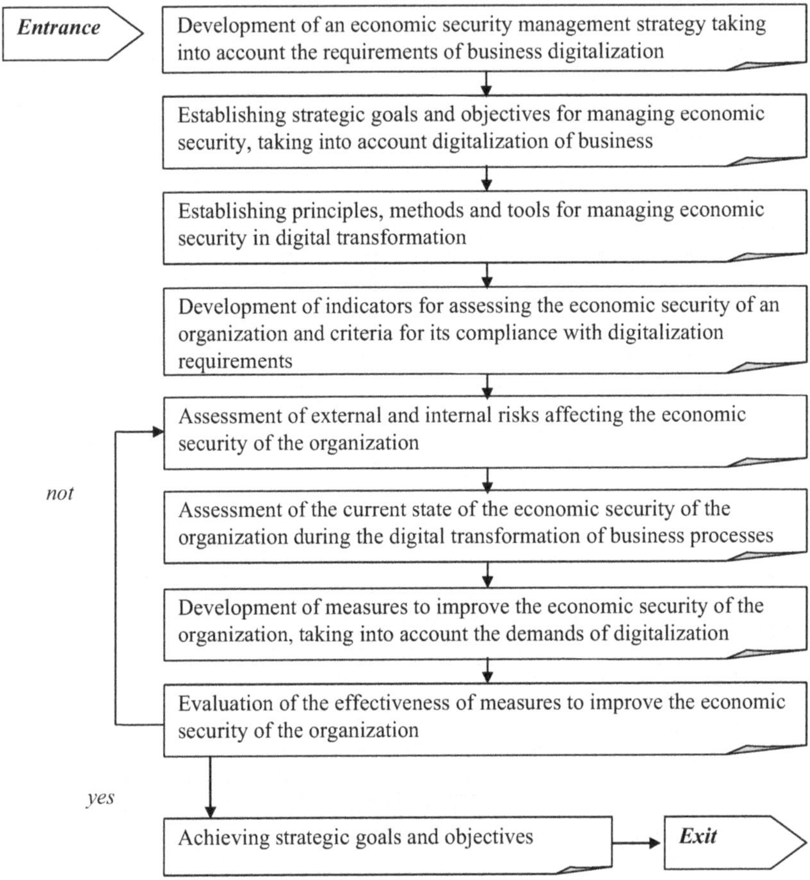

Fig. 5.3 Algorithm for managing the economic security of a company in the context of digitalization. (*Source*: *developed by the authors*)

transformation processes and ensuring the economic security of the subjects of the business environment entails the need for additional research and development in this area.

1. The definition of the term proposed in the chapter and the clarification of the elements of economic security in the context of digitalization expand the definitions and conceptual apparatus in this area of research.

2. The chapter highlights the key functional strategies based on preventive and operational measures that will ensure the economic security of the organization in the context of digitalization.
3. The conducted research contributed to the development of an algorithm for managing economic security that can be applied in the activities of modern organizations in the context of digitalization of business processes.

Currently, the results of the research are being implemented in the activities of small and medium-sized companies. The proposed tools will improve the economic security of organizations in the context of digital transformation.

References

Basuony, M. A. (2014). The Balanced Scorecard in Large Firms and SMEs: A Critique of the Nature, Value and Application. *Accounting and Finance Research, 3*(2), 14–22.

Biazzo, S., & Garengo, P. (2012). *Performance Measurement with the Balanced Scorecard. A Practical Approach to Implementation within SMEs*. Springer-Verlag Berlin Heidelberg.

Gong, Y. (2013). *Global Operations Strategy. Fundamentals and Practice*. Springer-Verlag Berlin Heidelberg.

Lawrie, G., & Cobbold, I. (2015). Development of the 3rd Generation Balanced Scorecard (Working Paper). *2GC Active Management*. Retrieved from http://2gc.eu/assets/files/resources/Papers/2GC-WP-201403-Evolution_of_the_BSC.pdf.

Malgwi, A. A., & Dahiru, H. (2014). Balanced Scorecard Financial Measurement of Organizational Performance: A Review. *Journal of Economics and Finance, 4*(6, July–Aug.), 1–10.

Rampersad, H., & Hussain, S. (2014). *Authentic Governance: Aligning Personal Governance with Corporate Governance, Management for Professionals* (pp. 65–78). Chapter 8—Corporate Balanced Scorecard. Springer International Publishing Switzerland.

CHAPTER 6

Modernization or New Engineering: Models of Leadership in the Global Civil Aviation Market

Anna Kolesnikova and Julia Kovalchuk

Introduction

Helicopters are currently operated, for both military and civil purposes, in more than 190 countries. Civil helicopters are used for carrying cargo or passengers, for medical and rescue missions, and for agricultural and other needs.

A. Kolesnikova (✉)
LTD "ChKalAvia", Moscow, Russia

Moscow State Institute of International Relations (MGIMO University), Moscow, Russia
e-mail: cfo@chkalavia.ru

J. Kovalchuk
Moscow State Institute of International Relations (MGIMO University), Moscow, Russia

Moscow Aviation Institute (National Research University), Moscow, Russia

I. Stepnov (ed.), *Technology and Business Strategy*,
https://doi.org/10.1007/978-3-030-63974-7_6

The civil helicopter market's genesis was towards end of the 1950s. Currently, the share of helicopters in the global market is more than 20% of all aviation units, with a positive trend due to increasing helicopter demand in emerging Asian, African, and Latin American countries.

The global civil helicopter market occupies a sustainable niche, originating from the design features that make helicopters indispensable across various fields of application. Experts believe demand from oil and gas producers to be the main driver for the civil helicopter market growth. Along with developing offshore hydrocarbon exploration and production technologies, the number of oil and gas production platforms has increased drastically within a short period of time. Consequently, the need for highly mobile aviation to carry passengers and cargo has expanded.

Today, there are several dozen helicopter manufacturers worldwide. Among them, despite recent years of proactive helicopter engineering in the Asian-Pacific Region (predominantly China), the USA, Europe, and Russia are the industry leaders, with their major manufacturers being:

- Bell Helicopter;
- MD Helicopters;
- Robinson Helicopter Company;
- Sikorsky (Lockheed Martin Corporation);
- Airbus Helicopters;
- Leonardo Helicopters;
- Russian Helicopters.

Helicopters are tech-intensive and science-based products. Due to cost-intensive design and production, several countries play a leading role here. Aviation industry development is primarily driven by advancing helicopter technologies for military purposes, which means a strong focus on upgrading machines' structural design; due to this, too, adjacent branches, inter alia civil helicopter engineering, are able to progress as well.

Experts predict a steady growth in manufacturing and using civil helicopters, due to the forecasted increase in demand for commercial transportation as well as operating in those industries where planes cannot be used. The main reason is a helicopter's flight performance: vertical takeoff and landing, maneuverability, ability to carry external loads, and so on.

Improving technologies to increase flight speed and range, whilst decreasing fuel consumption, will help helicopters occupy the part of the market where planes are mostly used now.

This chapter reviews the results of research in the upgrading and development of the global civil helicopters market.

Methodology

Considering specific features of the global market, modern trends, and advancing technologies, we have defined that the purpose of this research is to systemize main trends in civil helicopter development, and accordingly the main methods of bringing Russian helicopters to a new level, given the intense competition.

To solve these tasks, information from the following sources has been used: GAMA (General Aviation Manufacturers Association), reports of the major helicopter manufacturers (Robinson Helicopter Company, USA; Bell Helicopter, USA; Lockheed Martin Corporation, USA; Airbus Helicopters, France; Leonardo Helicopters, Italy; Russian Helicopters, Russia), reports by FlightGlobal, IBA (International Bureau of Aviation), and data retrieved from ITC Trade Map.

The statistical analysis (to process the data), the review article method, the systematic approach (to define the main trends and systemize them), and a comparative analysis are the methods that have served as the basis for this search.

Results

Among the aforementioned companies, Robinson and Airbus have the highest number of registered helicopters, with market shares of 24.7% and 24.3%, respectively, of the total amount of helicopters. Bell, the third-largest producer, has a share of 20.5%. Leonardo (8.4%), Russian Helicopters (7.7%), and Sikorsky (7.2%) appear to be far behind, according to FlightGlobal. The share of MD Helicopters, the last on the list, is 3.4%. The remaining 2.2% are formed by minor entities. The percentage provided by FlightGlobal represents the aircraft number produced by a certain company as a share in the total number of registered helicopters (RUAG 2020).

As with the manufacturing ratios, the distribution of aircraft in operation worldwide shows a dramatic difference between the North Americas and Europe compared to other regions, with over 60% registered helicopters for these two regions. In their report, FlightGlobal place the North Americas as the leader with 13,204 helicopters constituting 34.4% of the entire global fleet (10,814 in the USA and 2390 in Canada). Europe follows with 10,791 helicopters, or 28% (including 2879 in Russia, 1176 in the UK, 1007 in Italy). The Asia-Pacific region follows with a total of 18.6% (2089 in Australia and 1194 in China). The next positions are Latin America and Africa with, respectively, 4470 (11.6%) and 2037 (5.3%) registered helicopters. The Middle East has the fewest helicopters, with just 646, or 1.7% (RUAG 2020). It should be noted that the number of registered helicopters greatly differs, being a much higher figure, from the actual number of aircraft in use.

The North Americas and Europe are often deemed and treated by experts as a single market, which (as has been mentioned) is primarily due to the fact that these regions physically have the majority of registered helicopters. The other reason for this attitude, it is absolutely clear, is that the relevant headquarters and production facilities are all located in the United States and Europe.

According to the ITC Trade Map, more than half of the total exports of helicopters is attributed to three countries: the USA, Italy, and Germany (ITC 2020). This is perfectly explicable, considering the locations of global helicopter-building centers. France, the UK, and the Russian Federation are among exporting leaders as well. Regarding the countries importing helicopters, the USA, China, the UK, Australia, Thailand, Canada, and South Korea account for half of the imports. It is worth noting that the United States and the UK are among export leaders as well as among import leaders.

Prior to proceeding with a more detailed assessment of brands and marks forming the market structure, we would like to split the helicopters into types, with the main classification criteria being the maximum takeoff weight and the engine type and number. We begin with the engines because they serve as a clear distinguishing ground: helicopters can have either one engine or more, of either a reciprocating or a gas turbine type (Dudnik 2005).

Takeoff weight is slightly more complicated, as there are a lot of various cases. Most often helicopters are split into ultralight, light, medium, heavy, and super-heavy types. Therefore, helicopters need to be arranged into classes in order to analyze the brands and marks composition.

Materials published by IBA show that light helicopters with a single gas turbine engine are the most frequent model, with a global civil aviation market share of 61%. The market share of 36% is on equal bases formed by light helicopters with two gas turbine motors and medium helicopters. The remaining 4% are heavy and super heavy helicopters (Fallon 2019).

In their article, "World Helicopter Market", BART International have compiled a list of civil helicopter fleet in operation, specifying the mark and the relevant quantities. In the brand and mark tabulation provided herein, manufacturers are distinctly distributed by engine types. Robinson and Enstrom mainly produce reciprocating engine machines. 5000 Robinson R44 helicopters in service make it the most popular mark. Airbus, Bell, and Leonardo are more focused on producing turbine-driven helicopters, with Airbus dominating in this sector, according to BART. Airbus A350 is the most popular model, with a fleet share of more than 3000 helicopters. Among other producers, the bestselling machines are Bell 407, Bell 505, and AW-139 (Huber 2017).

JetNet, an American company, publishes an annual press release on the status of the global helicopter fleet in service, taking the engine type (reciprocating or turbine) as their basis. Considering the fleet dynamic evolution, a continuous growth is worth noting (Fig. 6.1).

The 2012–2018 growth rate made as much as 14.8%, mostly due to the increased number of gas turbine-driven helicopters, their share in the total figure rising by 4% from 65 to 69%.

Apart from the model list, the World Helicopter Market by BART International provides data on quantitative changes in the current global fleet structure. These dynamics show a trend of decreasing helicopter

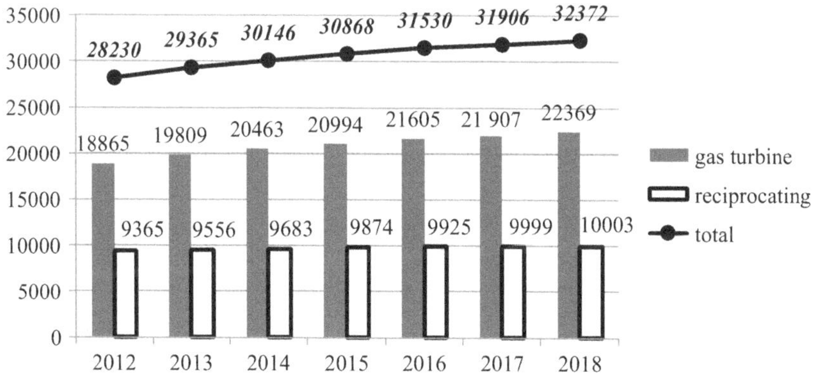

Fig. 6.1 Current status of global civil helicopter fleet in service, 2012–2018. (*Source*: compiled by the authors based on data (Butov 2019))

numbers in developed economies in the top ten countries by number of aircraft in operation. According to figures specified by BART International, the civil helicopter fleet has dropped by 3.7% in the Unites States, 7% in Canada, 3.8% in Italy, and 3.2% in Germany. Asia has shown a 5% increase, mainly due to China taking the lead (16%) (Huber 2017).

As seen from the quantity of helicopters on the global market, the growth is moderate but constant. Considering the market fluctuations cash equivalent, according to ITC Trade Map (2020), the total cost of helicopters exported worldwide suffered a massive decline in 2015 due to a nosedive in hydrocarbons prices. The 16.3% fall against 2014 was caused by decreased demand from oil and gas producers. This reduction trend in export cost quantities continued until 2017, resembling the market environment after the 2008–2009 recession; the helicopter market normally follows the oil market trend with a delay of a year or two.

According to a report by Russian Helicopters, the Russian market has been developing in line with the global market. Military helicopter production dominates—in 2016 the ratio of military vs civil rotorcraft was 91% to 9% respectively. 2018 saw an abrupt change in this ratio after a sharp rise in civil helicopters produced, to 35% (civ.) vs 65% (mil.). As the company plans, civil machines are to constitute as much as 40%. In 2016, only 6 out of 17 helicopters were exported. In 2019 customers recieved 160 machines, including 60 helicopters delivered to foreign customers (Boginskiy 2019).

Civil helicopters are manufactured by five entities: Kazan Helicopters, Kumertau Aviation Production Enterprise, Progress Arsenyev Aviation Company, Rostvertol, and Ulan-Ude Aviation Plant; all of these are parts of the Russian Helicopters holding company, the sole helicopter designer and fabricator. Three Design Bureaus also belongs to the holding: Mil Moscow Helicopter Plant (that designs Mi series helicopters), Kamov (designing Ka series helicopters), and VR-Technologies (developing the light multi-purpose VRT500).

Currently, the Russian share of the global civil helicopters market does not exceed 10% of the aggregate export quantities; still, most helicopters are bound for domestic clients.

According to the Federal Air Transport Agency, 2707 helicopters are state-registered as civil aircraft, of which 1830 were produced in Russia and 877 abroad. However, the number of helicopters actually flying is less than the specified figure. Among that, Mil Mi-8 (and its modifications) is the most numerous type. Robinson helicopters are the evident leader among foreign machines with 457 aircraft registered in Russia. Airbus Helicopters are in the second position (210 registered aircraft) (Ponteleev 2019). Leonardo and Bell have similar positions in the Russian market. Robinson R44, AS 350, AW189, and Bell-407 are the most popular.

Civil helicopter production in 2017 exceeded the 2016 values fourfold (65 machines), mainly because of the ongoing Medical Aviation program. With the state both the main client and main investor here, the program is implemented involving the Federal budget. Demand for Russian helicopters is sustained by state-owned leasing entities. Under the Medical Aviation development program, as much as 3.3 bln rubles were allocated from the Federal budget in 2017 and 4.6 bln rubles in 2018. 60 helicopters were supplied for medical aviation purposes within that period (29 in 2017 and 31 in 2018) (Lamzin 2019).

Another reason for increasing the domestic demand is the fact that the aircraft fleet in the Russian Federation is more or less "obsolete": as of April 2019, about 60% of the entire number of the registered aircraft were created more than 25 years ago (including 20% more than 35 years ago). Due to their closing lifetime, obsolete helicopters are stepwise put out of operation, to be substituted by new machines produced either in Russia or abroad. Until recently, due to the absence of medium- and light-class helicopters produced in Russia, the domestic market highly depended on imported machinery.

Taking the above grounds into account, the following conclusion can be drawn: civil helicopters are produced mainly to satisfy the domestic market needs. As mentioned above, the medical aviation program is the main driver for that, under which 21 other constituent entities of the Russian Federation are to be involved in 2020. By 2021, medical aviation services are to cover the country in full (Lamzin 2019). Another alternative to increasing demand in the Russian market is the Arctic development program.

In the 2013–2025 Aviation Industry Development, the Russian Federation state program, Helicopter Production is a standalone part, aiming to "form a highly competitive helicopter industry in Russia, with the products amounting to 19.4% of the global helicopter building market in 2025" (in accordance with the Strategy for the development of exports of civil aviation products of the Russian Federation for the period up to 2025, approved by the Government of the Russian Federation in 2017).

At present, as mentioned above, Russia's share in the worldwide exports does not exceed 10%. The main restrictions preventing the growth of

Russian export are limited product range (no light helicopters until recently) and difficulties in getting Russian aircraft certified. Consequently, both the European and the North American markets, being the regions with the majority of all aircraft in operation (more than 60%), are in essence inaccessible for Russian producers.

As assessed by the Russian Helicopters specialists, about 40% of the global market remains accessible for rotorcraft manufactured in Russia, except for the North Americas, the European Union, Saudi Arabia, Australia, and Japan.

In September 2017, the Civil Aviation Products Export Development Strategy was adopted by the Russian Federation Government, with a focus on exporting civil helicopters.

The types to be exported are limited to heavy (Mi-8/17, Ka-32) and super-heavy (Mi-26) helicopters. Though these types are most wanted by the market, exporting them is limited due to absence of EASA (European Union Aviation Safety Agency) or FAA (Federal Aviation Administration) certificates. Exporting Ansat, the new light twin-engine machine, is challenging due to severe competition in this class (AW109, H135 and H145). Consequently, the markets of the Asia-Pacific region, the CIS, and African states are deemed priority markets for exporting Russian light helicopters. The holding company facilities allow as much as 60 Ansat helicopters to be produced per annum.

The strategy provides for the following key measures to be taken by the Government to augment position of the Russian Federation on the global exports market:

- harmonizing Russian and foreign certification requirements to products, requirements to certifying the aviation designers and manufacturers, and standards for the certifying bodies and agencies;
- signing inter-governmental agreements with aviation authorities in potential buying countries on acknowledging type certificates issued by the Russian aviation authorities (in accordance with the strategy for the development of exports of civil aviation products of the Russian Federation for the period up to 2025).

It worth mentioning that technical advancements are ongoing and innovations are being implemented in a pro-active manner in the helicopter industry worldwide. Aviation is one of most cutting-edge, highly technological economic branches. Helicopter upgrade encompasses almost all elements of the design.

Using innovative technologies in engineering and fabricating new helicopters is one of the vital aspects to improve the competitive position in the international market. Another driver, apart from upgrading the technical performance and reducing the operational expenses, is continuously increasing flight safety requirements.

Composites and titanium and aluminum alloys used to produce the latest types of helicopters allow the machine weight to decrease. Modern engines are equipped with the dual-channel FADEC (Full Authority Digital Engine Control) system that reduces the need for the pilots to monitor the engine to a minimum and lessens fuel consumption. Implementing the six-blade rotor design ensures high thrust and cuts the vibration considerably. Installing an X-shapes tail rotor or a Fenestron allows the controllability to be improved and decreases the noise emission. Using innovative polycomposite rotor blades with improved aerodynamics allows the enhancement of the thrust and the speed, lowering the helicopter weight at the same time.

One the most numerous twin-engine heavy helicopters is the Mil Mi-8 along with its various modifications (there are more than 10 of them). These rotorcraft, having been produced for more than 50 years, are widely popular around the world. Due to the needs and development of the market, the technical outfitting of this helicopter type is constantly being retrofitted.

Upgrading the Mi-8/17 types ensures:

1. substituting the outdated equipment not complying to modern requirements with advanced equipment;
2. improving reliability;
3. improving ergonomic features;
4. improving the helicopter flight safety;
5. improving the flight performance.

In order to enhance the altitude features and cargo carrying capacity, to ensure operation in high-temperature and oceanic climate, to lower the gas temperature overshoot by 100–130 °C, TV3-117 (ТВ3-117) engines are substituted with VK-2500 (ВК-2500) engines. To add to the flight range, additional external fuel tanks are installed on both sides of the aircraft above the main tanks. To augment safety, the tanks shall be of a protected and suspended-type, to prevent fuel leaks in case of certain damage types or crash landings, thus decreasing the probability of fire. To ensure compliance with the UN requirements on providing safety for the crew and the passengers against firearms, ballistic protection is required for helicopters performing flights as part of peace-making missions. Polycomposite materials are considered one of the high-potential upgrade alternatives.

Mi-171A2 is the latest version of Mi-8/17, the world's most used russian twin-engine helicopter. Its cruise speed and maximum speed are 10% higher than serial Mi-8/17 machines, while the load-carrying capacity has been raised by 25% (Boginskiy 2019). These improvements are achieved due to the more efficient X-shaped tail rotor and the new composite-blade rotor, as well as an advanced airfoil section. Outfitting the Mi-171A2 with KBO-17-1 (КБО-17-1), a "glass cockpit" digital avionics suite incorporating both flight and navigation equipment and the general helicopter equipment with digital data display, allowed the crew number to be decreased to two persons. Using cameras improves the field of vision while working with external loads. Safety has been improved by utilizing up-to-date systems for avoiding impact against terrain (terrain avoidance), other aircraft, or other obstacles.

This helicopter type has already obtained certificates in India and Columbia, and is planned to undergo validation in PRC, South Korea, Brazil, Peru, Mexico and a number of other states.

Conclusions/Recommendations

The EU states and the United States are centers of global helicopter production. The standing of the Russian Federation in the international market can hardly be called strong. The country's share in the total export quantities in value terms is not more than 10%, even taking into consideration the fact that Russian helicopters occupy the most expensive class niches, that is, heavy and super-heavy classes. Consequently, looking at quantitative figures of the worldwide exports, Russia's share does not exceed 5%.

The advantages of the industry branch are design experience accumulated throughout the USSR period, the "aging" domestic fleet in operation, and a full cycle of standalone production segments unified under the Russian Helicopters holding company—engineering, fabrication, repairs, and maintenance. The downsides are a high dependence on state support, limited product range, lacking state-of-the-art technologies against the leading international producers, and issues with certifying Russian machinery abroad.

As seen from the data presented here, the industry is presently serving domestic demand in Russia. Therefore, the main tasks that manufacturers have are ensuring imports phase-out and enhancing competitive ability on the global market. As the Russian civil helicopter sector is actually controlled by the state, ramping up export supplies mainly depends on the possibility the state has to provide the industry with relevant assistance (both financial and political).

According to the forecast for the 2019–2028 period published by Forecast International, Airbus Helicopters is to be the industry leader in selling helicopters with a share as much as 20% in the worldwide exports, with Robinson to follow (17.3%), and Bell in the third place (13%). As the forecast shows, Russian Helicopters are to be just behind the leaders, with 12.7%. However, considering the cost aspect, the cash share of Russian Helicopters in the global exports is expected to rise to 17.3% (Jaworowski 2019).

Due to the absence of access to the leading markets formed by countries operating helicopters due to certification issues, Russia is building up partnerships and supply arrangements to Asia-Pacific regions. The development rate of that region's market as part of the global structure has been actively growing recently and, as experts say, the pace will be maintained.

Although challenges in the civil helicopter industry are quite serious, the major part of them can still be solved going forward. To widen the export sales channel for their products, Russian helicopter manufacturers have the following priority tasks to solve: simplifying the aftersales service, lowering the operational costs, developing new light and medium helicopters, and upgrading the existing types of helicopters using high-tech materials and additive manufacturing.

References

Boginskiy, A. (2019). New Year Address. *Russian Helicopter Magazine, 38*(3), 2 (in Russian).

Butov, A. (2019). *Market of Civil Helicopters.* Moscow: Higher School of Economics (in Russian).

Dudnik, V. (2005). *Helicopter Design.* Rostov: IUI AP (in Russian).

Fallon, A. (2019). IBA's Global Helicopter Market Update May 2019. *MRAeS*. Retrieved from https://ssusa.s3.amazonaws.com/c/308462937/media/5cdc115f41f82/Global%20Helicopter%20Market%20May%2019.pdf

Huber, M. (2017). Helicopter Fleet Report. *BART International, 6*, 48–51.

ITC. (2020). *Exporting and Importing Markets: ITC Trade Map*. Retrieved from https://www.trademap.org/Country_SelProductCountry_Map.aspx?nvpm=1%7c643%7c%7c%7c%7c8802%7c%7c%7c4%7c1%7c1%7c2%7c1%7c1%7c2%7c1%7c1

Jaworowski, R. (2019, May–June). The World Rotorcraft Market 2019–2028. *Vertical Flight Society's Vertiflite Magazine*.

Lamzin, M. (2019). Prospects for the Development of Air Ambulance and Medical Evacuation in the Constituent Entities of the Russian Federation. *The 1st Forum "Air ambulance"*, 4 October 2019. Retrieved from https://helicopter.su/meropriyatiya/forum-sanaviatsiya-2019/prezentacii-spikerov-foruma-sanaviaciya-2019/

Ponteleev, O. (2019). Helicopter Fleet of the Russian Federation. *The 11th International Conference "Helicopter Market: Realities and Prospects"* (in Russian).

RUAG. (2020). *World Air Forces 2020*. Retrieved from https://www.flightglobal.com/download?ac=66025

CHAPTER 7

Digital Twins Application in Managing the Scientific and Technological Development of High-Tech Industries

Vladislav Klochkov, Irina Selezneva, and Julia Kovalchuk

Introduction

In the scientific and technological development of high-tech industries, it is necessary to make management decisions—to determine the product strategy (what products to develop, with what characteristics, in what volumes to produce them), the process strategy (how to develop and produce products, according to what production technologies), and commercial and price policies (to what consumers, in what markets, and at what prices to sell products). It is also necessary to form a technology and innovation strategy (what product technologies and complexes to

V. Klochkov (✉) • I. Selezneva
V.A. Trapeznikov Institute of Control Sciences of Russian Academy of Sciences, Moscow, Russia

J. Kovalchuk
Moscow State Institute of International Relations (MGIMO University), Moscow, Russia

Moscow Aviation Institute (National Research University), Moscow, Russia

I. Stepnov (ed.), *Technology and Business Strategy*,
https://doi.org/10.1007/978-3-030-63974-7_7

develop to create promising products) as well as an organizational strategy of enterprises and industries (how to organize the development, production, sale of products, at what enterprises, what divisions should be there, etc.).

These decisions must be at least rational. It is meaningless to demand strict optimality according to certain formal criteria in practice; nevertheless, management decisions should contribute to achieving certain development goals (which should be at least partially or euphemistically formalized) to assess the degree of their achievement and the appropriateness of certain decisions. Moreover, the corresponding tasks of making rational decisions are becoming more and more complex. Their complexity increases over time and with improving management. Their intuitive judgment, as will be justified below, is almost impossible.

Methodology

For forming rational decisions in the high-tech sphere, the only possible methodological approach is calculation and complex multidisciplinary modeling (mathematical, computerized). The main tool for grounding and developing complex solutions is the so-called digital twins: complexes of computer models of controlled or developed products and systems. The development of appropriate models and methods is a complicated scientific problem which requires the application of various competencies, both in the sphere of mathematical modeling and information technologies. At first sight, support for adopting the relevant methods and technologies for the formation and justification of decisions should be in great demand. Modern management in the high-tech sphere must be "smart"—and for this, it must be based on digital twins.

At the same time, in reality "smart management" in the domestic high-tech industry is insufficiently demanded by decision makers (DMs), both within enterprises and in state administrative bodies. Voluntary, expert, intuitive approaches prevail, which often lead to the adoption of erroneous (at least according to the declared criteria) decisions. This chapter attempts to more strictly determine the need for "smart management" in the high-tech sphere and the systemic reasons for the current state of affairs.

Results

Digital Twin as a Means of Managing the Creation of High-Tech Products and New Technologies

A digital twin is a complex of computer models of a real object or product. In its turn, a model is always a simplified, schematized representation of the reality. The degree of simplification or, vice versa, specification depends on why these models are applied, and subsequently what decisions are justified and made with their help. It is necessary to remember that a digital twin is not an end in itself, but is only a means of improving the quality and speed of decision-making, a means of reducing risks and costs when creating sophisticated high-tech products. Its most significant quality is that it can be used to "play" with virtual models of products or systems instead of their actual implementation "in metal" and thus—avoiding long, expensive, and often dangerous trial and error—the best solutions can be chosen.

There are various types of digital twins, all solving different problems at different stages of the life cycle of high-tech products. A virtual representation of a product is at its most detailed upon the completion of design and development work (DDW), testing, and certification, when shifting to production. At this stage it is in fact already a detailed three-dimensional design model and four-dimensional work process model, and by the end of the DDW these are precisely optimal designs and processes—optimized with the help of digital twins.

Such "design" models are extremely accurate because such accuracy is required at this stage. However, digital twins should appear much earlier—at the very beginning of the stage of applied research, or the R&D of new technologies. Their creation at this stage, however, and their use in applied science, are still debatable characteristics.

Modern principles of the organization of applied R&D (Dutov and Klochkov 2019) imply the forward-looking creation of a scientific and technical back-log (STB). This means that decisions to create specific technical models are made only after the necessary technologies have been worked out and the best way to fulfill the targets has been chosen. The difference between the developed system of organizing the creation of new products and technologies and the traditional one is shown in Fig. 7.1.

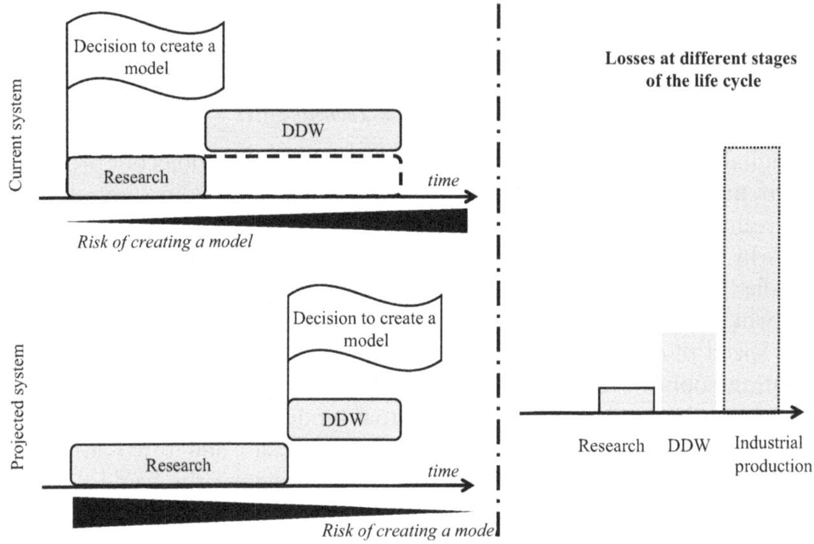

Fig. 7.1 Alternative systems for organizing the creation of knowledge-based products and new technologies. (*Source: created by the authors*)

However, if at the stage of creating a forward-looking STB a certain technical model is not available yet, it is not necessarily clear nor conclusive that a digital twin be created; there are, however, vital reasons why they should be.

Top-level Digital Twins as a Means of Justifying Requirements and Strategic Planning

With the creation of a forward-looking STB, the requirements for future models are first set only in the most general terms, in the form of top-level requirements meeting the set of targets. For example, strictly speaking, in the creation of a helicopter or plane, improved take-off and landing characteristics are not necessary—actually it is necessary to ensure the accessibility of remote and sparsely populated regions to transport. The achievement of such goals should be measured by certain indicators.

Components of products, products themselves, and their fleets in operation are only part of higher-level systems in which technology is used.

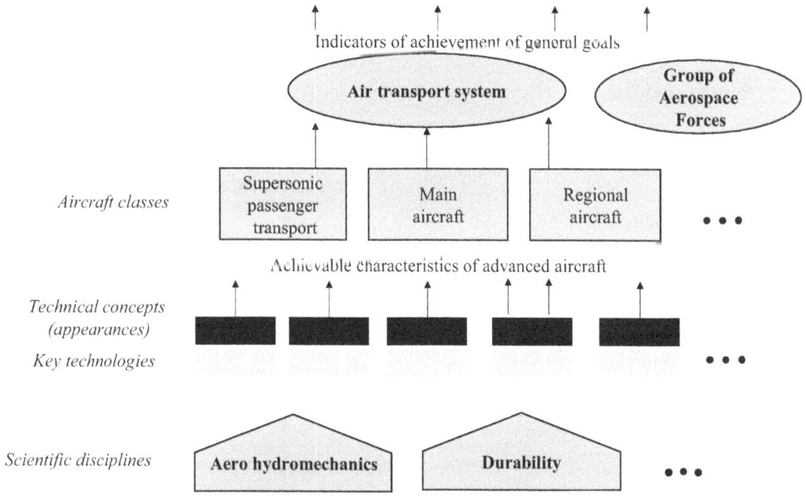

Fig. 7.2 Hierarchy of systems and their indicators (as exemplified by aviation). (*Source*: *created by the authors*)

The hierarchy of systems and the indicators that characterize them (using the example of aircraft engineering) is shown in Fig. 7.2.

From the very beginning, it is necessary to develop models of the super-system in which the future model will be used (for example, models of the transportation networks of the region), because it is with their help that it is possible to reasonably form the requirements for it. Such models do not reflect the design of future products at all, but, on the contrary, only their integral characteristics (for example, characteristics of future aircraft as a means of transport-loading capacity, speed, distance, requirements to air-fields, etc.) are used as input data. At the output there should be indicators of achieving the ultimate goal—for example, the transport accessibility of the territory. Figure 7.3 shows the hierarchy of models used to create new techniques and technologies. The models described here constitute the upper levels of this hierarchy.

Such system models are an essential part of the digital twin of the future product; it is the first "brick" at its base. The presence of a virtual top-level model enables, by varying the integral characteristics of future products, the more reliable determination of a framework of requirements for these characteristics (see Fig. 7.4). For example, they can be used to specify

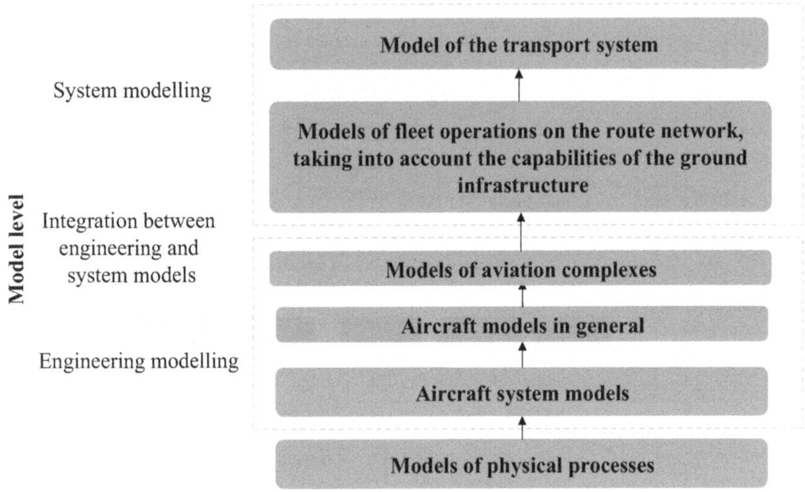

Fig. 7.3 Hierarchy of mathematical and computer models used in the creation of new aviation equipment and technology. (*Source: created by the authors*)

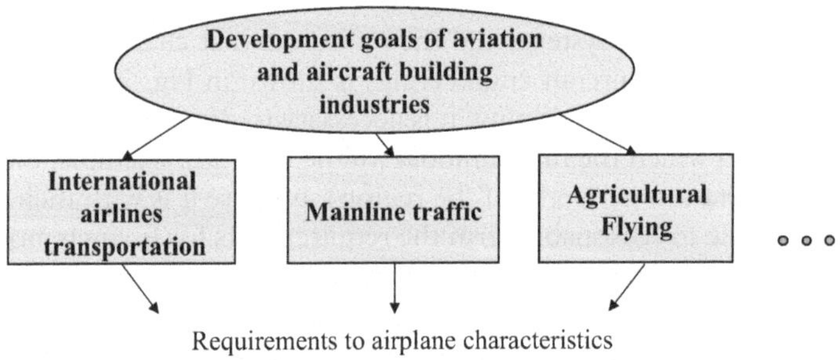

Fig. 7.4 Formation of the upper-level requirements for prospective equipment using super-system models (as exemplified by civil aviation facilities). (*Source: created by the authors*)

which ton-mile costs and cruising speeds will be acceptable for a prospective helicopter, and which ones will be acceptable for a plane that requires an airstrip (of one class or another), or other such predictions and calculations.

What is more, such a virtual twin of the upper level—a model of the targeted use of the future sample in the super-system—must be demonstrated to prospective customers. Firstly, their true requirements, reducing the risk of "not entering the market", can be clarified using it. Secondly, this model increases customer confidence in receiving a useful product. This largely explains why new products of leading foreign aircraft companies collect sufficient order portfolios (often even solid ones) for payback even before the start of a design.

In aircraft science, planning and forecasting horizons should exceed typical life cycles of a generation of technology. That is why, at the stage of creating a leading STB, it is necessary (for example, for airlines, as it is unclear how many of them will survive in 10–20 years or more) to take into account, strictly speaking, not so much the requirements of certain customers as more fundamental societal and state requirements. This is justified, all the more so, because even in market economies, applied R&D is financed mainly by the state.

A digital twin of the upper level (a complex of super-system models, or "a system of systems") at the R&D stage will be less detailed than the same digital twin required at the DDW stage. If an aircraft corporation, while creating a new product, needs to demonstrate the virtual operation of the future aircraft on the route network of certain airlines, then at the R&D stage it is only necessary to outline the future use of aviation for the next few decades. The accuracy of such a forecast may be low, but it is necessary, as businesses need to be able to quickly model future scenarios for the development of industry, changes in the socio-economic and demographic situation, natural conditions, and other future situations and scenarios.

Furthermore, if the "design" digital twin of the upper level helps aircraft companies more accurately choose their product strategy and aligning its parameters with future customers, then a similar "research" digital twin helps applied science choose the areas of scientific research and development for new technologies that are most relevant for the state and society. Aircraft companies have to ask numerous questions about their future—Where should the efforts of scientists be focused? Will it be necessary to fly faster, or will it be more important to make aviation of the future greener? and so on—these are typical questions that a top-level digital twin will help to answer at the R&D stage.

Digital Twins of Technologies and Appearances: A Means of Making Tactical Decisions in the Process of Applied R&D

How exactly target problems can be solved, and how to better solve them (faster, cheaper, etc.), will be shown by applied R&D. At first, it is necessary to consider a wide range of alternatives—not just individual technologies, but technical concepts, that is, the very appearance of future products. In this example, a short take-off and landing aircraft, helicopters, or other rotary-wing aircraft can be considered, with various aerodynamic design, power units, control systems, and so on.

The achievable characteristics of various technical concepts are first known only with great uncertainty—their assessment and specification is one of the main tasks of applied science. For each technical concept, a complex of models of general conceptual structures and their subsystems should be created and developed, being gradually specified at the same time. At the input of such models, there are the characteristics of the applied technologies: for example, the specific parameters of accumulators and fuel cells, which can be used in hybrid power units, material characteristics, and so on (see Fig. 7.5).

The presence of such integral models of various appearances makes it possible to virtually "run" different scenarios of technology development. For example, it is possible to predict which power plant unit will be more preferable in different cases, depending on future progress in the development of gas turbine engines, batteries, fuel cells, or other such technologies. The design parameters of different appearances can also be optimized because, for example, it is quite possible that a battery-powered aircraft

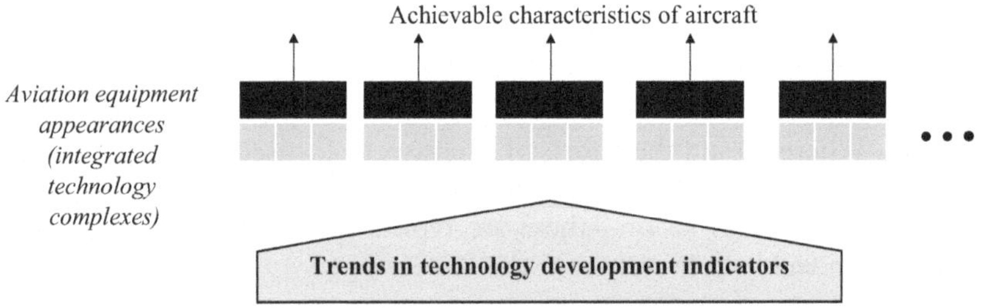

Fig. 7.5 Models of the appearance of prospective products and the influence of technologies on their achievable characteristics (as exemplified by aviation equipment). (*Source: created by the authors*)

will be optimal at short distances with a carrying capacity of up to a ton, but for heavy aircraft and long-distance flights, a hybrid power unit with a cruising gas turbine engine is better.

At first, there may be a lot of alternative technical concepts, or specific combinations of technologies. In order to effectively manage the process of conducting applied R&D, all the information about the achievable characteristics of alternative technical concepts must be stored and presented in digital form—otherwise it becomes unobservable. For example, it is necessary to have digital twins both for a prospective helicopter and an aircraft with short take-off and landing capability, each of them can have gas turbines, piston engines, hybrid power units, and so on. The number of possible appearances of future products, especially combinations of specific technologies, can reach the tens or the hundreds. When comparing them, it is impossible to rely on the intuition and the memory of even a brilliant scientist or engineer; besides, a formalized presentation of technology characteristics and technical concepts ensures transparency and objectivity in decision-making.

Therefore, at this stage of research, it is important to set out both a broad coverage of future products possibly appearing and possible combinations of technologies. At the same time, the required accuracy may be low at first—this is the difference between "research" digital twins and "design" ones.

In the process of applied research, as the achievable characteristics of different technologies and the appearances of future products are clarified, less viable and efficient technologies and their complexes are gradually eliminated, with instead the best alternatives selected. As their research is conducted, their digital twins are developing, becoming more specified and detailed. The technology readiness level (TRL) gradually increases (see Fig. 7.6) and the simplest analytical models are replaced by more detailed numerical models, then by experiment data banks that are increasingly close to reality. The simulated systems themselves also become more complex and closer to real products (i.e., if at first, for example, only a new wing was considered, then it is already included in the airframe, and then in the aircraft as a whole, with various systems; their interaction is taken into account).

Finally, the best appearances reach the stage of creation and testing by technology demonstrators. Then, the set of models of these technical concepts is replenished with real test data. Such a set of models, already verified in full-scale tests, is accurate and detailed enough to begin the design

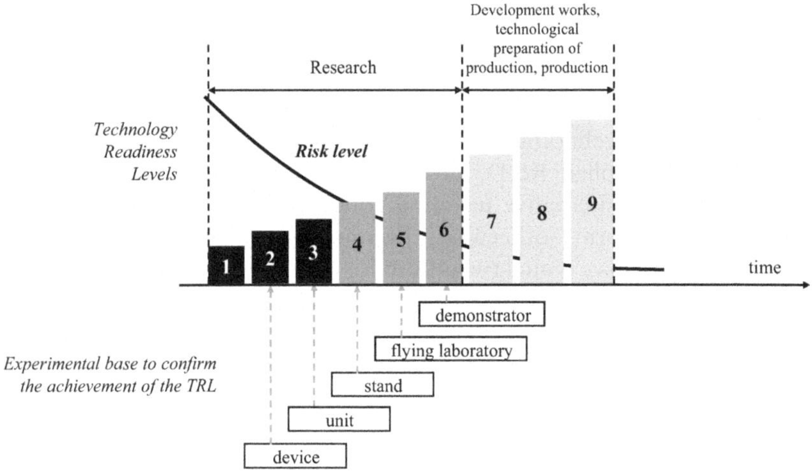

Fig. 7.6 Models for research and testing of technology readiness levels. (*Source: created by the authors*)

of a serial product on its basis—of course, this only actually takes place if its creation, based on the results of studies of the given concept, is considered "useful" (in the current geopolitical situation, under current market conditions, etc.). Figure 7.7 shows an "innovative funnel" that provides the gradual narrowing of the field of alternatives while increasing the TRL, cost, and complexity of research and testing.

Therefore, the digital twin of a technical concept, developed at the stage of applied research, turns to a digital twin of the product (or products of different classes and sizes, created on the basis of common technologies).

Digital Twins and Product Life Cycles in Technology Management

As this process demonstrates, the "tree" of digital twins of various technical concepts gradually narrows until it turns into a digital twin of a type of design adopted for serial production—but then, the digital twin of the product "branches out" again. Modern digital technologies (first of all, the so-called "Internet of Things" technologies) can be used to monitor in detail, on almost a real time basis, the state of each sample of the product in operation, and each sample must have its own "digital passport."

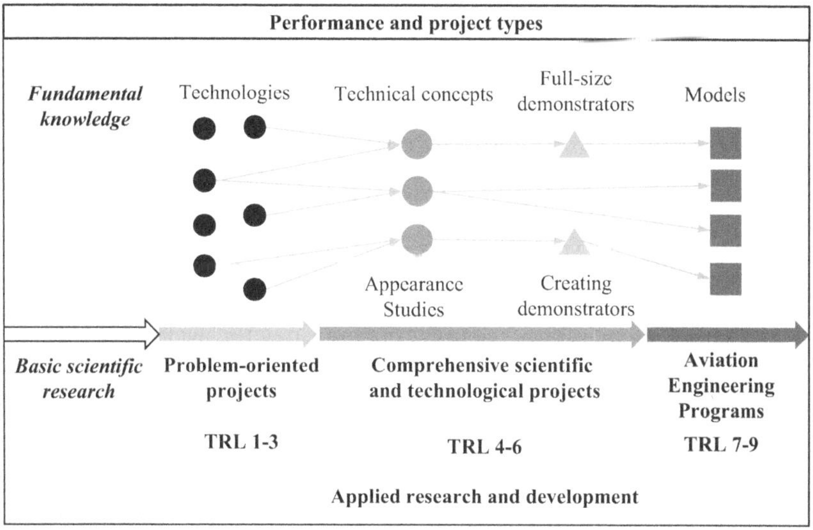

Fig. 7.7 Types of R&D and projects when creating STB. (*Source: created by the authors*)

Firstly, this opens up the possibility of optimizing the maintenance of the product fleet, organizing integrated logistic support for its use. When an aircraft is still in the air but there are already plans (to supply the necessary spare parts, do repair works, etc.), this makes it possible to reduce the necessary stocks, reserve capacity, and, most importantly, aircraft downtime.

Secondly, the knowledge gained in the process of production and use can be further taken into account in the modernization of this type of product, correction of possible designs, and production shortcomings. The synthesis of this knowledge is also valuable not only in DDW but also in the process of applied research, in the creation of new technologies, or in the formation of new requirements for future generations of products. That is, this locks the feedback loop between the stages of the product life cycle.

Locking the feedback loop between the production and use of products on the one hand and the creation of new products and technologies on the other is a non-trivial task. A huge array of data obtained in use, by surveying many sensors on a vast fleet of products, has often yet to be turned into knowledge, revealing patterns that are most often hidden and inconspicuous. Analysis of large amounts of data obtained during the production and use of products reveals the following hidden patterns:

- the dynamics of operation processes (intensity, seasonality, and other periodicity);
- actual operating conditions (including their differences from the assumed standard conditions);
- use of the product capabilities, sufficiency or insufficiency of their characteristics;
- regularities of various failures, prerequisites for aviation accidents, and so on.

The tasks of identifying such patterns and creating knowledge based on "raw" data can be solved by artificial intelligence technologies, automated analysis of large amounts of data, and pattern recognition using neural networks.

Besides, as a repository of data and knowledge about products and technologies, digital twins play an important role in knowledge management in the knowledge-based industry. In most mechanical engineering industries, the life cycles of products and technologies (running for decades) can be comparable or even exceed the period of active work by specialists. Today this creates significant problems, as the very viability of long-term projects critically depends on personalities—not even as holders of certain competencies who know certain areas of science and technology (who can create, calculate, and develop), but rather as knowledge holders who "remember where everything is"; these personalities are important not as scientific and technical workers but as "scientific and technical renters." This state of affairs is ineffective in terms of the speed of information processing, the speed of development, and decision-making; in the end, it is just dangerous. Entire industries and large-scale projects (of national defense or national economic importance) become extremely vulnerable to random and subjective factors. Besides, the following things have to be mixed (in management and financing):

- actual work in the field of applied research and innovation;
- maintaining the competencies of employees and teams with certain methods able to carry out new research and development;

- maintaining knowledge—even if it is almost not replenished in this area due to the exhaustion of its development reserves, of course it is necessary to continue activities, albeit routine.

The very technology of digital twins implies the elimination of the problems described. Knowledge and data are codified, then stored in a systematic way. Knowledge in the most formalized form—as mathematical models and methods—has standardized "inputs" and "outputs," interfaces. It makes it possible to:

- use them regardless of personalities (which reduces their "market power"—this is partly the reason for the hidden resistance to the introduction of the information technologies discussed here);
- choose models and methods for this purpose from available alternatives, replace them with better ones as they appear, and objectively compare their quality;
- use models and methods in different fields of science and technology (if they are suitable for their "inputs" and "outputs").

The latter means that digital twins—thanks to the objective formalization of the applied essence of models and methods (since in the standard form, it is written what they know and give)—open the way to a wide cross-industry integration, as well as the transfer of relevant knowledge and technologies (calculations, modelling, optimization, etc.) to different branches of the high-tech industry. Cross-sectoral barriers are reduced and the search for the necessary knowledge, methods, and models from various fields of science and technology is simplified. Such intersectoral integration and transfer of technologies are the most important means of ensuring the effective development of science and technology in Russia, taking into account severe resource restrictions, the relatively small capacity of accessible markets, and so on. Under such conditions it is especially important to increase the serial efficiency of the production of homogeneous products created on the basis of common technologies.

As depicted here, digital twins are one of the necessary conditions for the practical implementation of intersectoral approaches (Kovalchuk 2018). In the future, this opens the way to the formation of an effective flexible structure across the entire high-tech industry—a network in which competence centers and system integrators are distinguished, combining the necessary competencies as required. In such an industrial model there will no longer be industry barriers and their consequences, such as the unnecessary duplication of similar production capacities, product components, or research and development.

Thus, the system of interconnected digital twins, accompanying the entire life cycle, becomes an effective means of optimal management for the processes throughout the life cycle. Ultimately, this has the effect of reducing the cost and duration of processes, reducing risks, and improving the quality and competitiveness of complex knowledge-based products.

Digital Twins at Different Levels of High-tech Industry Management

The main tasks of decision-making in the high-tech industry and in the field of the public administration of its development can use digital twins across different levels of such management: at the intersectoral, sectoral, corporate, and engineering levels (Selezneva and Klochkov 2020).

The problems of making decisions at the engineering level are as follows:

$$k \rightarrow \max_x \mid I = fix, \tag{7.1}$$

$$\text{or}, Cp \rightarrow \min_x \mid k = k_r; I = fix, \tag{7.2}$$

k—an integral indicator of product quality;
x—product characteristics;
I—investment in research and development;
Cp—direct production costs of the enterprise;
k_r—the required level of product quality.

Tasks (7.1) and (7.2)—problems of a products' optimal design—are solved on the basis of digital twins of a high-tech product describing dependence of quality, competitiveness, cost of production, or other integral characteristics of the product on its design parameters.

At the level of a commercial enterprise, the task of making decisions in the short, tactical term looks like this:

$$= \left(p \cdot q - C_p\right) \rightarrow \max_{p,q} \mid q \leq V \tag{7.3}$$

Π—the current (margin) profit of a high-tech enterprise;
q—output volume (of course, if there is an assortment of products, this is a vector, but to simplify the recording you can omit the corresponding symbols);
p—product price;
v—production capacity.

Task (7.3)—the task of optimal tactical management—should be solved on the basis of digital twins of a high-tech enterprise, which include models of costs, revenues, and the profits of the enterprise as well as, possibly, other integral characteristics depending on the control parameters available to the head of the enterprise (here these are prices and products, its assortment).

In the long term, the corporate decision-making task is:

$$\mathrm{NPV} = p \cdot Q - Cp - Ic - It - I \rightarrow \max_{p,Q,V,\varphi,It,x}, \tag{7.4}$$

NPV—the net financial result of the project;
Q—total sales for the entire life cycle of a high-tech industrial project;
Ic—net investment in expansion of production capacity;
It—investment in improving production technologies;
φ—a parameter that reflects the organization of production (the impact of the organization of production on the cost of production can be seen in, for example, the works of Bajbakova (2014) or Klochkov (2006a)).

We believe that all the components of the expression (7.4) are considered for the entire planned period of the project implementation and are discounted; that is, they are given to the current point in time.

Task (7.4) should be solved on the basis of digital twins of a high-tech enterprise, including both models of the influence of organizing production on its costs and models of the influence of investment (in production capacities, in research and development) on the competitiveness of products, their cost, or production and sales volumes.

The decision-making task at the sectoral level is as follows:

$$\Delta BD = \left| p \cdot Q - Cc - W \cdot L - Ic - It - I \right| \rightarrow \min_{p,Q,V,L,\varphi,It,x} \mid L \geq Lr, \tag{7.5}$$

ΔBD—the increase in the deficit of the consolidated budget;
L—the employment of personnel;
Lr—the required level of employment;
W—required salary level;
Cc—direct production costs, with the exception of wages.

Task (7.5) should be solved on the basis of digital twins of the high-tech industry: that is, on the basis of models of the integral characteristics of the industry, including both the total revenue and total costs of high-tech enterprises, and the level of employment, depending on all the control parameters described above, as well as models of state subsidies of the industry and tax revenues from it.

At the interdepartmental, national economic level of public administration, it is necessary to solve the following problem:

$$\Delta BD_{\Sigma} = \Delta BD + D \rightarrow \min_{p,Q,V,L,\varphi,It,x} \mid L \geq Lr; s \geq s_r, \qquad (7.6)$$

ΔBD_{Σ} —the contribution of the entire complex (in the example under consideration, this is aircraft industry plus civil aviation) to changing the deficit of the country's consolidated budget (Klochkov and Gorshkova 2014);
D—civil aviation grants;
s—the quality of the final services provided;
s_r—the required level of the quality of the provided final services.

Task (7.6) should be solved on the basis of digital twins of the industry complex: that is, on the basis of models of integral characteristics of the sectoral complex (for example, models of total revenue and total costs of high-tech enterprises, models of the employment level, the volume of the output and the volume of the subsidies of the "final" industry depending on the required quality, and volume of the output of final services (in this example—air transportation)).

Thus, the tasks of managing the development of high-tech industry become more and more complex as the level of management increases. When moving to higher levels, the "outputs" of lower-level systems, which became integral decision-making criteria at those levels, become only one of the components of the generalizing criteria. Furthermore, the corresponding digital twins include the digital twins of lower levels only as elements.

Voluntarism and Intuitive Decision-making in the Russian High-tech Industry

Recently, to justify voluntarism in making responsible strategic decisions, appeals to the history of the Soviet high-tech industry and examples of ingenious designers of the past have often been heard. These appeals highlight how their intuition and experience literally made it possible to guess the right proportions and lines of contours of prospective products, or to evaluate visually that certain decisions are wrong because "ugly things do not fly." In this regard a few important aspects should be noted.

Almost all well-known general aircraft designers of the Soviet era had experience in aircraft modeling, the independent creation (i.e. development and manufacture) of gliders or other light aircraft, and, often, experience in flying them. They approached their most famous and successful projects through dozens of smaller projects (very often, as works on the history of domestic design bureaus and engineering schools note, unsuccessfully (Daffi and Kandalov 1999)). Besides, in the 1950s–1970s, the development of a number of new products of the international and domestic aircraft industry was accompanied by heavy losses (including due to erroneous design solutions), which, at the beginning of the twenty-first century, would already be considered unacceptable.

Identification, in terms of qualifications and experience, of people who now occupy responsible positions in the Russian and foreign high-tech industries (at this, positions are both purely managerial and "technical") with those historical personalities needs additional justification.

Today, technology is becoming more and more complex, its perfection is less and less visible, and modern high-tech products are no longer created by individual geniuses. Moreover, the extensive accumulated experience of Soviet designers worked precisely when creating equipment of the same technological structure. The modern era is characterized by frequent changes in scientific and technological approaches. Already during the transition to supersonic aircraft, designers faced a number of problems and dangerous phenomena, unfamiliar to aircraft manufacturers in the "subsonic" experience in principle. Without turning to science (which had to carry out a large amount of "catching up" research, eliminating the shortcomings of products that sometimes even went into operation (Daffi and

Kandalov 1999; TSAGI 1996)), design solutions led to systematic disasters, failures to achieve a given level of characteristics, and the system inefficiency of new aircraft.

In addition, some of these aspects were connected with the cost of errors and responsibility for errors. At present, the socially acceptable level of the impact of erroneous decisions is much lower due to significant scientific and technological progress. However, the "socially acceptable" responsibility of DMs for erroneous management decisions is also lower. Nonetheless, in the Soviet era, DMs were ready to hold great responsibility for the management decisions made and their consequences.

In the recent history of the domestic high-tech industry, a number of large-scale failures have been recorded, which are caused by voluntarism and conscious disregard for scientific recommendations (Dutov and Klochkov 2019); they also occur due to a number of erroneous decisions at all decision-making levels—from "technical" and design to systemic, defining the strategies for the development of high-tech sectors of the Russian industry. The following overview only illustrates typical cases, and by no means purports to be complete.

There are numerous examples of purely design miscalculations in the creation of new high-tech products in Russia, including in defense-related areas (Borisov 2017; Gusarov 2019). There has been failure (or even a fundamental non-fulfilment within the framework of the design decisions made, brought to light only after their implementation) to comply with the customers' requirements for product characteristics, systematic delays in progress, and overspending resources.

In the early 1990s, despite the presence of (at that time) quite modern civil aircraft and aircraft engines (aircraft of the Tu-204 and Il-96 families, engines of the PS-90 family), despite the main technical and economic characteristics largely not being inferior to foreign counterparts of the corresponding generation (and even offered at significantly lower prices), the Russian civil aircraft industry lost not only external markets but even its domestic market to its competitors. At this news, the responsible persons of the aviation industry and industry science ignored the opinion of potential customers and scientific recommendations (Kirpichev et al. 2006; Klochkov 2004, 2006b) in which it was even mathematically proved that the main problems at that time lay in the field of after-sales service.

Products that were officially planned as "breakthrough" (due to their capability of returning a significant share in the global and domestic markets to the Russian aircraft industry and ability to augment self-sustaining levels of production) have left such expectations unmet, and there is no reason to hope for this in the future. First of all, short-range aircraft of the Sukhoi SuperJet 100 family and medium-range aircraft of the MC-21 family (amongst others) are planned; however, at this, scientific analysis showed in advance that the declared "breakthrough" commercial goals of these projects are unattainable at the current level of technological development of the aircraft industry (Klochkov and Gusmanov 2007).

The socio-economic and natural-geographic specificity of the Russian Federation requires the creation of a sufficiently massive "aviation for Russia," whose needs will not be satisfied by imported products of a similar class. However, for almost 30 years of development in the modern Russian aircraft industry, no modern, efficient, and mass aircraft has been created for such regions. Local airlines have substantively degraded and have not recovered, despite being subsidized. Current attempts to develop and master the production of the relevant classes of aircraft are haphazard and chaotic (Vorobev 2019; Frolov 2019), in no small part because the conceptual problem has not yet been solved—what certain aircraft (their capacity, speed, flight range, etc.) and the air transport system of the respective regions should be like. The chaotic nature of the changing responses to these questions is due to the absence of any scientific justification. The risk of unsustainable decisions in this area is compounded by very limited resources. Therefore, even the task of "ensuring social stability" may not be achieved.

As can be seen from the examination of work carried out in support of strategic decisions on the development of the aircraft industry by the Accounts Chamber, the methodological level of this justification is very low. In fact, no scientific analysis (financial, engineering-economic, socio-economic, etc.) of the decisions made and their consequences was carried out. Of course, the corresponding digital twins were not created—except maybe digital twins of the lower, design level. Even then, they were not complex—for example, even when describing the flight performance of the aircraft, they did not touch upon their performance characteristics, let alone the parameters of the aircraft fleet.

Management Tasks Actually Solved in the Russian High-tech Industry

In principle, enterprises and industries can work at a loss but successfully solve the state tasks assigned to them, creating socially significant benefits at the expense of an acceptable level of subsidies (see Task (7.6) above). However, if they do not provide the required "output", their subsidies turn into a pure pay to industry workers, and it is much more profitable from the point of view of the state to abandon the imitation of production and scientific and technical activities. Thus, in the aforementioned Task (7.5), the following degenerate solution, which will in fact ensure the minimum loss of the state budget, is selected:

$$\Delta BD = W \cdot Lr, Ic = It = I = 0.$$

According to the authors, in fact, DMs in the high-tech sphere often solve localized problems of maximizing the amount of subsidies received in compliance with a number of restrictions. Moreover, these restrictions concern neither the real quality of the products created and produced, nor even the volume of their production. Instead they consist of formal compliance with existing legislation, namely the implementation of the action plan and the cash balance plan.

At the level of the national economy, this state of affairs leads to the stagnation of economic development (in which high-tech industries do not adequately participate either with their incomes or with their products used by other industries) and the degradation of the high-tech industry instead of its development. As a result, enterprises do not even try to create products useful for potential consumers that contribute to solving social problems or are competitive in the open market and profitable in production.

In its turn, the lack of demand for "smart management" in the Russian high-tech sphere leads to the degradation of the relevant competencies, or to the fact that the models and digital twins necessary to solve the problems described in this work have not been created at all—and most of them (with the exception of the simplest digital twins of the design level) are missing. To a large extent, the creation of digital twins is perceived in the Russian high-tech industry only as a fashion statement, since they are not in demand in the real process of management and decision-making.

Conclusion

To effectively develop knowledge-based products, it is necessary first of all to give a clear definition of the goals of creating these products from the upper level to the lower level and build digital twins for each level. This deconstruction of goals and models allows, from the very beginning, for the entire range of various design areas of future knowledge-based products to be covered, thus avoiding expensive errors. Then, in the course of applied research, the most viable, prospective models of elements of complex products are gradually selected, which create a specific appearance for the future product which will be verified in full-scale tests, and on its basis the design of a serial product begins. This is the way a detailed "design" digital twin is created. During the operation of the product, each sample must have its own "digital passport" updated on a real time basis. The analysis of the received data set, including "Big Data" received by means of data mining, will optimize the operation process, identify product shortcomings, and propose guidelines for future research.

The tasks of managing the scientific and technological development of the high-tech industry and the corresponding digital twins become more difficult as the level of control improves: from design tasks and digital twins to commercial and public (sectoral and intersectoral) levels. Even at the lower levels, these tasks are complex, due to the complexity of high-tech products themselves, their target use, and their development and production processes. Intuitive, expert shaping of rational solutions of such tasks is almost impossible. It is necessary to use digital twins of different levels and a developed toolkit of multidisciplinary mathematical modeling.

At the same time, taking the appropriate decisions is dominated by voluntarism, often covered formally by expert procedures. Although prominent designers and leaders of the Soviet era had successful experiences in intuitive decision-making, references to these scientists are incorrect and irrelevant under modern conditions. Voluntarist decisions lead to large-scale losses for the high-tech industry, for the national economy, and for national security in general.

It has been shown that, in fact, decision makers solve much more primitive problems that do not require mathematical modeling or real scientific justification. Therefore, digital twins, especially complex and high-level ones, remain almost unclaimed. However, they are the necessary way to effectively manage the high-tech industry in the current context.

References

Bajbakova, E. Y. (2014). Analysis of the Industry Organizational Structure Impact on the Cost Price of Science-Intensive Products. *Financial Analytics: Problems and Solutions, 35*(221), 29–39.

Borisov, Yu.I. (2017, March 9). Special Groundwork. *Military-Industrial Courier*. Retrieved from https://www.vpk-news.ru/articles/35468

Daffi, P., & Kandalov, A. I. (1999). *A.N. Tupolev—The Man and His Aircrafts*. Moscow: Moscow Worker.

Dutov, A. V., & Klochkov, V. V. (2019). *Management of Scientific-Technological Development of High-Tech Industry: Problems and Solutions*. Moscow: National Research Center "Institute Named after N.E. Zhukovsky".

Gusarov, R. V. (2019, April 15). Il-112—Long Road to the Sky. *AEX.RU*. Retrieved from https://www.aex.ru/docs/3/2019/4/15/2910/.

Frolov, A. (2019). Russia will Create a New Generation Aircraft for Local Airlines. *Politexpert.ru*. Retrieved from https://politexpert.net/154428-rossiya-sozdast-samolet-novogo-pokoleniya-dlya-mestnykh-avialinii.

Kirpichev, I. G., Kuleshov, A. A., & Shapkin, V. S. (2006). *Fundamentals of the Strategy for Creating Competitive Advantages of Russian Aviation Technique at the Present Stage*. Moscow: GosNII GA.

Klochkov, V. V. (2004). Organizational and Economic Analysis of the Competitiveness of Domestic Aircraft Engines. *Engineering Technology, 6*, 74–78.

Klochkov, V. V. (2006a). The Economic Efficiency Evaluation of Integration of Aviation Engine Building. *Flight, 7*, 28–33.

Klochkov, V. V. (2006b). *Organization of Competitive Production and After-sale Service of Aircraft Engines*. Moscow: Economics and Finance.

Klochkov, V. V., & Gorshkova, I. V. (2014). Problems of the Development Management of "Small Aviation" and Air Transport in Sparsely Populated Regions of Russia. *Regional Economy: Theory and Practice, 47*(374), 36–51.

Klochkov, V. V., & Gusmanov, T. M. (2007). Problems of Demand Forecasting for Perspective Russian Manufacture Passenger Aircrafts. *Problems of Forecasting, 2*, 16–31.

Kovalchuk, J. A. (2018). Newly Created Value Modeling in the Industry Based on "Digital Twin" Technology. *Economics and Management in Mechanical Engineering, 6*, 12–15.

Selezneva, I. E., & Klochkov, V. V. (2020). Problems of Decision Making in the Sphere of Innovative Development of the Russian High-Tech Industry. *Drukerovskij vestnik, 2*, 89–106. https://doi.org/10.17213/2312-6469-2020-2-89-106.

TSAGI. (1996). *TSAGI—Main Stages of Scientific Activity, 1968–1993*. Moscow: Science, Fizmatlit.

Vorobev, A. (2019, October 18). The Ministry of Industry and Trade Commissioned the Development of a New "maize" to the Mahmudov Plant. *Vedomosti*.

CHAPTER 8

Individualization of Approaches in Scenarios of Survival and Development for Companies in the Digital Environment

Zhaklin Sarkisyan and Maya Tikhonova

Introduction

There are more and more significant obstacles to modern economic growth. Macroeconomic trends are beginning to be reflected in the activities of both large companies and small- and medium-sized businesses. On the one hand, the digital transformation of business has become the source of modern development, as the successful decisions taken by individual companies have indicated that digital transformations are a key trend of

Z. Sarkisyan (✉)
Moscow State Institute of International Relations (MGIMO University), Moscow, Russia
e-mail: g.sarkisyan@odin.mgimo.ru

M. Tikhonova
Moscow State Institute of International Relations (MGIMO University), Moscow, Russia

SOGLASIE Insurance Co. Ltd., Moscow, Russia

I. Stepnov (ed.), *Technology and Business Strategy*,
https://doi.org/10.1007/978-3-030-63974-7_8

our time. On the other hand, the agenda of the next crisis has not been lifted, and we are expecting a depression, the scale of which is still unclear. At the same time, all processes were amplified by two more destructive processes. These include the strengthening of anti-globalization trends, including changes in public opinion, and the manifestations of a pandemic, which significantly worsened the business climate for most companies.

The effects of digital transformation, however, not only have a positive impact on many aspects of society but can also threaten the survival and development of companies trying to monetize digital advantages.

Therefore, the study aimed to establish the impact of digital transformations on the business environment, as well as to assess the possibility of a crisis in the companies' activities due to transformations, with additional consideration of the already identified threats to the external environment. As it turned out, the gig economy (as a result of digital transformation) also responded differently to the pandemic, not confirming its absolute advantage over the traditional model (Conger et al. 2020).

Besides, considering the historical perspective, it is obvious that the digital revolution, like any technological revolution, requires adapting all available business models and creating new institutions (Kochetkov 2019a). The difference between the digital revolution and previous such shifts is the fact that, along with a radical replacement of obsolete processes, modernization is also taking place ("digital transformation" in terms already accepted), which opens the door to formulating different scenarios of survival and development, ensuring the interaction of the old and the new.

At the same time, increasing technological transformations are transforming the crisis into a continuous phenomenon accompanying business; this is especially true for SMEs. As a rule, the imbalance between the business environment and the capabilities of a company affects the company's financial condition, which requires special solutions. In general, for further research, crisis management can be understood as a process that changes the company's activities based on the diagnosis of potential problems (Pearson and Mitroff 1993; Mitroff and Alpaslan 2003; Sahin et al. 2015). In any case, crisis management as a whole can be separated from ordinary management as sets of approaches, measures, and methods used in situations where managerial skills are no longer sufficient (Vašíčková 2019).

In our opinion, however, the classical methods of crisis diagnostics were based on the accumulation of historical experience, which the digital economy does not yet have. Therefore, we believe that in cases where known management methods are insufficient, it is necessary to individualize/differentiate tools to counter various threats. The well-known and widespread tools and approaches to crisis management for companies created in the context of previous technological updates do not take into account the specifics of the new digital arena.

The current stage is characterized by the significant growth of SMEs; therefore, crisis management tools for small and medium-sized businesses and large companies should be separated (Medaković and Marić 2019). The stages of small business development are the most important period in a company's life cycle, and it is this period that is most often affected by crises (Iborra et al. 2019).

It is known in the literature that crisis management contains from two (reactive and proactive management) to five major components (risk aversion, problem solving, anticipation, a reactive approach and an interactive approach) (Sahin et al. 2015). In our opinion, the reactive approach is most applicable to the digital economy, which we will focus on later. A reactive approach to crisis management is usually understood as a set of procedures and principles that help bring a business out of a crisis and stabilize it. This approach has a clear procedure and begins with identifying the crisis and creating scenarios for corrections. The proactive style of the digital economy is ineffective as there is a lack of historical experience that allows the formation of foresight algorithms.

Thus, it is shown that solutions to prevent crises require rethinking the theoretical background of crisis management and creating scenario tools to ensure sustainable development.

Methodology

The chapter contains a critical analysis of the existing practical and theoretical recommendations in well-known publications, which allows for the survival and development of a business during the digital transformation. An essential element of this analysis was to understand that the companies in the digital environment are heterogeneous, both in terms of creating development and survival and in terms of management.

Based on this understanding, it was established that there are two methodological approaches: (1) accumulating empirical data in the historical perspective, and (2) individualizing solutions, whereby recommendations are made whilst refusing to use the known trends of the recent past. We prefer the second approach; we are well aware that it is subjective, but we would like to underline the fact that there will be fewer errors associated with subjectivity in this historical interval than those associated with the business models of the previous technological mode for assessing threats.

A special place in assessing threats to company development is occupied by financial analysis (stability analysis), which enables making an express forecast. However, its role has become less important with the advent of new digital players. Moreover, the disparity between the results of financial analyses of companies from the previous order and those that emerged in the digital age requires that, at this stage, the predominant role of financial estimates should be methodologically abandoned and used only for reference. This current limitation of financial analysis will be lifted by the search for new relationships characterizing the activities of companies, although in anticipation of their appearance the universal character of financial instruments can mislead the researcher.

Undoubtedly, all of the above applies only to those sectors of the economy in which the prevailing technology (leader technology) is changing; therefore, as a basis for deciding on the need for individualization, it will be methodologically correct to confirm that new technological solutions begin to prevail in this area, which served the objective basis of the study. Moreover, the single company corresponding to the new one is enough to abandon the existing methods for diagnosing threats to the company development. Therefore, the authors did not set out to describe all the manifestations of digital solutions but rather relied on the known facts about digital scenarios.

The combination of subjective and objective views is most fully realized with a systematic approach, which can be considered a complex methodological solution in this study, the observance of the principles of which provided the result.

Results

The radicalism of digital transformations leads to the need to clarify the object of study and classifications for most economic areas. While an essential feature of traditional production was integration into the industry, which allowed for structuring management approaches, today, the object of study should be established relative to the "digital" criterion.

From our point of view, it is advisable to distinguish three types of companies: industrial companies that arose in the previous era of public relations, companies completing the digital transformation, and companies of a new type created as an answer to digital challenges. A similar approach is presented in Kochetkov (2019b), where only two types of companies—"old industrial" and "new digital companies"—are considered. At the same time, E. P. Kochetkov believes that one of the threats to "old-industrial" companies is "new digital" companies.

In our opinion, considering two types of companies is not enough, since it does not fully describe the actual processes in society. In our opinion, attention should be paid to the symmetry of the threat—not only companies of the "new type" pose a danger to the "old industrial" companies, but also those "old industrial" companies compete very successfully with the new formation.

As a result of the analysis of scientific publications and systematization of approaches, we distinguish three types of companies (as three historical stages of business development in a particular segment) and eight subtypes (as possible scenarios).

It should be noted that SMEs, as a rule, refuse digital transformation, implementing a new business model in a new company, while large companies prefer reforms. It can be stated that it is necessary to ensure a company's readiness for a crisis at the level of strategic decisions. In the digital environment, crisis management cannot yet prevent a crisis, but companies can use it more efficiently with minimal losses.

When assessing threats, we propose considering three types of companies: (1) industrial, (2) transformable, and (3) newly created (Table 8.1).

Attribution to ***industrial*** companies implies two features: length of creation time and attitude towards material resources. There are two subtypes of classical industrial companies: those focused entirely on material production and/or those focusing on the provision of services, including information processing. The expected survival scenario for them is to provide digital access to material resources replacing the sale of products with the provision of services (servicization). Digital access is provided by creating platforms. Therefore, the individual criterion for assessing the survival scenario is the success of platform solutions.

SMEs managed by their owners have other survival scenarios: entering an ecosystem that provides marketing (Amazon, for example) or (with a

Table 8.1 Characteristics of the company types for assessing threats from the digital environment

Company classification attribute	*Subtype*	*Large companies*		*SMEs*	
		Applicability	*Expected scenario*	*Applicability*	*Expected scenario*
1. Maintaining an industrial approach	Material nature of production	+	Digital access Digital transformation	+	Entry into the ecosystem Terminating activity
	Services/ information processing	+	Digital transformation	+	Segment expansion
2. Digital transformation	Successfully completed	+	Competition with new digital	-	Not applicable
	Unsuccessfully completed	+	Bankruptcy or takeover	-	Not applicable
3. Creating a new digital company	Digital content	+	Development due to segment growth	+	Explosive growth
	Digital access	-	Development through consumer growth	+	Takeover or bankruptcy
	Digital business model	+	Development through the growth of consumers and suppliers	+	Implementing individual parts of the ecosystem

Source: Created by the authors

shrinking market) bankruptcy. For companies traditionally focused on information processing, the only way out is the digital transformation or leaving the market (regardless of the company's size). Therefore, to adjust the scenarios, one should consider the availability of the market segment and its dynamics.

Companies that have chosen a digital transformation strategy and are transforming their business processes under the newly selected business model (Stepnov and Kovalchuk 2020) should be considered as *transformable* companies. However, the digital transformation carries with it threats of undermining stability and bankruptcy, and therefore two subtypes should be distinguished: successful and unsuccessful transitioning to the digital economy. At the same time, companies close to restructuring business processes should be attributed to the same type. The fact that digital transformation suggests updating all business subsystems does not require justification. Nonetheless, additional costs and errors in anticipating market dynamics can prevent companies from adapting to the digital economy. For example, General Electric, Ford Motor, and Procter & Gamble have performance indicators with mixed dynamics and do not inspire optimism for a long time (Table 8.2).

Successfully transformed companies will continue to work competing with both companies from the first group and those newly created ones. It should be noted that these companies are, as a rule, more burdened with tangible assets than new digital ones. This reduces their chances of survival in the new environment.

Table 8.2 Net profit of companies, $ million

Index	*2016*	*2017*	*2018*	*2019*	*Dynamics for 4 years*
General Electric Company	8831	-8490	-22,354	-4979	-156%
Ford Motor Company	4596	7731	3677	47	-99%
Procter & Gamble Company	10,508	15,326	9750	3897	-62%

Source: Compiled by the authors based on the financial statements of Ford Motor Company, Ford Motor Company, Procter & Gamble Company

Access:

https://www.ge.com/investor-relations/events-reports

https://shareholder.ford.com/investors/financials-and-filings/default.aspx#annual

https://s1.q4cdn.com/695946674/files/doc_financials/2019/e28f717a-9858-69a1-8783-00c4604463cd.pdf

The newly ***created*** digital companies are becoming the most appropriate response to business (Kamolov and Stepnov 2020). The number of SMEs significantly exceeds large companies, but the risk of their going bankrupt significantly exceeds that of large companies. Nevertheless, despite the attractiveness and market demand for the newly created companies, they have a negative sign in terms of survival scenarios, due to the intangible nature of their main income-generating assets, which requires special tools to manage them.

Newly created digital companies should be divided into three subtypes: those digital offering primarily digital content or communications (like Zoom), platform-like intermediaries between consumers, goods, and services (Avito, Booking), and those acting as an add-on for industrial companies (Tesla).

The classic logic of crisis management was that the growth of companies served as an indicator of a way out of the crisis (i.e., after implementing a scenario, a financial analysis was mandatory, and an improvement in indicators implied a way out of the crisis). Applying bankruptcy forecasting models is one of the simplest and most accurate ways to predict enterprise bankruptcy, but unfortunately it does not work with the digital environment due to the lack of necessary experience.

Accordingly, it was financial diagnostics that served as the criterion (the basis for identifying the threat). We understand by crisis diagnostics the use of various (usually financial) methods for assessing the state of a company and identifying the characteristics of a crisis. Crisis diagnostics is very important because through it a person can assess the real state of the company and make decisions for its future work. It rarely happens that the same symptoms appear in several companies. Therefore, it is argued that crisis diagnosis is a complex process that identifies some of the various symptoms determining the company's problems (Meiste and Jakstiene 2015).

However, for digital companies, diagnostics of their financial situation begins to give false results when comparing the identified types of companies and competitors. For the first time in the entire history of businesses, a paradoxical situation has arisen: the market model of a new company type does not fit into the traditional theory of corporate finance and unprofitable activities have long been accompanied by a continuous increase in business capitalization. This is because today, digital companies can show significant losses alongside the growth of capitalization, which leads to a break in the historically formed causal "financial condition–crisis" relationship.

If the market believes that company A has the potential for value growth (and it grows) if there is a loss, then analysts can draw the same conclusion concerning company B, which has the potential for value growth but is unprofitable at the moment (Fig. 8.1).

However, such a conclusion without an individual study of the company's activities may be a mistake. The losses (or a high debt burden) can lead to a crisis having a significant negative impact on the company's activities, and the intangible basis of the business will lead to disaster, as it will not ensure the protective sale of assets (as loss coverage), as was the case in the industrial era.

Therefore, we conclude that an assessment of a company's financial condition based on the prevailing balance sheet proportions cannot reflect all the features of its growth. This is primarily since the intangible component of the new types of business cannot be capitalized in the balance sheet (by accumulating assets), except by increasing the excess of cash. In our opinion, this is one of the reasons for the rapid growth in companies' market value—as compensation for the accumulation of tangible assets in traditional business models. In this case, we believe that only two indicators from the previous approaches to diagnostics need to be preserved, which provide an objective measure of threats: the debt burden of the business and the dynamics of demand growth.

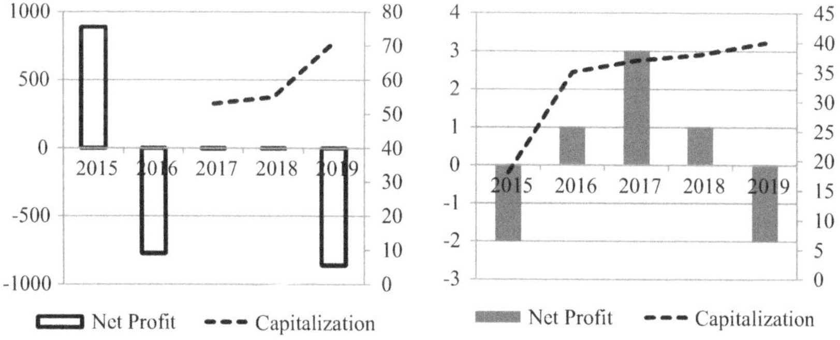

a) Tesla, billion dollars

b) KAMAZ, billion rubles

Fig. 8.1 Indicators of net profit and capitalization of companies. (Source: Developed by the authors based on company data from: https://quote.rbc.ru/company/)

One of their most important components of survival scenarios is state support. Traditionally, states have focused on supporting companies of the third type. Taking all other types of companies, intervention by the state during a crisis is not in demand, preferring the work of market mechanisms. Within the crisis theory framework, it is also essential to determine what scenarios companies and small business owners use to survive an unexpected work interruption.

With the task of government intervention being much more complicated than simply eliminating crisis-related problems, it is also important to look at long-term goals, namely to understand whether the state seeks to replace market-based survival mechanisms or it presupposes market marjoram. Governments can provide short-term assistance, but it should be assessed whether the business model of supported companies and small- and medium-sized enterprises will be changed or not, taking into account the fact that one-time support can prevent unnecessary bankruptcy now but does not exclude future problems. In other words, if a company identifies a threat of bankruptcy (based on diagnostics), then receiving state support leads to working, as usual, hoping that market conditions will improve. Nonetheless, an understanding of the digital transformation suggests that market conditions for Type-1 companies are unlikely to get better. Therefore, non-personalized sectoral support is a dangerous phenomenon, similar to deferred demand—deferred bankruptcy, with the expectation of continued government support.

Government policy is aimed at creative destruction to bring market mechanisms in line with changing demand and reduce budget spending on individual companies. As part of business support, the government must be sure that a change in survival scenarios must be a prerequisite. Therefore, the scenarios should be supplemented by a new typology for companies including three additional classification features (Fig. 8.2): (1) companies with a low debt burden and maintaining demand; (2) companies with stable demand, but with difficulties servicing accumulated debts; and (3) companies with a reduction in demand. It makes no sense to support the first and third groups relying on independent scenarios for the first group and bankruptcy procedures for the third one. From the point of view of the state, the second group has priority.

In this case, the degree of individualization/differentiation should be selected as follows:

Type of company	Demand	Debt load	Diagnostics	State support	Scenario
industrial	shrinking	low	individual	possible	survival
		high	No	No	bankruptcy
	stable	low	mass	Yes	development
		high	individual	Yes	survival
	growing	low	individual	No	development
		high	individual	No	survival
transformable	shrinking	low	mass	No	bankruptcy
		high	No	No	bankruptcy
	stable	low	mass	Yes	development
		high	individual	Yes	survival
	growing	low	mass	No	development
		high	individual	No	survival
new digital	stable	low	mass	Yes	development
		high	individual	Yes	survival
	growing	low	mass	No	development
		high	individual	No	survival

Fig. 8.2 Possible options for combining the selected types of companies, diagnostics and government support. (Source: Created by the authors)

- an individual approach for large companies (to clarify, if a company can be assigned to the second group);
- a differentiated sectoral approach for SMEs (with emphasis on the second group), so the sectoral approach can be replaced by a consideration of associations.

But, at the same time, markets cannot quickly ensure structural transformation without their bankruptcy mechanism; therefore, the states protecting business and workers must understand that finding stability will be protracted. The only reasonable criterion for postponing bankruptcy proceedings to a later period is the growing threat to the financial sector.

Thus, we conclude that—according to our approach—there are at least three groups of arguments justifying a departure from the established methods of crisis management in favour of individualizing scenarios: the heterogeneity of companies, the unreliability of financial diagnostics of digital companies, and the inconsistency of state and market crisis regulation.

Conclusion

Digital progress leads not only provide for success and the emergence of new business leaders but also to the emergence of problems, including methodological ones. This chapter shows that new problems are caused by the impotence of existing tools for predicting threats to company survival in the digital environment. It is undeniable that the very fact of creating companies indicates the possibility of ending their existence, so constantly monitoring threats to the activities of companies ensures their survival and future digital progress.

For further use of the conclusions obtained in the chapter, it is advised to follow the sequence of actions.

Firstly, the presence in the segment of all three company types must be established: those of the old structure, those who have undergone (or are completing) a digital transformation, and those that appeared in the digital age.

Secondly, the financial diagnostics (and its comparability) for various types of companies must be critically used, realizing that the smaller historical experience distorts the conclusions drawn. Standard financial reporting procedures (in terms of financial stability) create cognitive dissonance when unprofitable companies successfully place their shares on the stock exchange. This allows us to talk about the divergence of the value and analytical approaches, but does not allow us to conclude in favour of one of them.

Thirdly, it is vital to understand that governments will refuse to individualize as much as possible and apply mass support methods for such companies, acting as an "insurance company" for the segment as a whole.

Fourthly, new threats must be shown (for example, approval or disapproval by social groups) for companies in the digital environment. Until new criteria for their success are historically confirmed, it is possible to argue that such companies will have a higher degree of instability.

Fifthly and finally, based on the above assumptions, the chapter concludes that crisis management should abandon universal models and more widely implement individualization, otherwise this will lead to two types of problems: either (1) an unreliable assessment of sensitivity to various threats, or (2) an unreliable assessment of competitors in the digital environment.

To solve this dilemma, it is recommended that scenarios that take into account both financial and non-financial indicators be individualized.

This approach will allow us to more correctly assess threats to the future stability of companies. Further research in this area should lead to finding a balanced indicator of company sustainability and updating the crisis management methodology.

References

Conger, K., Satariano, A., & Isaac, M. (2020, March 18). Pandemic Erodes Gig Economy Work. *The New York Times*. Retrieved from https://www.nytimes.com/2020/03/18/technology/gig-economy-pandemic.html.

Iborra, M., Safón, V., & Dolz, C. (2019). What Explains Resilience of SMEs? Ambidexterity Capability and Strategic Consistency. *Long Range Planning*, 16 December, no. 101947. https://doi.org/10.1016/j.lrp.2019.101947.

Kamolov, S., & Stepnov, I. (2020). Sustainability through Digitalization: European Strategy. *E3S Web Conf.*, 208 (2020), 03048. https://doi.org/10.1051/e3sconf/202020803048.

Kochetkov, E. P. (2019a). Digital Transformation of Economy and Technological Revolutions: Challenges for the Current Paradigm of Management and Crisis Management. *Strategic Decisions and Risk Management, 10*(4), 330–341. https://doi.org/10.17747/2618-947X-2019-4-330-341.

Kochetkov, E. P. (2019b). Digital Transformation of the Economy: The Confrontation of 'Old' Industrial and 'New' Digital Companies (Aspects of Crisis Management). *Journal of Management Research, 5*(3), 23–30.

Medaković, V., & Marić, B. (2019). Crisis Management in SMEs: Empirical Study in Bosnia & Herzegovina. *Annals of the Faculty of Engineering Hunedoara, 17*(3), 183–186.

Meiste, R., & Jakstiene, S. (2015). Crisis Diagnosis in Anti-Crisis Management Process in a Company. *Oeconomia Copernicana, 6*(4), 49–58. https://doi.org/10.12775/OeC.2015.0.028.

Mitroff, I. I., & Alpaslan, M. C. (2003). Preparing for Evil. *Harvard Business Review, 81*(4), 109–115.

Pearson, C. M., & Mitroff, I. I. (1993). From Crisis Prone to Crisis Prepared: A Framework for Crisis Management. *The Executive, 7*(1), 48–59. https://doi.org/10.5465/ame.1993.9409142058.

Sahin, S., Ulubeyli, S., & Kazaza, A. (2015). Innovative Crisis Management in Construction: Approaches and the Process. *Procedia, Social and Behavioral Sciences,* (195), 2298–2305. https://doi.org/10.1016/j.sbspro.2015.06.06.181.

Stepnov, I. M., & Kovalchuk, Yu. A. (2020). Measuring Value Created by Business Models in the Sharing Economy. *Upravlenets – The Manager, 11*(5), 58-69 (in Russian). http://doi.org/10.29141/2218-5003-2020-11-5-5.

Vašíčková, V. (2019). Crisis Management Process—A Literature Review and a Conceptual Integration. *Acta Oeconomica Pragensia, 27*(3–4), 61–77. https://doi.org/10.18267/j.aop.628.

CHAPTER 9

Artificial Intelligence in Public Governance

Sergey Kamolov and Kirill Teteryatnikov

Introduction

According to the findings of Oxford Insights, artificial intelligence (AI) technologies are predicted to add US$15 trillion to the global economy by 2030 (Government Artificial Intelligence Readiness Index 2019). AI may not just contribute to the technological development in various industries but completely change the public services delivered by the executive branch of power. In many countries of the world the governments are already implementing AI in their operations in order to improve efficiency, save time and money, and deliver better-quality public services. In 2017, Oxford Insights created the world's first Government AI Readiness Index, which allows to better understand the current capacity of governments to exploit the innovative potential of AI. The 2019 Government AI Readiness Index scores the governments of 194 countries and territories

S. Kamolov (✉)
Moscow State Institute of International Relations (MGIMO University), Moscow, Russia

K. Teteryatnikov
ANO Research and Expert Analysis Institute of Vnesheconombank (The Bank for Development and Foreign Economic Affairs), Moscow, Russia

I. Stepnov (ed.), *Technology and Business Strategy*,
https://doi.org/10.1007/978-3-030-63974-7_9

according to their preparedness to use AI in the delivery of public services. The overall score is comprised of 11 input metrics, grouped under four high-level clusters: governance; infrastructure and data; skills and education; and government and public services. The data was derived from a variety of resources, ranging from deep research into AI strategies of more than 40 countries, to databases such as the number of registered AI start-ups on Crunchbase, to indices such as the UN eGovernment Development Index.

As could be expected, countries with strong economies, good governance, and innovative private sectors dominate in the top 20. Singapore comes first, followed by the United Kingdom, Germany, the USA, Finland, Sweden, Canada, France, Denmark, and Japan. There are no Latin American or African countries in the top 20. China, which is well known for its advances in implementing AI in public service delivery, has turned out to find itself on the 20th place although China has deployed the National Key Research and Development Plan's key special projects, such as intelligent manufacturing; issued and implemented the "Internet +" and AI Three-Year Activities and Implementation Program, releasing a series of measures from science and technology research and development; and promoted applications and industrial development and other aspects (AI Policy and China Realities of State-Led Development, Oct. 2019).

According to the Next Generation Artificial Intelligence Development Plan, approved by the State Council of China in July 2017, China's widespread use of AI in education, medical care, pensions, environmental protection, urban operations, judicial services, and other fields has already greatly improved the level of public service quality, enhancing the people's quality of life. AI technologies can accurately sense, forecast, and provide early warning of major situations for infrastructure facilities and social security operations; grasp group cognition and psychological changes in a timely manner; and take the initiative in decision-making and reactions—which will significantly elevate the capability and level of public governance, playing an irreplaceable role in effectively maintaining social stability. Thus, the Chinese government sees the AI as a vehicle to provide better governance to the Chinese people, using AI to drive smart cities, smart government, smart manufacturing, and forming the infrastructure for a smart society.

Meanwhile, Russia is 29th (between Iceland and Portugal) in the 2019 Government AI Readiness Index, which made us go deeper into the methods applied in measuring success of AI in public governance.

Methodology

This research is focused on the formulation of objective evaluation criteria of AI in public governance, as well as on applying the developed methodology to assessing the readiness of Russia to implement AI solutions on the federal, regional, and municipal levels. The approval of AI Strategy for Russia (Decree of the President of the Russian Federation No. 490 dated October 10, 2019 "On the Development of Artificial Intelligence in the Russian Federation") laid a legal basis for evaluating the willingness of state machinery and residents to deep transformations related to IA, which is crucial for paving the way for such changes.

To substantiate the degree of readiness of Russian State for implementing AI solutions, we have collected and categorized regulatory documents on the topic, ascertained the experience of integration of AI solutions into the national development programs, and also checked the potential of project management measures specified in corresponding roadmaps.

To achieve the objectives of the study, that is, making substantiated recommendations of the subject, we have used such methods as comparison, as well as expert, statistics, and content analysis. The analytical sample of our study included the Federal Government, 23 Russian Regions, and 100 Russian cities with a population of up to 33 million people. At the municipal level, we searched for regulatory documents directly or indirectly related to the intellectualization of urban spaces of each city included in the sample.

Results

First of all, analyzing international experience of assessing the government AI readiness we came to the conclusion that almost all abovementioned indexes are methodologically limited to their type: research (surveys and/or questionnaires), composition of other indexes, analysis of quantitative data, and qualitative expert analysis. Each of these types has its own advantages and disadvantages. None of them are perfect.

Second, the AI definitions adopted in AI Strategies in more than 30 countries (Canada, Singapore, China, Kenya, Denmark, France, etc.) differ greatly by its content (Heumann and Zahn 2018). Even the international consultants have different approaches. Thus, for example, Accenture defines AI as a range of technologies that "extend human capabilities for perception, comprehension, action, and learning" (Accenture 2017), and

McKinsey sees AI as "the ability of machines to display human-like intelligence" (McKinsey 2017). Naturally, with such dissimilar definitions, the characteristics that make up these definitions' elements will also differ greatly (A Definition of AI: Main Capabilities and Scientific Disciplines 2019).

Third, indicators used within indexes also come in three types, depending on the nature of what the authors call the AI: indicators that directly characterize the level of AI development—such as the number of AI startups in the country; indicators that directly affect the potential for AI development in the country—such as the number of high-performance supercomputers from the TOP 500 list; indicators that indirectly influence the potential for AI development in the country—such as the level of "digitalization of the economy and society" in the country.

Fourth (the last, but not the least), different indicators, characteristics, and other indexes from a very wide range of sources are used to calculate AI indexes (sometimes incomplete, contradictory, or incomparable).

These factors make it very difficult to make a correct and consistent comparative analysis of the current and potential AI development in most countries of the world, including Russia. This is largely a result of missing or insufficient data. The best-performing region, on average, is North America, while the worst-performing regions are Africa and the Asia-Pacific. But while the USA is closely watching Chinese and Russian AI progress in the security and defense areas (2016–2019 Progress Report: Advancing Artificial Intelligence R&D 2019; Wright 2019), those countries are making rapid advances in quite peaceful areas, China—in industrial production, Russia—in AI research, regulation, and big data.

The Index highlights the current inequality in AI readiness between global governments, with higher-income countries predictably doing better in the rankings than middle- and lower-income countries. Given that we are on the cusp of seeing widespread AI implementation across a number of sectors, including public services, this should serve as a timely reminder of the ongoing inequality of access to AI technologies, which will only deepen the gap between the developed and the developing countries.

More than 40 countries have already adopted national AI strategies in order to take advantage of the opportunities of AI in industrial production, services, and public governance. The Russian Government has also followed suit and is going to adopt an action plan designed to serve as a road map for implementing the National AI Strategy we have already mentioned. Like many other AI strategies in the world, the Russian Government is trying to take a comprehensive approach, covering implications of AI for research, balance between research and business development, employment, education, and regulation to name just a few of the most important issue areas.

However, the strategy has been criticized for not defining clear and measurable objectives. The lack of concrete goals and clear indicators of success is symptomatic for many strategy papers and announcements in Russian digital policy. Definitions of clear goals are missing as are policies to monitor progress and measure success. Politicians and citizens are therefore often left wondering what precisely the Government is trying to achieve, and whether there is any progress. The Government is still trying to divide responsibilities between the Ministry for Economic Development and the profile Ministry for Communications. Defining success indicators naturally would require the development of cross-departmental goals, which lays the foundation for tracking progress and thus creates the conditions for an effective implementation of the AI Strategy.

The Russian AI Strategy defines artificial intelligence as a set of technological solutions that allows simulating human cognitive functions (including self-learning and search for solutions without a predetermined algorithm) and gets results when performing specific tasks that are comparable, at least, with the results of human intellectual activity. The complex of technological solutions includes information and communication infrastructure, software (including those that use machine learning methods), processes and services for data processing and search for solutions. The main goal of the strategy is ensuring the growth of the welfare and quality of life of its population, ensuring national security and law enforcement, ensuring the sustainable competitiveness of the Russian economy, including leading positions in the world in the field of AI.

There are 6 objectives for AI development in Russia:

(a) Support for scientific research in order to ensure the advanced development of AI;
(b) Development of software that uses AI technologies;
(c) Improving the availability and quality of data necessary for the development of AI technologies;
(d) Increasing the availability of hardware necessary for solving AI problems;

(e) Increasing the level of AI qualified personnel and the level of awareness of the population about possible areas of use of AI technologies;
(f) Creating a comprehensive system for regulating public relations arising from the development and use of AI technologies.

Having accurate, understandable, and objectively measurable KPIs is a key condition that is necessary (but not sufficient) for the success of AI strategy. Most national AI development strategies we have analyzed require 4 types of KPIs:

- Initial KPIs (quantitative and qualitative) that assess the status and potential of both the country and the resources available for implementing the AI development strategy (for example, the amount of funding for the implementation of the National AI Strategy and flexibility and efficiency of managing article-by-article funding the AI research).
- Target KPIs (quantitative and qualitative) that evaluate the result—how far the goals set in the strategy have been achieved (for example, the number of AI patents filed in a particular year and completeness and elaboration of accepted standards in the field of AI).

Having analyzed the goal and tasks of the Russian AI Strategy, we have come to the conclusion that neither quantitative nor qualitative KPIs are applicable to them. The achievement of a goal formulated as above can neither be confirmed nor denied. Therefore, everything depends only on the personal will of those who make the assessment—senior public officials.

Conclusion

The original KPIs for the six so-called tasks of the Russian AI National strategy are either missing or are so vague that it simply makes no sense to even try to evaluate such KPIs as "having a strong natural science school", "having competencies in the field of modeling" or "winning international school Olympiads", regardless of what task these KPIs were assigned by the developers of the Russian AI Strategy. Most of other KPIs are formed according to a remarkable pattern—"increase in the number of X" or "significant growth of X" (where X is "organizations", "results", "citation index", etc.). Moreover, it does not matter how much these "numbers" are planned to increase. And even if they do not increase but decrease, it cannot be checked since the initial quantitative KPIs for these "quantities" are not named.

Target KPIs are named in the strategy in a similarly non-specific and immeasurable way. Thus, new Russian microprocessors developed during the execution of the strategy "should be widely represented" in the Russian and international markets, Russian universities "should occupy leading positions in the world in AI", "by 2024, necessary legal conditions must be created to achieve the goals, objectives, and implementation of the measures provided for in this Strategy", "by 2030, the Russian Federation should have a flexible system of legal regulation in the field of AI", and so on.

We believe that the Federal, Regional, and Municipal action plans designed to implement the National AI Strategy should list exact targets that the appropriate power bodies would like to achieve in public governance with the help of AI. Moscow, as one of the world leaders in the digitalization of municipal life, is preparing to introduce an experimental legal regime (regulatory sand box) for the development of AI with the participation of large IT companies from July 1, 2020. The draft law on conducting a corresponding five-year experiment was submitted to the State Duma on February 7, 2020.

A new bill should be developed in response to President Vladimir Putin's address to the Federal Assembly on January 15, 2020, "to ensure the creation of its own standards and the development of technologies that determine the future, in particular artificial intelligence technologies". The new law would significantly encourage the introduction, development, and use of AI technologies, ensuring technological sovereignty in the field of AI and, as a consequence, ensuring the viability of Russian business and economy, improving the quality of life of citizens of Russia, security, and defense potentials of the state.

In light of the above, AI has become a focal area of strategic target for public governance and a key driver of economic development. It can bring solutions to many challenges, from treating diseases to minimizing the environmental impact of farming, from national defense and security to culture and education. If the state does not pay due attention to this industry, Russia risks missing the opportunity for a technological breakthrough. The global market for technological solutions based on AI will be divided among competing countries, first of all the USA and China, which will make it difficult for Russia to successfully develop strategically important sectors of the economy and slow down its development.

However, socio-economic, legal, and ethical impacts of implementing AI strategy have to be carefully addressed from the point of view of efficiency of both public and private investments in corresponding projects. National systems of measurable and controllable performance results should become part of AI development strategy.

References

2016–2019 Progress Report: Advancing Artificial Intelligence R&D. (2019, November 19). Retrieved from https://www.whitehouse.gov/wp-content/uploads/2019/11/AI-Research-and-Development-Progress-Report-2016-2019.pdf/.

A Definition of AI: Main Capabilities and Scientific Disciplines. (2019). High-Level Expert Group on Artificial Intelligence. Retrieved from https://ec.europa.eu/digital-single-market/en/news/definition-artificial-intelligence-main-capabilities-and-scientific-disciplines.

Accenture. (2017). Boost Your AIQ—Transforming into an AI Business. Retrieved from https://www.accenture.com/_acnmedia/accenture/next-gen-5/event-g20-yea-summit/pdfs/accenture-boost-your-aiq.pdf.

AI Policy and China: Realities of State-Led Development. (2019). *Stanford-New America DigiChina Project*. Retrieved from https://fsi-live.s3.us-west-1.amazonaws.com/s3fs-public/digichina-ai-report-20191029.pdf.

AI Strategy for Russia. (2019). (Decree of the President of the Russian Federation No. 490 dated October 10, 2019. 'On the Development of Artificial Intelligence in the Russian Federation'). Retrieved from http://publication.pravo.gov.ru/Document/View/0001201910110003.

Government Artificial Intelligence Readiness Index. (2019). Retrieved from https://ai4d.ai/wp-content/uploads/2019/05/ai-gov-readiness-report_v08.pdf.

Heumann, S., & Zahn, N. (2018). *Benchmarking National AI Strategies*. Stiftung Neue Verantwortung. Retrieved from https://www.stiftung-nv.de/sites/default/files/benchmarking_ai_strategies.pdf.

McKinsey Global Institute. (2017). Artificial Intelligence—The Next Frontier. Retrieved from https://www.mckinsey.com/~/media/McKinsey/Industries/Advanced%20Electronics/Our%20Insights/How%20artificial%20intelligence%20can%20deliver%20real%20value%20to%20companies/MGI-Artificial-Intelligence-Discussion-paper.ashx.

Next Generation Artificial Intelligence Development Plan. (2017). Approved by the State Council of China in July 2017. Retrieved from https://www.newamerica.org/cybersecurity-initiative/digichina/blog/full-translation-chinas-new-generation-artificial-intelligence-development-plan-2017/.

Wright, N. (2019, February). *AI: China, Russia and the Global Order*. Retrieved from https://www.airuniversity.af.edu/Portals/10/AUPress/Books/B_0161_WRIGHT_ARTIFICIAL_INTELLIGENCE_CHINA_RUSSIA_AND_THE_GLOBAL_ORDER.PDF.

CHAPTER 10

Global Navigation Satellite Systems as Digital Solutions for Smart Cities

Sergey Kamolov and Grigory Tarasov

Introduction

The role of global navigation satellite systems in the development of smart cities is a highly relevant topic, attracting more and more attention of the expert and academic communities.

The city is the most important subject of economic, sociocultural and political development in the world. For example, with only 16% of the population of France living in Paris, this city produces one-third of the GDP of the French Republic and more than 5% of the GDP of the European Union.

The active growth of cities and agglomerations is accompanied by a steady increase in systemic problems for city authorities, including logistics, housing, communal, socio-economic and environmental issues. The

S. Kamolov (✉)
Moscow State Institute of International Relations (MGIMO University), Moscow, Russia

G. Tarasov
Institute of Smart Cities Comparative Studies, Moscow, Russia

I. Stepnov (ed.), *Technology and Business Strategy*,
https://doi.org/10.1007/978-3-030-63974-7_10

fact that they are unresolved negatively affects the life of both the urban population and the welfare of the world as a whole because 80% of world GDP is produced by cities.

One of the approaches to solving modern urban problems is the "Smart City Concept", an important role in the implementation of which is played by global navigation satellite systems that ensure functioning and inclusivity of the management and technological elements of a smart city.

In 2018, Carlo Doride, CEO of the European Agency for Global Navigation Satellite Systems emphasized the crucial role of GNSS technologies in his study on the use of space technologies in smart cities. According to Doride, the key element of a smart city is information and communication technologies, the development of which depends on space technology, including global navigation satellite systems that provide accurate identification of the location of an object in space. The modern functionality of personal gadgets (smartphones, tablets, electronic watches) is largely based on the capabilities of GNSS: from obtaining information about the traffic situation to transmitting coordinates to emergency services. Moreover, according to Carlo Doride, a number of smart technologies are completely impossible to implement without GNSS, such as the Internet of things or unmanned transport management (Dorides 2018).

The general theoretical part of the study is based on the views formulated in the research of Russian and foreign authors, including scientific articles "On the epistemological essence of "smart cities" (Kamolov 2019) and "Smart City—Hype and/or Reality?" (Finger 2018). The data of the European GNSS Agency is of particular analytical value for this study since it allowed us to formulate reasonable conclusions about the features of the value chain that is emerging in the global GNSS market and the downstream segment of the global space market (European GNSS Agency 2017).

The goal of our study is to analyze the prospects of using global navigation satellite systems in smart cities. To achieve the above goals, the authors identified the following research tasks:

1. Reveal the concept of smart city;
2. Explore the key characteristics of GNSS;
3. Analyze the downstream segment of the GNSS market, including the value chain; and
4. Define the scope of application of GNSS in smart cities.

Methodology

When carrying out the present study, some methods of analysis, measurement and forecasting were used. The main body of research includes work with statistical data on the development of key GNSS segments, followed by the modeling and formalization of the data obtained.

The study involved bibliometric data analysis, which comprises the use of statistical logical-linguistic methods to study scientific articles, reports, journals and regulatory documents. In particular, citation analysis was used to determine the frequency of use of particular phrases and terms. Thus, the dynamics of publications of scientific papers on the problems of smart cities was studied and specific examples of the GNSS application in the urban environment were established.

Results

1. Smart City

The urban population of the world is growing steadily. The UN experts state that currently 55% of people live in cities and by 2050 the urban population will reach 68% (United Nations 2018). This is also confirmed by the data of specialists who observe a steady growth in urban agglomerations with over one million inhabitants (The World Bank 2018). Urbanization is accompanied by an increase in the load and pressure on existing urban utilities and social infrastructure, on the effectiveness of which the further prosperity of cities depends (Kamolov 2019).

One approach to addressing these new challenges in the development of urban agglomerations is the concept of "Smart City". The growth of interest in this idea began in 2010, when a scientific discussion was actively spreading in the expert community. At the same time, there is still no single terminological apparatus, as well as a generally accepted understanding of the problems of the "Smart City". This is due to the fact that the concept of "Smart City" is dealt with by specialists from various fields—ecology, sociology, construction and management—who consider the development of smart cities through their own professional prism (Finger 2018). Under conditions of categorical uncertainty, it is advisable not to create the only correct interpretation of the phenomenon of "Smart City" "by all means", but to study the stages of development of this phenomenon and formulate the basic principles that a smart city should meet and be in conformity with.

Russian practitioners were able to identify the universal principles of a modern smart city based on a detailed study of a wide range of smart city projects (including Portuguese PlanIT, South Korean Songdo, Barcelona, City of London and Rio de Janeiro) (Kamolov 2019):

1. Citizen-centered design;
2. Sustainable and scalable urban infrastructure;
3. Self-regenerating city resources;
4. Comfortable and safe environment;
5. Economic efficiency.

The implementation of the above-mentioned principles may indicate the ongoing qualitative changes in the urban process management system. A similar approach to the perception of smart city issues is adopted in the European Union, where "Smart City" refers to a territorial entity within which a high level of security and operational management of the city are provided. Moreover, traditional channels of interaction and communication have reached a new level of efficiency through the use of digital and telecommunication technologies integrated into the transport infrastructure and housing system (OECD 2019).

2. GNSS: Concept and Performance Criteria

One of the most important areas for the development of a smart city is digital and telecommunication technologies that provide the automatization of urban processes and control systems with real-time information about the situation in the city. A special role in the implementation of digital and telecommunication technologies in the urban environment is played by global navigation satellite systems.

At a fundamental level, the global navigation satellite system is a solution for providing the user with autonomous geospatial information about the position of bodies related to land, air and water spaces. GNSS consists of three key elements:

1. In-orbit satellites;
2. Signal streams from a satellite to the Earth;
3. Ground-based infrastructure for receiving signal from satellites.

The functional model of the global navigation satellite system relies on the following algorithm. A ground-based GNSS receiver determines the position of a particular satellite in orbit and determines the time it takes to receive a satellite signal, which allows the receiver to calculate its position on the Earth. It is important to note that a GNSS receiver can only interact with satellites that are above the horizon—usually a group of 6 to 12 satellites. If the GNSS receiver encounters an obstacle while receiving a signal (for example, high-rise buildings), it automatically switches to interacting with another available satellite.

European experts identify the following key criteria for GNSS effectiveness (European GNSS Agency 2017):

1. Availability. The time during which a sufficient number of satellites is capable of transmitting a signal to the Earth.
2. Accuracy. It is important that GNSS provides the most accurate information about the location of an object.
3. Duration. Continuity and stability of the signal coming from the satellite to the Earth.
4. Reliability. The level of confidence in the data that was obtained as part of the use of a particular GNSS system.
5. Location time. The response time of the receiver after it is turned on.
6. Security. Stability against attacks on the processes of signal transmission and reception.
7. Authenticity. Confidence that the consumer is receiving a signal from a reliable source.

3. GNSS Geographical Breakdown

Established during the Cold War, the Global Positioning Systems (GPS) and the Global Navigation Satellite System (GLONASS) were the initial phase of the global navigation satellite system creation.

Today the geography of the GNSS development and its core elements are not limited by Russia and the territory of the United States. Many countries are actively involved in the development of GNSS technologies, and we see how various levels of the global GNSS market are shaped (global, regional and local):

1. International navigation satellite systems: GLONASS (Russia), GPS (USA), Galileo (EU), BeiDou (China).
2. Regional navigation satellite systems: QZSS (Japan), IRNSS (India), specific elements of BeiDou (China).

3. GNSS Augmentation: WAAS (USA), EGNOS (EU), MSAS (Japan), GAGAN (India), SDCM (RF), SNAS (China).

The United States is leading the global GNSS industry, controlling 29% of the market, followed by the EU countries (25%) and Japan (23%). These regions concentrate the largest number of GNSS equipment producers, navigation services providers and the so-called system aggregators (European GNSS Agency 2017).

4. GNSS: Value Chain

The result of the intensive development of GNSS was the formation of the downstream segment of global space market, within which GNSSs are an important link in the chain of operations for providing services to the end consumers (for example, providing data for a consumer's digital device to create a route from point A to point B). The main elements of the downstream market value chain are (Fig. 10.1):

Component manufacturers		System integrators		Added-value service providers		GNSS applications users
Qualcomm	USA	Toyota	JP	Google	USA	Mass Market Users, Professional Users, Users With Special Needs, Retailers
Broadcom	USA	General Motors	USA	Here Global ●	DE	
Mediatek ●	CN	Garmin	USA	Pioneer	JP	
Trimble Navigation	USA	Ford	USA	Denso	JP	
Hexagon	SE	China First	CN	Microsoft	USA	
u-blox ●	CH	Volkswagen	DE	Boeing ●	USA	
STM ●	CH	Samsung Elec.	KR	Ericsson ●	SE	
Cobham	UK	Apple	USA	Garmin ●	USA	
Furuno Electric	JP	Nissan	JP	Clarion	JP	
Topcon ●	JP	Honda	JP	Tomtom	NL	

● New Entrants in the Top 10

Fig. 10.1 Top-10 companies across the value chain based on 2015 revenues. (*Source*: European GNSS Agency (2017). *GNSS Market Report*, p. 12. https://www.gsa.europa.eu/system/files/reports/gnss_mr_2017.pdf)

1. Component manufacturers. The leaders are American companies Qualcomm and Broadcom—in total they account for up to 40% of revenues in the industry;
2. System integrators. This group comprises automobile concerns and smartphone vendors, which operate in the GNSS technology market from outside of their core industries (for example, automobile manufacturing);
3. Manufacturers of value-added services. With the help of GNSS, consumers are provided with value-added services.

It is expected that the annual growth in the development of GNSS value-added services during the period from 2015 to 2025 will be 20%, and after 2025 it will stabilize to an average of 9.6% (European GNSS Agency 2017). The total revenue from the use of GNSS technologies in 2019 amounted to 150 billion euros; it is expected to grow up to 325 billion euros by 2029.

It is important to note that the structure of GNSS producers is heterogeneous and specific. On the one hand, most of the companies in this area are small enterprises, and on the other hand, only a few large companies dominate in turnover and profit distribution of this market (Stepnov et al. 2019). This is confirmed by the turnover data of companies in the field of creating equipment for receiving satellite signals. Thus, in 2015, five companies accounted for almost 60% of the total GNSS equipment market turnover.

5. *Industry Segments and Applications*

The main segments of the market (by gross revenue criterion) are geolocation and road services. Together they account for 93% of the market, and this structure will remain until 2025 (see Fig. 10.2), due to the significant development of unmanned vehicles that have occurred recently.

Another important incentive for the development of the GNSS end-use market is the direct integration of the GNSS receivers into smartphones and other gadgets, which makes it possible for a much larger number of people to use the satellite signal in different spheres of life. As part of the implementation of smart city projects, we see the highest potential for the use of GNSS technologies in the following areas:

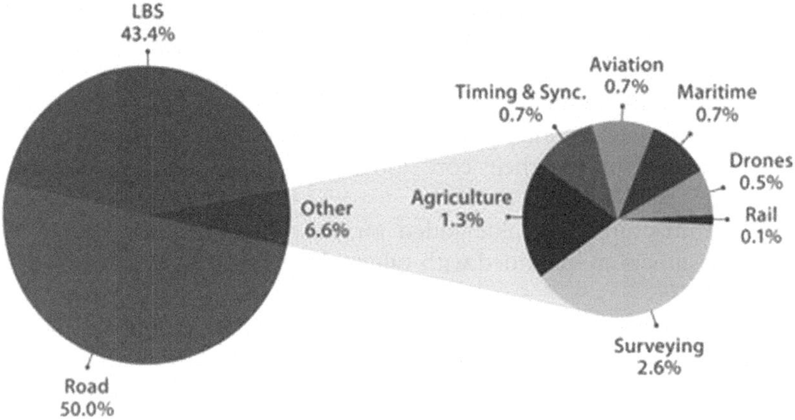

Fig. 10.2 Cumulative Revenue (2015–2025) by segment. (*Source*: European GNSS Agency (2017). *GNSS Market Report*, p. 11. https://www.gsa.europa.eu/system/files/reports/gnss_mr_2017.pdf)

1. *Road Traffic.* In addition to providing drivers with accurate information about the situation on the road, as well as their location, space technology is at the heart of the development of unmanned vehicles, which depends on a stable and accurate signal between traffic participants. Satellite systems are relatively inexpensive and effective solution to the problem of unavailability or signal insufficiency for the development of unmanned vehicles. For example, the City of London was one of the first to equip buses with satellite signal receivers, which allowed to reduce the number of traffic jams by 20%. In the capital of Iceland, Reykjavik, with the help of GNSS, a "priority" system for the green signal on the road for ambulance and public transport was installed (European GNSS Agency 2017).
2. *Shipping.* GNSSs provide safer shipping and are indispensable in ports where cargo ships in a limited space must efficiently carry out loading and unloading activities. These systems are especially relevant in a situation where modern ports do not have time to provide enough room for maneuver of cargo ships, which creates additional difficulties in matters of security and time for the implementation of the necessary cargo handling.

3. *Air Traffic.* GNSS is a new stage in the development of systems for providing accurate information for pilots about flight conditions and the location of the aircraft, which makes the flight safer and more comfortable. Moreover, GNSS creates conditions for the development of regional aviation infrastructure, since the system does not require large financial costs for installation at small regional airports, which makes them more affordable, including for servicing large aircraft that previously had to avoid landing at airports with poorly developed navigation and dispatch systems (European GNSS 2018).
4. *Railway Connection.* The use of GNSS can make the process of moving trains more efficient, safe and well-coordinated. For example, in the EU, thanks to GNSS, the costs of developing railway infrastructure have been reduced, since to accurately track the location of the train, it is enough to install a special system in the driver's cab that "connects" the train to the satellite. This solution not only reduces the cost of the development of railway infrastructure but also facilitates the process of coordinating the movement of trains and reduces the likelihood of emergencies. In Russia, for example, an integrated train safety system has been developed that uses GLONASS and GPS signals to better determine the location of trains.
5. *Search and Rescue.* The European GALILEO system allows specialists to reduce the time it takes to find people in trouble or missing from 3 hours to 10 minutes, which is extremely useful for overcoming the consequences of natural disasters and other emergencies.
6. *Mapping and Spatial Planning.* Based on GNSS technologies, the process of studying the terrain for planning and developing infrastructure is accelerated and simplified (EIP-SCC 2018). For example, in Prague, the local authorities are implementing a program to analyze the situation in different parts of the city that are experiencing a shortage of certain infrastructure (for example, public transport), which is based on receiving information from a satellite.
7. *Agriculture.* GNSSs allow modern agriculture to be more efficient, safer and financially sound. In particular, farmers can track via satellite information on where to increase/decrease the use of fertilizers, leading to a better output. In the EU, a system of "virtual pens" for livestock has been successfully used: cattle are equipped with sensors that allow tracking the movement of animals, and, if necessary, assist them if they leave the space allotted for their grazing.

8. *Streamline-based Waste Management.* A program for using satellites is being implemented in the French municipalities to reduce the time and cost of local authorities for the disposal of organic waste. Moreover, according to the authorities of the English city of Exeter, after equipping the garbage collection machines with satellite systems, it was possible to optimize the costs of garbage collection by 470 thousand pounds since the start of the program (European GNSS Agency 2017).

Conclusion

As a result of the study, an ontological analysis of the concept of "smart city" was carried out. Smart City means urban space, where the quality of services provided by the city authorities to citizens and process control are brought to a new level. Moreover, the criteria that a smart city must meet have been defined:

1. Citizen-centered design;
2. Sustainable and scalable urban infrastructure;
3. Self-regenerating city resources;
4. Comfortable and safe environment;
5. Economic efficiency.

In this article, we studied the basic characteristics of GNSS: the origin, the development of global navigation satellite systems, the principles of operation, and performance indicators across the regions of the world.

A holistic view of the value chain in the global GNSS market has been shaped, which includes manufacturers of equipment, value-added services and system integrators mainly represented by major automobile producers and smartphone vendors. The downstream segment of the GNSS market was investigated, which includes geolocation and road services, technologies in the field of land, air and sea navigation, agriculture, urban waste management, search and rescue capabilities and spatial planning. The achieved goal of the study—an analysis of the prospects for the use of global navigation satellite systems in a smart city—develops and supplements the provisions of the concept of a space economy in relation to sustainable urban development and the role of GNSS in urban agglomerations (Yanik 2019).

The complex of challenges related to urbanization, including ecology, housing shortages, access to utilities and limited socio-economic opportunities, requires bringing the quality of process management in the urban environment to a whole new level, which can be achieved through the implementation of the principles of smart city and governance based on the large-scale application of information technologies.

The implementation of the Smart City concept is impossible in isolation from the use of GNSS technologies since they underlie the functioning of many controls of smart cities, the effectiveness and functionality of which depend on the quality of satellite signals. The need for GNSS will only grow in the coming years, as evidenced by the rapid development of the downstream space technologies, its financial performance and the interest of private companies to invest in the development of GNSS.

It should be emphasized that despite the dominant role of geolocation and road services in the GNSS market, we see a real growth potential for segments such as rail, air and sea communications, agriculture, spatial planning, mapping, wastes disposal, search and rescue services. These areas will continue to develop and in the foreseeable future will constitute a significant share in the smart technologies market.

References

Dorides, C. des. (2018). *How Space Technologies are Driving the Future of Smart Cities.* Retrieved from https://cities-today.com/industry/how-space-technologies-are-driving-the-future-of-smart-cities/

EIP-SCC. (2018). *Cities are Reaching into Space to Solve Urban Challenges.* Retrieved from https://eu-smartcities.eu/news/cities-are-reaching-space-solve-urban-challenges-and-save-money

European GNSS. (2018). *EGNOS for Aviation.* Retrieved from https://www.gsa.europa.eu/library/videos?search=&field_video_gallery_topic_tid=1112&field_video_gallery_language_value_1=en&sort_by=field_video_gallery_date_value&sort_by=field_video_gallery_date_value

European GNSS Agency. (2017). *GNSS Market Report.* Retrieved from https://www.gsa.europa.eu/system/files/reports/gnss_mr_2017.pdf

Finger, M. (2018). Smart City—Hype and/or Reality. *IGLUS Quarterly*, no. 4. Retrieved from https://iglus.org/wp-content/uploads/2019/05/IGLUS-Quarterly-Vol-4-Issue-1-1.pdf

Kamolov, S. (2019). Epistemological Essence of "Smart Cities". *Innovazii i investizii*, no. 1 (in Russian). Retrieved from http://innovazia.ru/archive/?ELEMENT_ID=16041

OECD. (2019). *Smart Cities and Inclusive Growth*. Retrieved from https://www.oecd.org/cfe/regional-policy/OECD-Roundtable-on-Smart-Cities-and-Inclusive-Growth_Issues-Note.pdf

Stepnov, I., Kovalchuk, J., & Gorchakova, E. (2019). On Assessing the Efficiency of Intracluster Interaction for Industrial Enterprises. *Studies on Russian Economic Development, 30*(3), 346–354. https://doi.org/10.1134/S107570071903016X.

The World Bank. (2018). *Population in Urban Agglomerations of More than 1 million (% of Total Population)*. Retrieved from https://data.worldbank.org/indicator/EN.URB.MCTY.TL.ZS

United Nations. (2018). *Revision of World Urbanization Prospects*. Retrieved from https://www.un.org/development/desa/publications/2018-revision-of-world-urbanization-prospects.html

Yanik, A. (2019). To the Concept of "Space Economy". *Trendi I Menedgement, 1*, 51–66. https://doi.org/10.7256/2454-0730.2018.1.25708.

CHAPTER 11

The Digital Trade Route to an Economic Space in the Eurasian Economic Union: Institutions and Technology

Kobilzhon Zoidov and Alekxey Medkov

Introduction

Both the development of transport and transit systems (TTS), and the digital transformation of the carriage industry, are the most vital directions taken by EEC member-states, and the integration community in general, for the innovational development of their national economies. With this in mind, the aim of the chapter is to identify the main and the most relevant areas of digitalization in the transportation industry, since it is the most advanced industry in its field, on the basis of a systematic analysis, the

K. Zoidov (✉)
Institute of Economics and Demography, Academy of Sciences of the Republic of Tajikistan, Dushanbe, Tajikistan

Market Economy Institute of the Russian Academy of Sciences, Moscow, Russia

A. Medkov
Market Economy Institute of the Russian Academy of Sciences, Moscow, Russia

I. Stepnov (ed.), *Technology and Business Strategy*,
https://doi.org/10.1007/978-3-030-63974-7_11

theory of evolutionary institutionalism, the theory of manufacturing, the technological balance of the national economy, and a historic analysis.

Areas of digital transformation that enjoy governmental, organizational, and commercial support remain the main focus of the chapter. Efforts from both the government and businesses are, above all, directed at forming a single digital platform for transportation companies, with the aim of fulfilling the country's transit potential, making trade routes as technologically advanced as possible, and developing transportation channels, specifically by means of utilizing tracking mechanisms for goods.

According to Ditrich, the minister of transportation of Russia, "the most important factor in the transportation system's development is its digitalization and it is this point that is included in the complex long-haul infrastructure development and expansion program. Our mission is to create a single digital transportation platform with the use of Russian-developed software and with access to transportation services in a 'single window'". In fact this will signify the creation of a "green" digital channel, where the carriage of goods is safe and uninterrupted thanks to the electronic navigation seal subject to control by GLONASS and "Platon" systems. Circulation of documents in an electronic form will ensure fast and high-quality processing and faster checkpoint passage. A multi-module digital carriage exchange market will become available for companies and the passengers will be able to purchase a fully functional e-ticket for different modes of transport (Pletnev 2018).

Another important area is the implementation of electronic documents, advanced communication procedures upon the arrival of goods about the goods' characteristics, unmanned documents processing, and control technology, which, in turn, has been met with discontent on the part of governing bodies exercising control, motivated by the potential automation of their employees' work duties. Experts note that "by simplifying the circulation of documents and transitioning into an electronic form, by modernizing infrastructure and perfecting its logistics practices, Russia will be able to achieve a significant increase in railway transportation volumes towards China" (Kober 2018a).

It was in 2015 that the Chinese project "One belt—one way" began its transformation into the "Digital silk road". According to Bannikova, the head of the Russian Government's Analytics Centre Foreign Economic Policy Department, "this concerns not just transportation as an industry, but also the development of digital technology and IT". For example, within the "Digital silk road" project, propositions have been made to create "such communication channels (the aim of which would be the development of inter-state communication by means of online and voice data transfer) as China–Mongolia–Russia, and the new Eurasian channel which will be laid on land and will pass through, among others, Kazakhstan, Russia and Belarus" (Kudryavtseva 2018).

Digital transformation is especially relevant in the process of developing modern trade routes and is beginning to be utilized widely in transit carriage of goods. Starting from July 1, 2018, a decree of the Russian President has allowed the transit carriage of "sanctioned" goods through Russia into other states. As a result, Akimov, Deputy Head of Government, instructed several federal agencies to facilitate such carriages on an organizational and institutional level, more specifically to prepare proposals on creating a system of transit carriage supervision.

Furthermore, in order for seal-press devices to function properly, cloud data storage, as well as internal storage technologies, could be utilized. For the carriers' convenience, and for the purposes of their adaptation, no installation fees and no fines for the misuse of seals have been imposed on carriers. Moreover, a piece of software called "GLONASS-Transit" has been developed, the purpose of which is to process all the information it receives from electronic seals and to direct the said information to supervisory bodies.

Within the "Digital economy" program and its subprogram "Digital transportation and logistics", plans have been made to develop digital systems integration solutions in the field of transportation and logistics within the EEC. The digitalization of the transportation industry may serve to raise its economic efficiency by 35%.

However, it should be noted that modern trade routes may only become an integral part—indeed, a driving force—of both national economies and the integration community as a whole if they are based on high-tech industrial and agricultural development with the use of internal technical and technological advancements.

List, who developed protectionism theory, pointed out that "trade originates from factory manufacturing and land usage and no country in the world will be able to develop both its domestic and foreign trade options without first bringing these two base industries to perfection. There once used to be individual cities or city-alliances with the capacity to trade on a wide, intermediary basis with the help of foreign factories and farmers; however, with the creation of powerful farming, manufacturing and commercial states even the notion of intermediary trade in its

Hanseatic form became unthinkable. In any case, such trade is by its very nature so unreliable that it hardly deserves any attention as opposed to trade that has its roots in the country's own industry" (List 2017).

The TTS digital transformation of EEC member-states must also be conducted on the basis of their own development projects, the need for which is becoming more and more relevant, taking into account the strict economic sanctions imposed on Russia by Western countries. This area, like none other, requires the wide use of a particular competitive advantage that Russia possesses, namely human resources, as well as a high level of scientific advancements in the transportation industry along with logistics universities graduates and transportation engineers.

Maslov, Head of the Higher School of Economics Oriental Studies Department, notes that

> nowadays, in order for IT to become a driving force behind economic growth, the technology has to be selective and innovational and that is something that we possess. What's more, it has to be simple and easy to use. That, in turn, is going to pose a problem, which is why the implementation period in Russia might stretch to infinity, even though the government tries to make it run faster through small and medium sized businesses support programs. Despite all this the most interesting of the Russian projects tend to flow overseas because many think that they are easier to be realized there. (Kolbina 2018)

On the other hand, it should be taken into account that the unfurling Fourth Industrial Revolution, in the opinion of academic Akaev, "will lead to a new dawn of local mass consumption goods industry. This is especially vital for developing countries … industry can be transferred to our towns and villages which will get rid of great transportation expenses" (Akaev and Akaeva 2019).

With that being said, an unavoidable decline in transportation has to be balanced out by its intense digitalization based on national (intra-integrational) developments and innovations in manufacturing.

Methodology

The study utilizes a systematic analysis, the theory of evolutionary institutionalism, the theory of manufacturing and technological balance, and a historical analysis.

The aim of the study is to analyze the main organizational and institutional problems in the development of digital trade routes in the economic space of the Eurasian Economic Union (EEU).

Results

With regard to this, the main areas of digital transformation of trade routes in the EEC economic space must be analyzed. Table 11.1 lists all of the aforementioned areas.

Implementation of Electronic Navigational Seals ("Smart" Seals) and Electronic Way Bills

For the purposes of increasing the volume of transit carriage of goods and raising its efficiency and profitability in the EEC, an electronic way bill has to be uniform for all states—Russia, Kazakhstan, and China. Currently, car carriers have no such way bill. Further improvements to the carriage process entail the implementation of a uniform electronic carriage document on the Polish and German routes, which would allow carriage from a loading point to an unloading point without any institutional barriers.

Transit carriage of goods control with the use electronic navigational seals ("smart" seals) will help to secure tracking opportunities for the movement of goods in the EEC. An electronic navigational seal is, in itself, an onboard computer, storing the live information necessary for carriage of goods, as well as information on the goods' whereabouts and security.

As for railway transportation, electronic seals must—apart from providing a tracking mechanism—prevent any unauthorized opening of the containers and carts, which serves as a means of digital security in the carriage process. One of the main competitive advantages that this railway carriage has is the relatively high degree of safety regarding the carriage process. One of the reasons behind such a high degree of safety is the "Security train" project, which utilizes satellite geographical positioning technology. Electronic seals are used primarily in areas with high theft levels, as well as in the carriage of dangerous and expensive goods, for example, electronics and alcohol.

An interesting and important organizational and institutional problem in the field of implementing electronic seals and organizing the transit of sanctioned goods through Russia in accordance with the President's

Table 11.1 Main areas of digital transformation of trade routes in the EEC economic space

№	*Area of digital transformation*	*Implications of the area*	*Effect upon the functionality of the trade route*
1.	Implementation of electronic navigational seals and electronic way bills.	Unification of electronic way bills in the Eurasian economic space. Establishment of tracking mechanisms for goods and transactions, ensuring compliance with speed and technical parameters.	Increase in competition by enhancing carriage transparency and maximizing the efficiency of supervisory authorities' work, ensuring the safety of carriage and goods.
2.	Digitalization and automatization of customs and other control operations.	Providing information to border security authorities about the goods' characteristics, implementation of unmanned customs units and other operations.	Seamless border crossing, time reductions for non-stop supervisory provisions, lowering corruption risks.
3.	Use of autonomous (unmanned) vehicles powered by digital technology.	Implementation of special lanes on roads, formations of autonomous convoys of heavy cargo vehicles, development of high-sensitivity detectors that would detect foreign objects in the convoy's path.	Reduction of logistic costs, reduction of empty runs and overemployment as well as management expenses, reduction of insurance allocations.
4.	The development of "smart" rolling stocks.	Spread of unmanned vehicle controlling technologies. Transition from rolling stock and infrastructure repairs as per regulations to repairs based on the state of the vehicle. Implementation of predictive diagnostics.	Reduction of trade route usage costs, in terms of both the carriage process itself and infrastructure maintenance.
5.	Increase in the railways' transportation capacity.	A transition from a centralized auto-blocking system to a non-traffic-light status quo with potential implementation of dynamic block-members.	Increase in the railways' transportation and carriage capacity without building new railways.
6.	Automatization and digitalization of internal processes.	Implementation of electronic services aimed at providing easier access for clients to carriage services, improvement of internal processes.	Increase in accessibility and comfort of transportation services consumption on trade routes.

Source: Developed by the authors

Decree of July 1, 2018, was presented by Ilchenko, the project manager of "Aurora Logistics" LLC:

> "Following this decree, all operators have taken action but have encountered some difficulties. The Ministry of Transportation, the Ministry of Industrial Trade, the Federal Customs Office, and other agencies were instructed to develop an electronic seal handling procedure manual, but this document is as of yet non-existent. Earlier in 2014, a procedure manual was developed for transit goods coming from Ukraine under GLONASS seals into and through Russia, which is why the old seals are utilized way more frequently than new ones, thanks in large part to the existing procedure manual. There is no way to know who installs the new seals, who stores them while waiting for a handling manual and nobody understands how to handle them, the technology simply does not exist. This is pretty much how it looks like. As the goods cross the Russian border, a seal is installed and is then de-installed at the end point—as it leaves the Russian border. It is unclear as to who is responsible for the installation and de-installation. A station worker takes the seal, proceeds to the railway, looks for the right cart, installs the seal, signs the protocol, comes back, inputs all the data into a computer and sends it on the Federal Customs Office. According to a worker at the station "Smolensk-Sortirovochnyi", the procedure takes from 60 to 90 minutes. This is due to the fact that it requires a large amount of walking and there is simply not enough personnel. Besides, there is as of yet no list of transit goods subject to mandatory sealing. There is also no way of knowing the customs offices' role in all of this".

This large quote demonstrates the complexity and the inconsistency of digitalizing the railway transit carriage, which necessitates the establishment of manufacturing and technological balance. Implementing advanced technology usually entails the spread of manual labor, a need for human resources, and more physical human movement. The reason behind this inefficiency is the flawed nature of the organizational and the institutional basis for trade routes in the Eurasian economic space.

Controlling the temperature inside carts and containers throughout the whole route is the task of electronic seals in the carriage of temperature-sensitive goods (refrigerated carriages).

In 2018, a series of test multi-module contained goods carriage procedures were carried out along the Japan–Russia–EU route. A classic 40-feet container carrying retail goods was equipped with vibration, humidity, and temperature detectors, which are especially necessary in the carriage of goods produced by Japanese companies due to their high added value. The speed of the movement of the goods, and the aforementioned parameters, can be controlled independent of the carrier with the help of "Russian Railways" PLC information systems, as well as GLONASS and GPS navigational devices (Taranets 2018).

Digitalization and Automatization of Customs Operations and Other Control Operations

The digitalization and automatization of customs and other control operations serves to ensure that search procedures are conducted without stopping the vehicle. An information system registers and checks the customs declaration and authorizes release.

Digital sealing of goods moving across the country will make it possible to:

- Provide the consignor and the consignee with information about the actual whereabouts of the goods, their speed of movement, and their status.
- Provide the supervisory authorities working at the border with information about the type and the characteristics of the goods.
- Form a risk assessment profile for goods and consignors.

With this in mind, a portion of the goods will be allowed to cross the border through the "green channel", which will serve to increase delivery speed and reduce transportation expenses. As part of the project of constructing digital trade routes ("green channels") between Asia and Europe through Russia, the Federal Customs Office launched a pilot project in 2018 aimed at monitoring transit car carriage between Russia, Kazakhstan, and China with the use of electronic navigational seals. The joint Russian and Chinese navigation system GLONASS/Beidou has been tested on car routes passing through the Russia–PRC border checkpoints of Kraskino–HunChun and Poltavka–Dun Nin.

According to Yakovleva, the deputy head of Informatization Department of "Russian Railways" PLC,

> should an appropriate governmental ordinance be enacted, our company is ready to further develop the joint transit goods tracking project. "Russian Railways" PLC is taking part in developing a new service, which is meant to

> increase the quality of first-hand information used for carriage planning and forecasting, in large part thanks to the use of electronic sealing devices. The Russian Federal Customs Office conducted an experiment with the use of electronic sealing devices on cars and the experiment was called a success. All we need is a governmental ordinance and afterwards we will work on improvements to our automated systems, which will allow to increase the quality of various control procedures, including the delivery times control, route deviations monitoring, goods safety control, as well as to more accurately pinpoint the carts' location etc. Once again, all we need is the enactment of the appropriate documents. (Mozharovskaya 2018)

Electronic seal technology will be implemented in the "Russian Railways" PLC corporate digitalization program. All initial information about the goods is recorded on the device during the container sealing process. As the goods cross the Russian border, the data are collected remotely. In this case, border patrol, internal revenue offices, and customs offices will be able to receive all the required data electronically without having to open the container, check their own databases, and calculate the cargo charge and value added tax. This technology will serve to make transit operations a lot easier and to supervise the movement of containers up to their leaving the border.

Automatization of the Carriage Process, Use of Autonomous (Unmanned) Vehicles Powered by Digital Technology

It is estimated that by 2030 the use of autonomous unmanned vehicles will reduce almost half (47%) of all logistics expenses thanks to the digitalization and automatization of logistical processes, and largely (80%) thanks to personnel cuts. Unmanned heavy vehicles will be able to deliver goods 2.5 times faster than manned vehicles, due to the truck drivers' rest stops. The implementation of artificial intelligence in logistics will allow the reduction of empty runs, the reduction of administration and managing costs (Kamolov and Stepnov 2020), and the reduction of insurance payment sums. A fully automated loading, storage, and unloading system will also raise the efficiency of companies involved in transportation and logistics (Russian Railways-Partner 2018).

In order to implement autonomous carriage of goods by car and by railway, the following criteria have to be met:

- The addition of special lanes on roads.
- The formation of autonomous heavy vehicle convoys alongside mechanisms for their interaction with other vehicles on the road.
- The creation of additional protective barriers along railways.
- The creation of high-sensitivity detectors allowing a train to be notified in advance of any foreign objects in its path.
- Amendments to the existing legislation.

On July 10, 2018, the Australian company Rio Tinto launched an unmanned train carrying 28,000 tons of iron ore, originating in the extraction site and going to the port town of Cape Lambert, for a stretch of 280 kilometers. The transportation was under remote surveillance by the operators in a special center located 1500 kilometers away from the place of transportation. The operator designated a route, and, afterward, the computers installed in the operational center and on the train took control of the train while simultaneously monitoring the goods' safety (Aleksandrova 2018).

Producing a "Smart" Rolling Stock

Railway Transport

Old trains operated on the basis of analogue electric circuits. Traction rolling stocks, currently being developed, feature an improved microprocessor control and unit diagnostics system. In the near future, live transmission systems of diagnostic data on the train's state will be widely implemented.

The main advantages of using modern control systems are: limiting the train control functions to a single person, easing the train driver's burden thanks to autopilot, and telemechanical alert systems that turn the train driver into an operator. Besides, a telemechanical alert system is implemented.

Positioning devices include visual, light radar, and radar odometers, as well as machine sight, with their main function being to use the video surveillance systems to identify any objects with their precise coordinates. Implementation of complex systems is expected to allow the position of the rolling stock to be precisely located on various sections of the railway, and to give a serious push to development of unmanned transportation technology.

Trains are equipped with automatized and automatic control systems, including diagnostics, autopilot, and global GPS/GLONASS two-way communication positioning.

Transition from the interval rolling stock service to service-when-necessary means implementing broad self-diagnosis functions. The "Uralskie Lokomotivy" company, in particular, receives live diagnostic data (about 700 parameters) on every part of the rolling stock with the help of a specially developed program "UL-Service" (Kober 2018b). It is now time to develop a single database that accumulates operational information and information on the machinery's work. Predictive diagnosis is thought to be promising, as it will make it possible to predict the happening of events and to prevent potential problems.

It is not only information on the state of the rolling stock that is collected, but also external data about the surrounding infrastructure; for example, the technicalities of railway switches and their electric components are noted. This serves to cut infrastructural surveying and control costs.

Electric trains' security systems have the ability to automatically engage brakes should the train exceed the speed limit; they are also able to choose the braking mode themselves depending on the situation and to process the traffic light indicators.

The CEO of the Sinara Group, Khodorkovskiy, notes the obvious advantages of train servicing digital transformation: an increase in the train's technical availability rate, a more precise repair assessment, and an estimate of the spare parts needed for repairs.

To summarize, it is important to remark that a "smart" train concept includes artificial intelligence and being equipped with the necessary devices and systems that allow the train to function autonomously:

- Automatic instruction receivers.
- All-mode autopilots system.
- Videotaping and self-analysis systems that record everything happening onboard the train and on the surrounding infrastructure, self-diagnosis, predictive data analysis systems utilizing neural self-learning technology, operation modes intellectual self-analysis systems.
- In-motion obstacle detectors.
- Automatic rolling stock connecting mechanism.
- Other equipment and software allowing the transformation of a train into a single intellectual mechanism (Zubov 2018).

Digital transformation of the rolling stock and the surrounding infrastructure allows for the transition from "as per regulation" repairs to repairs based on the train's state. The "smarter" a traction rolling stock, the more alarm, centralization, and blocking devices the surrounding infrastructure requires, and the less manpower it needs to be serviced. Technology with the potential to raise transportation efficiency is to be tested on the Northern Latitude railway, and is expected to be spread to the entire railway system.

The junction and freight cart parts diagnostics system, as is currently in use, provides the operators with data on the freight cart's wheels when they are close to falling into disrepair. This allows quick decisions to be made to fix any detected flaws and, thus, to raise train park managing efficiency.

Car Transport

The "Platon" system is an example of car digitalization; it is a fee charging system aimed at heavy vehicles with a maximum approved weight capacity of 12 tons. With this comes the problem of verifying the data and its status. This is a key question for all of our government information systems currently collecting data by operation of law.

Heavy vehicles are expected to be equipped with axis strain detectors. By 2024, new legislation will be enacted which would impose the mandatory installation of detectors on vehicles weighing more than 3.5 tons. By the end of 2021, the Industrial Trade Ministry and the Ministry of Transportation are to prepare modifications to the Customs Union technical regulation, which would prohibit heavy vehicles not carrying such detectors to cross the Russian border. Old vehicles will not have detectors installed on them; however, car manufacturers will be required to install them onto new vehicles from 2023 onward.

Water Transport

One example of digital transformation in water transport is digital technological operations control, as used in harbors. For example, an active investor into the Russian economy, DP World (of the UAE), controls 78 sea terminals in 40 nations around the world with the help of digital technology; the control center, however, is located in Dubai, where the work of harbor equipment is monitored by 30 workers (Ermolenko 2018).

Aircraft
"Aeroflot" utilizes digital technology, in particular the Internet of Things technology, whereby planes transmit data to earth through a satellite mid-flight, said data including aircraft condition data. In February 2018, an automated airworthiness maintenance, servicing, and repair system, "AMOS", was implemented. This has allowed aircraft to stay in the air for up to 12 hours a day. The company is currently actively implementing artificial intelligence: the need for such development is linked to predictive servicing and repairs (when the want for repairs can be predicted based on which countries and airports the planes visit).

Telecommunication as a Means of Increasing Railway Transportation Capacity

Interval train traffic regulation is meant to increase railways' transportation and carriage capacity without constructing additional railways. With this comes the need to switch all centralized auto-blocking systems currently in use into no-traffic-light mode, which could potentially mean the implementation of mobile block-sections and data radio transmission technology, which will lead to speed increases. Signals for the oncoming train are emitted from the back of the train currently ahead, which allows the oncoming train to move at a distance less than 1 kilometer from the train ahead. Siemens AG company's experience is evidence that controlling trains through digital technology, incorporated into the entire national railway network, is already more than enough to increase transportation capacity by up to 50% (Kadik 2018).

Automatization and Digitalization of Internal Processes

Saraev, CEO of "TransContainer" PLC, believes that "the main problem for cargo owners is the complexity of carriage services order system. Nowadays cargo owners are meant to specialize in the field of transit carriage simply to apply for carriage. Our task is to make a simple, clear, and an affordable service. Digitalization may be closer and more affordable for customers and a transition to digital services lowers the risk of problems with documents" (Ermakova 2018).

In order to solve those problems, "Russian Railways" PLC is developing electronic services aimed both at enabling easier access for customers to carriage services and at improving internal processes. Some standard operations, such as empty carts clearance, are already conducted automatically.

Conclusion/Recommendations

The digital transformation of the transportation and communication system, and of modern trade routes, is a necessity, especially in the area of e-commerce. It is noted that this market segment is extremely promising for transportation and logistics companies: for an online store, the price of logistical processing is one of the main competition factors, and let us not forget that online-stores, unlike industrial cargo owners, are willing to outsource this process. Despite the appeal of the service to logistics operators, it has a low profit margin and becomes profitable only with bigger volumes. This model works only if there is a high enough level of processes automation, including setting up communication means with online-store customers (Perechneva 2018).

Integrating informational and communicational systems in the Eurasian economic space will help to establish electronic communication between "Russian Railways" PLC and the Russian Customs Office; in transit across Russia into EU countries, this will enable the planned transition to fully electronic documentation by 2020. Electronic document circulation solves the problem of points of delivery being too far from customs offices locations; it also lifts the need to physically move paper documents between these two points, which would normally take several days.

"Russian Railways" PLC subsidiaries and affiliates are also implementing electronic means, designed to modernize the carriage process. For example, JSC "Ulan-Bator Railway" (JSC "UBZD"), which services the China-Mongolia-Russia economic channel, started producing electronic way bills for empty carts, moving as part of forming trains and heading for Russian border stations of Naushki and Solovyevsk. The company is actively implementing paperless technology in order to expand Mongolia's transit potential.

The implemented informational technology has helped to make the seamless inter-module carriage from Yokogama to Moscow through the Vladivostok sea trade harbor possible. Transportation of containers carrying Japanese auto spare parts and accessories, including transportation by sea and by rail, was conducted as part of the "Intertran" project.

The project combines all customs offices' and harbors' databases, shipping companies' bills of lading, all railway way bills into one electronic package. Thanks to "Intertran", the time it takes to fill out all the documents is reduced by four days. During the first stage of the project the technology will be available for import carriage and it will then be expanded to transit carriage of goods from Asian countries into Europe (Belov 2019).

"Intertran" technology includes paperless clearance of up to 30 operations with the involvement of the sea line operator, the carrier (here: "Russian Railways" PLC), the customs offices, the consignors, and the consignees. Previously, fragmented automated operations had been combined into a single process. Thanks to electronic and digital signatures, loading and unloading points have become the places where documents are filled in. As a result, the documentation of the cargo at the harbor now takes up to 21 hours, as opposed to five days.

Rodionova, deputy head of branch of "Nomur Research Institute Ltd." JSC, believes that "when we speak of digitalization, an important word springs to mind—platform. The capitalist takes a backseat and the platforms enter the stage" (Rodionov 2018). Applied to TTS, this means the formation of innovational and industrial trade route belts.

The development of digital technology is accompanied by the rising problem of cyber-security: the logistics market players are subjected to cyber-attacks, and the processing of large data volumes increases the risk of losing control. The growth of transnational e-commerce poses hidden threats to the economy: in particular, it may lead to base erosion, want of certification requirements, or to a lack of employment opportunities.

References

Akaev, A. A., & Akaeva, B. A. (2019). *Kyrgyzstan in the Digital Economy Era on the New Silk Road*. Moscow: URSS.

Aleksandrova, K. (2018, August 24). For the First Time in the World, a Long-Distance Cargo Was Transported by a Drone Train. *Russian Railways-Partner*. Retrieved from http://www.rzd-partner.ru/zhd-transport/news/vpervye-v-mire-gruz-na-dalnee-rasstoyanie-perevez-poezd-bespilotnik/.

Belov, P. (2019, September 4). The First Container Train with Full Electronic Support Was Sent from Vladivostok. *Russian Railways-Partner*. Retrieved from https://www.rzd-partner.ru/zhd-transport/news/iz-vladivostoka-otpravlen-pervyy-konteynernyy-poezd-s-polnym-elektronnym-soprovozhdeniem/.

Ermakova, K. (2018, October 3). Myths Will Dispel the Index. *Gudok*. Retrieved from http://www.gudok.ru/newspaper/?ID=1437348&archive=2018.10.03.

Ermolenko, M. (2018, September 12). DP World Offered to Digitalize Technologies in the Port of Taman. *Russian Railways-Partner*. Retrieved from http://www.rzd-partner.ru/wate-transport/news/dp-world-predlozhili-tsifrovizovat-tekhnologii-v-portu-taman/.

Kadik, L. (2018, October 3). By Plane, Train, or Car. *Gudok*. Retrieved from http://www.gudok.ru/newspaper/?ID=1437333&archive=2018.10.03.

Kamolov, S., & Stepnov, I. (2020). Sustainability through Digitalization: European Strategy. *E3S Web Conf.*, 208 (2020), 03048. https://doi.org/10.1051/e3sconf/202020803048.

Kober, P. (2018a, June 25–July 1). Manna of the Middle Kingdom. *Expert Ural*, no. 27(769). Retrieved from http://expert.ru/ural/2018/26/manna-podnebesnaya/.

Kober, P. (2018b, July 2–8). Trains are a Private Company's Business. *Expert Ural*, no. 27(769). Retrieved from http://expert.ru/ural/2018/27/poezda%2D%2D-delo-chastnoj-kompanii/.

Kolbina, L. (2018, July 2–8). Korea Gives The Signal. *Expert Ural*, no. 27(769). Retrieved from http://expert.ru/ural/2018/27/koreya-daet-signal/.

Kudryavtseva, E. (2018, October 23). 'Belt' Added Russia Points. Interview with the Head of The Department for Foreign Economic Activity of the Analytical Center Under the Government of the Russian Federation. *Gudok*. Retrieved from http://www.gudok.ru/newspaper/?ID=1439869&archive=2018.10.23.

List, F. (2017). *National System of Political Economy*. Moscow: Chelyabinsk, Socium.

Mozharovskaya, A. (2018, December 21). Russian Railways Can Join the Project for Joint Tracking of Transit Cargo. *Russian Railways-Partner*. Retrieved from http://www.rzd-partner.ru/zhd-transport/news/rzhd-mozhet-podklyuchitsya-k-proektu-po-sovmestnomu-otslezhivaniyu-ranzitnykh-gruzov/.

Perechneva, I. (2018, July 16–August 12). The Difficulties of Transportation. *Expert Ural*, no. 29–32 (771). Retrieved from http://expert.ru/ural/2018/32/trudnosti-perevoza/.

Pletnev, C. (2018, November 21). All on the Same Platform. *Gudok*. Retrieved from http://www.gudok.ru/newspaper/?ID=1443463&archive=2018.11.21.

Rodionov, A. (2018, November 27). Mobility as a Service. *Gudok*. Retrieved from http://www.gudok.ru/newspaper/?ID=1444163&archive=2018.11.27.

Russian Railways-Partner. (2018). *Self-driving Trucks Will Help Reduce Logistics Costs by Almost Half*. Retrieved from http://www.rzd-partner.ru/auto/news/bespilotnye-gruzoviki-pomogut-pochti-v-dva-raza-sokratit-raskhody-na-logistiku/ (дата обращения: 25.09.2018).

Taranets, I. (2018, September 12). More Volume Means Better Rates. *Gudok*. Retrieved from http://www.gudok.ru/newspaper/?ID=1434505&archive=2018.09.12.

Zubov, A. (2018, November 14). Reliability and Autonomy. Interview with the Deputy Chief Engineer of the Traction Directorate, a Member of the Working Group on the Preparation of Those Requirements, K. Nikolsky. *Gudok*. Retrieved from http://www.gudok.ru/newspaper/?ID=1442628&archive=2018.11.14.

CHAPTER 12

Digitalization as Objective Factor of the Substitution of the Labor by the Capital

Vladimir Osipov, Yuan Lunqu, Liu Dun, and Geng Yuan

Introduction

The policy pursued by many states on the formation of the prerequisites for the transition to a digital economy undoubtedly serves the purpose of increasing the national and international competitiveness of their countries, but at the same time, the issue of the impact of the introduction of information technologies on socio-economic processes is on the agenda. The volumes of scientific papers are such that even a simple enumeration of them will occupy a rather large space. We restrict ourselves to the most

V. Osipov (✉)
Moscow State Institute of International Relations (MGIMO University), Moscow, Russia
e-mail: vs.ossipov@inno.mgimo.ru

Y. Lunqu • L. Dun
Beijing Jiaotong University, Beijing, China

G. Yuan
Capital University of Economics and Business, Beijing, China

I. Stepnov (ed.), *Technology and Business Strategy*,
https://doi.org/10.1007/978-3-030-63974-7_12

important, in our opinion, works that have a significant impact on the vector of discussion. So undoubtedly the following research are very important: Pissarides, C.A. (2000, 2013, 2016); Coldwell, D.A.L. (2019); Gómez-Plana, A.G. and Latorre, M.C. (2019); Krämer, H. (2019); Curran, D. (2018); Frey C.B. and Osborne M.A. (2013); Srnicek N. and Williams A. (2016); Ford M. (2015) etc.

Despite the abundance of fears for the future welfare of society and proposals to overcome the "attendant evil" of digitalization, the identification of the causes of a new round of the struggle between labor and capital has not yet been thoroughly worked out. Of particular concern is the continuous increase in structural unemployment arising under the influence of scientific and technological progress and the replacement of living human labor with robots, machines, programs, and other IT facilities (Osipov et al. 2017). In this regard, the issues we are developing are relevant and require deep scientific understanding.

Global consequences for society and the economy were considered in the works of such scientists as Brynjolfsson, E., McAfee, A. (2014) and C. Schwab (2016).

Based on the research of the selected authors, we will evaluate the impact of digitalization on the labor market and consider its features and development trends using the countries of the European Union as an example. International integration in the modern world is a powerful lever of political and economic pressure on the world stage (Konina 2018); the European Union (EU) created in the early 1990s, which includes today 28 countries, is no exception. We will intentionally ignore the BREXIT process, because, firstly, its future is uncertain, and secondly, it does not affect the past economic performance of the European Union (Díaz Dapena et al. 2019).

As a result of the integration processes, a single market was created, which allows unimpeded movement of capital, labor, goods, and technology. Occupying key positions in the global structure, the European Union has a strong influence on the entire European region, North Africa, and Eastern countries, imposing its foreign economic policy. In this regard, it is of interest to conduct a study aimed at identifying the laws that determine the economic power of the Union; for this, the quantitative econometric apparatus for identifying and measuring relationships is best suited. In the framework of the analysis, we hypothesize the identification of the quantitative effect of labor and capital factors on the resulting indicator.

Considering the reaction of the Eurozone economy to the entry of new members and the impact of this transition on the accession countries, the scientists listed come to the disappointing conclusions that the countries that enter do not make a significant contribution to the overall economy and are a kind of market for the founding countries of the Union.

Methodology

The methodology of institutional analysis and the general theory of systems were used in the chapter to identify and justify the connections of elements of systems.

Despite the merits of the selected scientific works, they have one drawback, which is the lack of econometric models describing the influence of socio-economic factors on the functioning of the economy of the European Union. In this regard, the relevance of econometric modeling of the impact of macroeconomic indicators on the GDP of the EU member states is only increasing.

As a source of information, the statistical data of the World Bank database was selected, which aggregates information on all countries of the world on a single methodological basis, which makes it possible to conduct cross-country comparisons in comparable conditions.

Before proceeding directly to the identification and modeling of relationships, relying on statistics from the World Bank, we will consider the structure and dynamics of GDP, which is a key indicator of the system of national accounts. This approach will establish the role of the European Union in the global economy, as well as identify the role of individual countries in the formation of all-Union macro-values.

The data presented in Fig. 12.1 indicate a significant contribution to the global GDP of the three selected players, which together form more than 50% of world income. The leader is the United States, in second place with the EU, but it is worth noting the decrease in specific gravities in the reporting period compared to 2000, which is under pressure from China, which during the period under review showed a tremendous increase of 11.6 percentage points. According to the results of studies by specialists of the International Monetary Fund, the Chinese economy since 2014 overtook the United States in terms of GDP in terms of purchasing power parity (but not in nominal terms). Thus, the EU is gradually losing its leading position in the world (Osipov 2019b).

The data in Fig. 12.2 indicate significant volatility in the growth rate (decrease) of GDP, since a period of recovery almost always follows a

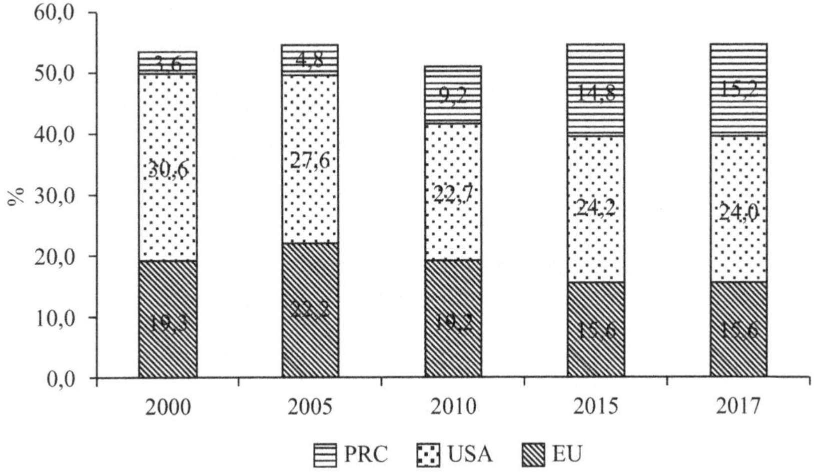

Fig. 12.1 The share of large countries in world GDP, in % of global GDP. (*Source: compiled according to the World Bank*)

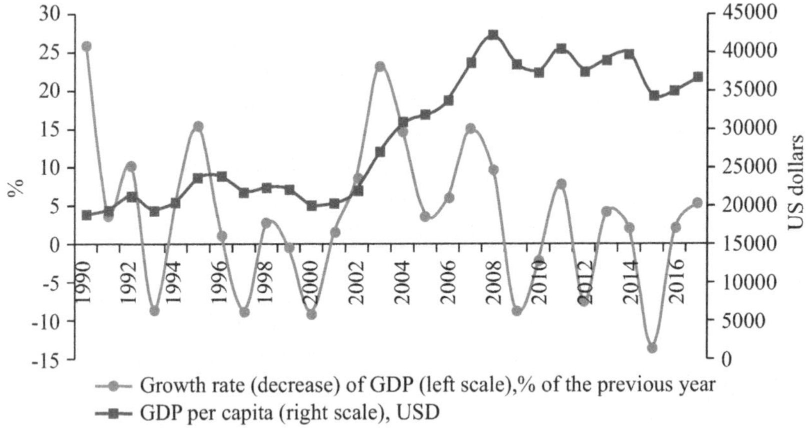

Fig. 12.2 GDP growth rate and GDP per capita dynamics of the European Union. (*Source: compiled from the World Bank*)

period of decline. In general, for the period under review, the coefficient of oscillation was 92%, and the average value is 4 percentage points.

GDP per capita until the early 2000s was not high and amounted to about 20,000 dollars per person, after 2006 the value increased to 40,000, but over the past ten years there has been a downward trend, an average of 430 dollars per year.

The values presented in Fig. 12.3 indicate the dominance of the three countries of Germany, Great Britain, and France; in the aggregate, three countries account for more than 50% of the GDP of the entire EU. The countries that joined the EU after the 2000s have practically no effect on the economy of the Union.

To illustrate the effectiveness of the economy of individual countries that are members of the community, we turn to the data presented in Table 12.1.

The data in Table 12.1 clearly illustrates the effectiveness of individual countries, so the highest value of GDP per capita is observed in Luxembourg, while the share of services and foreign trade in GDP in this

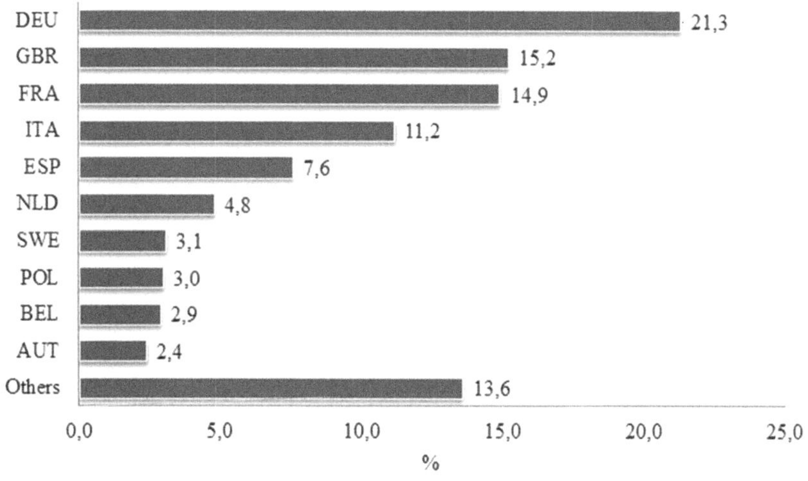

Fig. 12.3 GDP structure by countries of the European Union in 2017, %. (*Source: compiled according to the World Bank*)

Table 12.1 Comparative characteristics of the member countries of the European Union in 2017

Countries	GDP per capita	Labor ratio	Macro indicators in% of GDP of the country				
			Industry	Agriculture	Services	Import	Export
AUT	47290,9	0,52	25,3	1,13	62,8	50,8	53,9
BEL	43323,8	0,44	19,8	0,62	68,8	84,3	85,1
BGR	8031,6	0,46	24,5	3,74	58,3	64,8	66,3
HUN	14224,8	0,48	26,4	3,31	54,9	82,3	90,1
GBR	39720,4	0,51	18,6	0,52	70,1	31,9	30,5
GRC	18613,4	0,45	14,8	3,53	68,9	34,3	33,2
DEU	44469,9	0,53	27,6	0,63	61,9	39,7	47,2
DNK	56307,5	0,53	27,6	1,15	65,9	48,2	55,2
ITA	31953,0	0,42	21,4	1,92	66,3	28,2	31,3
IRL	69330,7	0,47	36,4	0,92	55,3	87,9	120,0
ESP	28156,8	0,49	21,6	2,59	66,4	31,4	34,1
CYP	25233,6	0,52	9,9	1,81	75,7	67,8	63,8
LUX	104103,0	0,48	11,6	0,28	78,9	194,0	230,0
LVA	28156,8	0,51	19,5	3,40	64,4	61,8	60,5
LTU	16680,7	0,52	26,4	3,09	60,3	79,3	81,3
MLT	26946,0	0,47	12,5	1,16	72,0	125,4	136,1
NLD	48223,2	0,53	17,5	1,86	70,4	74,8	86,5
PRT	21136,3	0,50	19,4	1,90	65,2	42,1	43,1
POL	13811,7	0,48	27,9	1,68	58,3	49,4	53,4
ROU	10813,7	0,45	30,1	4,37	56,2	43,6	41,4
SVN	23597,3	0,48	28,8	1,82	56,4	72,6	82,2
SVK	17605,0	0,51	31,0	3,25	55,9	92,9	96,3
FRA	38476,7	0,45	17,4	1,51	70,2	32,0	30,9
FIN	45703,3	0,49	24,0	2,32	60,1	38,1	38,6
HRV	13294,5	0,44	21,8	3,29	58,5	49,1	51,3
CZE	20368,1	0,51	33,5	2,19	54,2	72,2	79,5
SWE	53442,0	0,53	22,1	1,10	65,2	41,1	45,3
EST	19704,7	0,52	23,5	2,46	60,4	73,5	78,0
Note: saturated green indicates the maximum values in the column; saturated red indicates the minimum values in the graph.							

Source: *compiled according to the World Bank*

Note: saturated green indicates the maximum values in the column; saturated red indicates the minimum values in the graph country is also maximum. The countries of Eastern Europe, which entered the EU last, show insignificant results, since their GDP per capita is minimal (the smallest value in Bulgaria is 8000 dollars per person), while the share of agriculture in GDP is high, and is at the level of 3% (Rapacki and Prochniak 2019).

The labor force coefficient is approximately the same in all countries and varies around 0.49; that is, almost half of the inhabitants are employed in the economy or are ready to work.

Of the features, one can also point out high values of services, from 54.2% of GDP in the Czech Republic to 78.9% in Luxembourg, as well as foreign trade (both import and export).

Based on the data obtained, we evaluate the influence of the main factors (labor and capital) on the variation of GDP per capita in 2017; that is, we tested our hypothesis about the prevalence of the capital factor over the labor factor. To do this, we turn to the construction of the Cobb-Douglas production function. The choice of this particular model is determined by significant analytical capabilities: firstly, the transition to logarithms makes it possible to level the dimensionality of the economies of the countries in question; that is, we pass to a comparable form; secondly, the parameters of this function have a clear economic interpretation; they are elasticity coefficients; thirdly, the sum of the parameters of the production function is an independent indicator called "returns to scale" in the economic literature.

The classic form of the Cobb-Douglas production function is as follows:

$$Y = AK_i^{\alpha} L_i^{\beta} \tag{12.1}$$

где Υ—volume of production;
K—capital costs;
L—labor costs;
A, α, β—desired equation parameters.

Obviously, with regard to macroeconomics, other indicators should be taken, so for the role of the effective indicator (Υ) we will choose the GDP, K—gross capital formation (the only characteristic of reproducible capital in the World Bank's indicator system), and L—the number of the labor force of the participating country.

The relationship between the three variables is quite high, so the correlation coefficient in the *Y*&*K* link is 0.99, and for *Y*&*L* it is 0.97, which indicates a direct strong relationship between the dependent and independent variables.

As a result of evaluating the model parameters in the statistical package of STATISTICA programs, we obtain the following results (Table 12.2).

According to the data presented in the table, the obtained model is statistically significant by the Fisher *F*-test and Student *t*-statistics, while 98.9% of the variation of the resultant variable is described by the variation of the factors included in the model.

The interpretation of the parameters is as follows: with an increase in labor force in the EU countries by an average of 1%, GDP will increase by only 0.096%, in turn a capital increase of 1% will lead to an increase of 0.911%. It turns out that the labor factor practically does not play a key role in the growth of the Union economy. The resulting pattern does not contradict the logic, since the Union with its open borders policy is not threatened by personnel shortages, the countries of Eastern Europe also made a significant contribution to the labor market by providing highly professional workers (and for unskilled and/or low-paid jobs, citizens of Ukraine and Belarus proved to be useful, from which there is also a leak of labor). Refugees from North Africa in the early 2010s provided the EU labor market with a huge "army" of low-skilled workers who are ready to do any job for a minimum wage.

The sum of the coefficients $a + b$ gives a value of 1.007, which is of course higher than unity, but still not so much as to consider the return on

Table 12.2 The results of the estimation of the parameters of the Cobb-Douglas production function for 28 countries of the European Union in 2017

Variables	*Equation parameters*	*Standard error of equation parameters*	*Student t-test*	*p-level of significance*
Free member of the equation	2.290	0.589	3.887	0.001
LN(L)	0.096	0.058	1.669	0.108
LN(K)	0.911	0.052	17.665	0.000

Source: compiled by authors

Note: calculated by the author in the STATISTICA package; parameters are statistically significant at 10% level; R^2=0.989; $F(2.25)$=1101.3 p<0.05

the scale increasing, rather it is constant, that is, an increase in costs is accompanied by an equivalent increase in output.

The obtained model is statistically significant and it can be used for modeling. We are using variables *K* and *L* values of the USA, China and the Russian Federation in 2017. As a result, we obtain the response of the model presented in Table 12.3.

The constructed model approximates the actual data quite well, so in Germany the actual value of GDP in 2017 is US$3.7 trillion, and forecast values are in the range from US$3.0 to 3.9 trillion.

It is logical that with a significant population and the volume of capital accumulation, GDP will be huge, as in China, US$27.9 trillion (the actual value is only 12.2); that is, considering the fact that the PRC economy is still at a stage of development (albeit rapid), we can state the presence of growth reserves. Similar conclusions can be drawn by considering the Russian figures -2.1 forecast, against US$1.6 trillion. If Russian Federation with its potential was integrated into the European community, the economic indicators would be much higher.

Having previously described the two most important economic and demographic trends—the constant population growth of the planet, which is already approaching eight billion people, as well as the participation of labor and capital factors in the creation of European Union GDP (the Cobb-Douglas model showed that the importance of capital participation is ten times higher than labor)—the problem remains unresolved, what to do with those people who are engaged in jobs that can be algorithmized, that is, divided into simple operations and automated, that is, with those who lose out in the near future due to digitalization and robotics (Osipov 2019a)?

Table 12.3 GDP modeling results for various values of factors *K* and *L*

Indicators	*USA*	*China*	*Germany*	*Russia*
Work force, million people	163.5	786.7	43.5	75.6
The accumulation of capital, trillion US$	3.7	5.3	0.7	0.4
Point forecast of GDP, trillion US$	16.6	27.9	3.4	2.1
The lower confidence limit of the forecast, trillion US$	13.6	21.2	3.0	1.7
The upper confidence limit of the forecast, trillion US$	20.4	36.8	3.9	2.5

Source: *compiled by authors*

Note: calculated by the author in the STATISTICA package

Results

We must recall the classic of economic science A. Smith and his theory of the division of labor. Then put his arguments on today's reality, we get a paradoxical situation when, as the degree of specialization increases, different types of activities or individual operations become easier to automate. Therefore living labor will be displaced from such operations (Stroiteleva et al. 2019; Osipov et al. 2018; Bogoviz et al. 2019).

Robotization and digitalization allow capital to abandon the labor factor almost completely, but at the same time achieve high profits from production and sale of goods. That is, the pace of production of goods is maintained, while the labor factor is gradually being squeezed out of the production process. When introducing e-government technologies, the public administration system can also get rid of some of the civil servants who are responsible for performing routine standardized operations—issuing documents, registering legally significant actions, and adopting algorithm-regulated decisions on certain issues in social and economic activities (some functions have already been transferred to electronic view, and to obtain public services, a citizen does not need to communicate with public servants, the service is performed by the machine) (Osipov 2016).

It turns out that the achievements of technological progress, digitalization, and robotization prevented the creation of new jobs, but in fact made the labor factor much less important in the production function.

The research of the economic situation of the European Union and the influence of macroeconomic factors on it allows us to draw the following conclusions:

1. The share of European Union GDP on a global scale is large (third place in the world), but there is a tendency to decrease in specific gravity over time; the reason for this is the growing Chinese economy.
2. The growth rate (decrease) of EU GDP is characterized by significant volatility in the interval 1990–2017, which indicates the instability of the Union economy.
3. The dominant roles in the EU economy are played by three countries: Germany, the UK, and France; the rest of the countries, in particular the countries of Eastern Europe, are assigned secondary roles; in fact, they are markets and suppliers of labor.
4. The accession of the postsocialist countries to the European Union in the 2000s certainly had a positive impact on the growth of their

economic indicators, in contrast to Russia, Ukraine, Belarus, and Kazakhstan, which are the largest countries of the ex-USSR and the population is 2–3 times higher, but at the same time, agriculture and, most importantly, industry are minimized.

5. An econometric modeling of the impact of labor and capital on the GDP of the EU countries showed that the first factor does not have a significant impact on economic development, while the return on scale can be described as constant.
6. Identified possible solutions to the problems of ensuring the well-being of the population after digitalization have both pros and cons, but, nevertheless, their combination can help solve the problem of incomes of the population who lost their jobs due to robotization of jobs.

References

Bogoviz, A. V., Osipov, V. S., Chistyakova, M. K., & Borisov, M. Y. (2019). Comparative Analysis of Formation of Industry 4.0 in Developed and Developing Countries. *Studies in Systems, Decision and Control, 169*, 155–164.

Brynjolfsson, E., & McAfee, A. (2014). The Second Machine Age: Work, Progress, and Prosperity in a Time of Brilliant Technologies. *New York Times.*

Coldwell, D. A. L. (2019). Negative Influences of the 4th Industrial Revolution on the Workplace: Towards a Theoretical Model of Entropic Citizen Behavior in Toxic Organizations. *International Journal of Environmental Research and Public Health, 16*(15), 26–70.

Curran, D. (2018). Risk, Innovation, and Democracy in the Digital Economy. *European Journal of Social Theory, 21*(2), 207–226.

Díaz Dapena, A., Rubiera-Morollon, F., & Paredes, D. (2019). New Approach to Economic Convergence in the EU: A Multilevel Analysis from the Spatial Effects Perspective. *International Regional Science Review, 42*(3–4), 335–367.

Ford, M. (2015). *Rise of the Robots. Technology and the Threat of a Jobless Future.* New York: Basic Books. A Member of the Perseus Books Group.

Frey, C. B., & Osborne, M. A. (2013). *The Future of Employment: How Susceptible are Jobs to Computerization?* Working Paper. Oxford Martin School.

Gómez-Plana, A. G., & Latorre, M. C. (2019). Digitalization, Multinationals and Employment: An Empirical Analysis of Their Causal Relationships. *Jahrbucher fur Nationalokonomie und Statistik, 239*(3), 399–439.

Konina, N. (2018). Issues of Modern Geoeconomics. *Mezhdunarodnye Protsessy, 16*(2(53)), 186–196.

Krämer, H. (2019). Digitalisierung, Monopolbildung und wirtschaftliche Ungleichheit. *Wirtschaftsdienst, 99*(1), 47–52.

Osipov, V. S. (2016). Project-Functional Structure of Management for Public Administration. *Public Administration Issues, 3*, 219–230.

Osipov, V. S. (2019a). The Rise of Unemployment in the Cyber Economy. The Cyber Economy. *Contributions to Economics*, Part F2, 105–116.

Osipov, V. S. (2019b). To Characteristic the Uneven Economic Development of the European Union. *Russian Economic Journal, 6*. https://doi.org/10.33983/0130-9757-2019-6-63-73.

Osipov, V. S., Skryl, T. V., Blinova, E. A., Zeldner, A. G., & Alexeev, A. N. (2017). Institutional Analysis of Public Administration System. *International Journal of Applied Business and Economic Research, 15*(15), 193–203.

Osipov, V., Zeldner, A., & Skryl, T. (2018). Making the Smart City: Technologies, Experiences, and Future Perspectives. *MATEC Web of Conferences*, vol. 212, ICRE.

Pissarides, C. A. (2000). *Equilibrium Unemployment Theory*. Cambridge, MA: The MIT Press.

Pissarides, C. A. (2013). Unemployment in the Great Recession. *Economica, 80*(319), 385–403.

Pissarides, C. A. (2016). *Dynamics of Unemployment, Vacancies and Real Wages with Trade Unions*. In Book “Trade Unions, Wage Formation and Macroeconomic Stability”, pp. 244–261.

Rapacki, R., & Prochniak, M. (2019). EU Membership and Economic Growth: Empirical Evidence for the CEE Countries. *European Journal of Comparative Economics, 16*(1), 3–40.

Schwab, K. (2016). *The Fourth Industrial Revolution*. World Economic Forum.

Srnicek, N., & Williams, A. (2016). *Inventing the Future. Postcapitalism and a World without Work*. New York and London: Verso Books.

Stroiteleva, T. G., Kalinicheva, E. Y., Vukovich, G. G., & Osipov, V. S. (2019). Peculiarities and Problems of Formation of Industry 4.0 in Modern Russia. *Studies in Systems, Decision and Control, 169*, 145–153.

PART II

Spurt of Economic Systems

CHAPTER 13

Investment in the Modernization and Reconstruction of Industrial Equipment. An Evaluation of Multiplier Effects in Russia

Nina Goridko and Elena Krasina

Introduction

While directing active efforts toward the introduction of digital technologies in all areas of activity, it should not be forgotten that the basic sectors of the modern Russian economy are sectors based on industrial technologies. Moreover, the regression calculations of multiplier effects conducted previously show that it is too early for individual regions, even industrialized ones, to set the task of total transition to information production (Goridko and Nizhegorodtsev 2018). Furthermore, the restructuring of the national economy in general and its transition to a new technological platform at once are almost impossible. Here, the introduction of

N. Goridko (✉)
V. A. Trapeznikov Institute of Control Sciences RAS, Moscow, Russia

RUDN University, Moscow, Russia

E. Krasina
V. A. Trapeznikov Institute of Control Sciences RAS, Moscow, Russia

I. Stepnov (ed.), *Technology and Business Strategy*,
https://doi.org/10.1007/978-3-030-63974-7_13

information and communication technologies (ICT) into the service sector is the most active; for industrial enterprises, digitalization has been introduced more in the form of organizational innovations and has affected management functions most significantly, supply functions in some ways, and, to a very small extent, the material production sector.

Nevertheless, the increasing market requirements for the differentiation of production due to individual consumer preferences, the accuracy of products' technical characteristics, and their reliability stimulate industrial enterprises to upgrade their equipment and update fixed assets by means of modernization and reconstruction. These mechanisms, which originate from individual levels of the production chain and gradually change the entire technological process, can act as drivers of increased production, contribute to the improvement of product quality and increased productivity, and thus stimulate the introduction of innovative technologies.

In the context of rapid scientific and technological progress, enterprises need to spend effectively their own funds and attract third-party borrowed money to implement their strategies and maintain competitiveness. Investment should be aimed at expanding opportunities, encouraging the modernization of the existing technological base and creating innovations. In recent decades, Russia has been in a state of instability, and the investment impetus affects production in a particular way. The purpose of this research is to analyze the impact of investment in fixed assets in general and in the processes of its modernization and reconstruction, as well as machinery and equipment, on the growth of the national economy.

Effective investment management in the modernization and reconstruction of fixed assets will make it possible to save production resources, reduce product unit costs, develop the enterprise as an economic entity, and even contribute to the economic growth of the country in general to increase competitiveness in international markets. The process of upgrading fixed assets is not always smooth; usually it is accompanied by a number of problems, without solving which the effect of technical re-equipment can be diminished (Antonyan et al. 2017; Pyrog and Stelmakh 2016).

Methodology

To assess the effectiveness of modernization, different scientific schools use different methods and tools. Accordingly, at the enterprise level, the proposal was to use the difference in discounted flows of such indicators as revenue and income as an indicator of efficiency (Guseva and Shevchenko 2015); assessment of the reduction of the flow of taxable profits is estimated in Rokunova and Angelova (2013). The analysis of discounted flows as a basic method of assessing an investment project was carried out using various software tools (Shishorin et al. 2014). The regression factor analysis of repair and reconstruction performance was used in the research of Biryukov et al. (2019).

The regional aspect of the efficiency of investment in technological innovations was discussed in Dementiev (2019). At this, the issue of the productivity paradox was considered, which is expressed in the fact that the introduction of new technologies is accompanied by a long-term slowdown in resource productivity.

Regression modeling and calculating multipliers provide an opportunity to assess which part of the investment accounts for the effect on long-term horizons exceeding the duration of one industrial cycle, and reveals patterns that make it possible to predict future investment and return on it.

In macroeconomics, this concept is measured as a change in a certain dependent variable (e.g., the volume of GDP) per one unit change in an external exogenous variable (in this research, total investment and investment in certain parts of capital) (Samuelson and Nordhaus 2009), where investments can be both public and private.

The multiplier was first suggested by R.F. Kahn in 1931 to calculate the quantitative relationship between the increment of investment and the associated increase in employment in a particular sector of the economy, which subsequently stimulates employment in other sectors producing consumer goods (Kahn 1931).

Later, J.M. Keynes investigated the multiplier in identifying the interdependence between the increase in the investment scale and the increase in that income which changed depending on the variation in the number of units of labor, revealing that changes are taking place but in the same direction. Keynes considered income, not employment, as an endogenous variable. With an increase in total investment, income increases by *m* times (Keynes 1935):

$$\Delta Y = \Delta Y0 + m * \Delta I \tag{13.1}$$

where ΔY = the increment of the GDP of the current year compared to the previous year;

$\Delta Y0$ = the autonomous increment of GDP, independent of the change in investment inflows (which cannot be explained by the change in investment inflows);

m = the multiplier showing to what extent an increment of investment leads to an increment of the GDP of the current year;

ΔI = the increment of investment of the current year compared to the previous one.

The multiplier reflects the dynamics of economic cycles and other changes in the situation; its value is inversely proportional to the volume of savings. Keynes has refuted the traditional theory that savings will contribute to economic growth; he proved that, with an increment of autonomous investment during technical re-equipment, gross income will increase, unemployment will decrease, and employment and public activity will increase.

The accelerator ("catalyst") reflects an opposite effect—a coefficient showing a possible increase in investment due to the previous increase in GDP; this can be calculated by the formula:

$$\Delta It = \Delta I0 + h * \Delta Yt - 1 \tag{13.2}$$

where ΔI_t = the increment of investment of the current year;

ΔI_0 = the constant showing what investment increment will be if GDP does not change compared to the previous period;

h = the accelerator showing how the increment of the GDP of the last year affects the increment of investment in the current year;

ΔY_{t-1} = the increment of the GDP of the previous year.

Results

Assessment of Russia's National Competitiveness

The possibility of attracting investors and building mutually beneficial partnerships largely depends on the reputation of the country, which is conditioned by financial stability, foreign economic activities, market openness, the level and quality of labor productivity, the innovativeness of the benefits produced, and the degree of modernization of the processes implemented. The Global Competitiveness Index (GCI), the value of which consists of component variables covering a wide range of business climatic factors that determine the viability and attractiveness of countries at different stages of economic development, was identified by experts as a priority methodology for assessing competitiveness on the international level.

On the basis of statistics provided by Knoema Enterprise Data Solutions (2020), it is possible to analyze the dynamics of Russia's GCI gap compared with the leading countries of the world (Fig. 13.1).

Figure 13.1 shows that Russia's competitiveness is well below the level of more successful countries. However, the GCI index increased by 2.59 points in 2017 and went to 65.62 in 2018; thus Russia was ranked 43rd (in the second half of the list) (Schwab 2018). The leading places in the ranking are held by the United States, Germany, Switzerland, and Japan. The United States, according to the World Bank, is number one in terms of GDP production in 2018, while China takes the second place (World Bank 2020). Economists associate such significant characteristics of these two countries with their growth of labor productivity in such sectors as trade; it is in this sphere that information technologies have been improved (Rogatnykh 2006). Russia ranks only 83rd in the product market ranking (Schwab 2018).

In addition to generalized factors (infrastructure; a fundamental set of political, legal, and social rules; the role of the state; education; business;

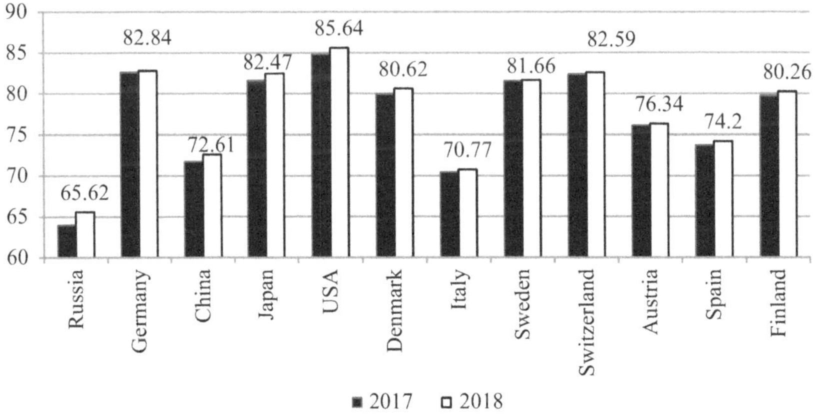

Fig. 13.1 Global Competitiveness Index (GCI) by country, 2017–2018. (Source: Compiled by the authors based on Knoema Enterprise Data Solutions (2020))

market efficiency), the GCI forms macroeconomic indicators, the scientific and technical level of the technological system, and innovation of technologies (Rogatnykh 2006; Goridko and Choroyu 2019).

The chronic low profitability of enterprises in basic industries, even in achieving the desired output and quality results and cost reduction, can destabilize investment and undermine competitiveness (Porter 2011). Priority financial decisions will be made in favor of "uniqueness," which makes it necessary to revise and adjust the current strategy and restructure the system with the subsequent modernization of production and business processes.

Innovation is a crucial characteristic for the formation of the GCI, as it implies the development and creation of innovation, labor automation, and a maximized use of information and communication technologies and services (Stepnov et al. 2019). Research, design, and development work lead to more efficient processes and are able to meet the market demand which plays a significant role in transforming new knowledge into products of practical value and improving the quality of life (Romer 1990).

Investment Performance Analysis

It is possible to improve the level of innovations using mechanisms for improving the level of education of personnel, differentiating competencies. Awareness of new technologies, products, projects, understanding, processing, and implementation, and the dissemination of this information, form the basis of human capital, which is intensively used in R&D and leads to a high level of production (Hanushek and Woßmann 2010). However, the innovative capacity of workers is not sufficient for production based on the equipment used. Worn out or outdated machines of increased energy intensity, alongside the use of outdated raw materials, will be barriers for the production of high-quality unique things (Çalışkan 2015).

Productivity growth and an increment of the stock of effective capital are also directly related to technological changes which will stimulate accumulation and affect the increase in production per hour worked (Romer 1990; Goridko and Krasina 2018). Using the statistics of the Federal State Statistics Service (2020), we will make a histogram of the volume of the gross domestic product of the Russian Federation (Fig. 13.2).

The graph (Fig. 13.2) shows that the highest increment of GDP was observed in 2006 and 2007—8.2% and 8.5% respectively. In 2009 this

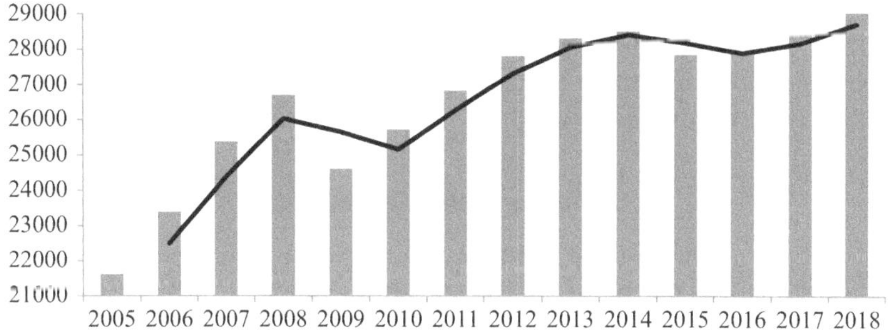

Fig. 13.2 Dynamics of Russia gross domestic product (GDP), 2005–2018, in fixed prices of 2005, billion rubles. (Source: Compiled by the authors based on Federal State Statistics Service (2020))

sharply dropped by 7.8% (the worst result for the G8 countries). In Russia, the year 2009 was a year of recession—the crisis took place as a result of the global financial decline and the deterioration of the investment climate, and was accompanied by an increase in unemployment and the devaluation of the ruble. Anti-crisis measures contributed to a 4.5% increase in gross output in 2010, but in 2013 growth rates slowed down considerably to 1.8%, and in 2014 to 0.7%. The economy of the Russian Federation depends on the global energy environment, and when the cost of oil falls, the economic situation also worsens.

In 2015, experts attributed the 2.3% decrease in GDP to Russia's actions against Ukraine, which pushed many countries (Japan, Canada, the United States, New Zealand, Australia, etc.) to impose economic sanctions. The GDP deflator for this year was 7.2%. Conducting a protectionist economic policy, imposing snapback sanctions provoked a sharp outflow of capital from the country. Russia lost an important source of financial resources, and this partially explains the insignificant GDP growth rate in recent years: in 2016 it was 0.33%, in 2017 1.63%, and in 2018 2.25%.

However, what is productive for highly developed countries is not always effective for developing countries, since they are characterized by many nuances (the difference in factors affecting technology, namely: the size of the target market, the type and amount of energy used, the capacity of the production unit, the nature and quality of the raw materials, the volume of business, the level of development of infrastructure facilities, the organization of the production process, etc.) (Çalışkan 2015).

According to the information base (Federal State Statistics Service 2020), we have made a scatter plot of the relationship between GDP increment and investment (Fig. 13.3). The graph confirms the impact of capital outflows on GDP increment (2009, 2015–2016).

Assessment of Multiplier Effects

Using the modifications of Formula (13.1), we have analyzed the impact of investments in technological changes on the economic growth in Russia using regression modeling. We will consider the GDP increment (ΔY) as a dependent variable, and the increment of investments in fixed assets (ΔK), modernization/reconstruction (ΔIm), machines/equipment (ΔIe) as independent ones.

The linear regression equations have the form:

$$\Delta Y = \Delta Y0 + m * \Delta K \tag{13.3}$$

where ΔY = the GDP increment for the current year compared to the previous year;

ΔY_0 = the autonomous GDP increment, independent of changes in investments in fixed assets;

m = the multiplier showing the extent to which an increment of fixed investment generally leads to an increment of GDP;

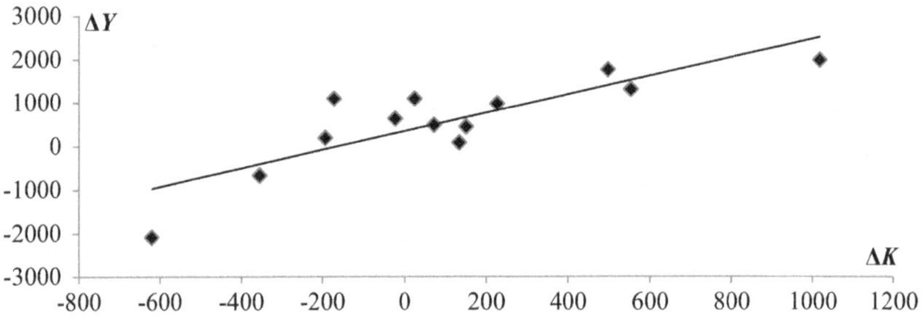

Fig. 13.3 Correlation field for the relation between capital investment increment (ΔK) and GDP increment (ΔY), billion rubles. (Source: Compiled by the authors based on Federal State Statistics Service (2020) and World Bank (2020))

ΔK = the increment of the volume of capital investment of the current year compared to the previous one.

$$\Delta Y = \Delta Y0 + m * \Delta I^{m} \tag{13.4}$$

where ΔY = the increment of GDP for the current year compared to the previous year;

ΔY_0 = the autonomous increment of GDP, independent of changes in the volume of investments in modernization and reconstruction;

m = the multiplier showing how much the increment of investment in this direction will lead to an increment of GDP;

ΔI^m = the increment of the volume of investment in the modernization/reconstruction of the current year compared to the previous one.

$$\Delta Y = \Delta Y0 + m * \Delta I^{e} \tag{13.5}$$

where ΔY_t = the increment of GDP of the current year compared to the previous one;

ΔY_0 = the autonomous increment of GDP, independent of investment;

m = the multiplier showing how much increased investment in machinery and equipment stimulates GDP increment;

ΔI^e = the increment of investment in machines/equipment of the current year compared to the previous one.

For clarity and interpretable regression results, it is recommended to use a long series of data with long-term time horizons. This research uses the statistical baseline data of 2005–2018. With regard to the allocation of the part of investment aimed at reconstruction/modernization and invested in machinery/equipment, starting in 2005, this year was selected as the base year. The current data of the Federal State Statistics Service in value terms (Federal State Statistics Service 2020) are adjusted to the base year of 2005 by deflation using the GDP deflater (World Bank 2020). The received increment of the time series is presented in Table 13.1, wherein:

$$\Delta Y = Yt - Yt - 1 \tag{13.6}$$

where Y_t = the GDP of the current year;

Y_{t-1} = the GDP of the previous year.

Table 13.1 Dynamics of increment indicators of GDP, capital investment, investment in modernization/reconstruction, and investment in machinery/equipment, billion rubles

Year	*GDP*	*Capital investment*	*Investment in modernization/ reconstruction*	*Investment in machinery/equipment*
t	ΔY	ΔK	ΔI^m	ΔI^e
2006	1771.98	497.65	79.23	181.66
2007	1987.44	1015.99	182.61	327.67
2008	1319.17	553.17	158.27	148.06
2009	-2081.68	-620.54	-273.16	-258.05
2010	1107.29	24.55	24.85	44.97
2011	1105.72	-172.15	-7.82	-66.13
2012	992.37	225.56	53.80	68.40
2013	500.61	71.69	-22.47	87.48
2014	198.19	-193.35	-106.54	-196.15
2015	-657.96	-355.40	-66.50	-355.39
2016	91.71	133.39	-24.84	44.26
2017	455.54	150.47	14.64	156.21
2018	640.39	-23.11	-33.24	32.44

Source: Compiled by the authors based on Federal State Statistics Service (2020) and World Bank (2020)

Similar to Formula (13.6), the indicators ΔK, ΔI^m, ΔI^e (Table 13.1) are calculated.

According to Table 13.1, we have built correlation fields in order to preliminarily determine the direction and tightness of the connection between the increment of GDP volume (ΔY) and the increments of investment in modernization/reconstruction (ΔI^m), as well as in machines/equipment (ΔI^e) (Fig. 13.4).

Figures 13.3 and 13.4 show that the closest connection is between GDP increments (ΔY) and modernization/reconstruction investment increments (ΔI^m). All the three correlation fields have a positive relationship between variables.

Several adequate models were also obtained, explaining the impact of exogenous variables ΔK, ΔI^m, and ΔI^e on ΔY with significant parameters; their equations and basic statistical characteristics are presented in Table 13.2.

The correlation coefficients for all models exceed 60%. Model (3), predictably, has the greatest explanatory power: in it, investment in

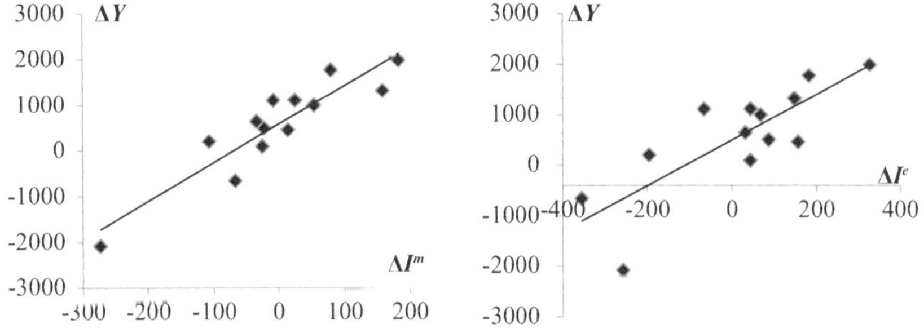

Fig. 13.4 Correlation field for the relation between increment of investments in modernization/reconstruction (ΔI^m), increment of investment in machinery/equipment, and GDP increment (ΔY), billion rubles. (Source: Compiled by the authors based on Federal State Statistics Service (2020) and World Bank (2020))

Table 13.2 Models reflecting the impact of increment of investment in the modernization/reconstruction and investment machinery/equipment on Russia's GDP investment, 2006–2018, billion rubles

N	*Models*	R^2	*Standard error*	*F statistic*
1	$\Delta Y = 357.51^{*} + 2.13^{***}\,\Delta K$	0.70	606.98	26.18
2	$\Delta Y = 2.334^{***}\,\Delta K$	0.69	684.20	26.33
3	$\Delta Y = 585.34^{***} + 8.44^{***}\,\Delta I^m$	0.84	449.25	56.87
4	$\Delta Y = 497.07^{**} + 4.497^{***}\,\Delta I^e$	0.64	665.78	19.90

Source: Modeled by the authors based on Federal State Statistics Service (2020) and World Bank (2020)
*the regression coefficient is significant at the level 0.1; **the regression coefficient is significant at the level 0.5; ***the regression coefficient is significant at the level 0.01

reconstruction and modernization act as a regressor. The 83.79% variation in Russia's GDP increment in 2005–2018 can be explained by the change in investment in modernization/reconstruction, the 70.41% variation by the change in total investment, and the 64.4% variation by the change in investment in machines/equipment (Table 13.2). Thus, the importance of reconstruction and re-equipment of production for the Russian economy and its impact on long-term economic growth indicators is proven again.

The free term autonomous GDP has quite high values in Models (1), (3), and (4); this suggests that an annual GDP increment (ΔY) will represent an average of 357.51, 585.34, and 497.07 billion RUB respectively in the prices of 2005 if the variables under review ΔK, ΔI^m, and ΔI^e are equal to 0; that is, there will be no investment, and at this, the increment is explained by the influence of other factors not described in the model.

In Model (1) the free term is significant: at the significance level of more than 5%, it was excluded from this equation, as a result of which Model (2) without the free term was received. It is assumed here that all GDP increments can be attributed to an increment of capital investment.

A special description is required by the multiplier (m)—the coefficient by which in the received model's investment increments of various kinds are multiplied: ΔK, ΔI^m, and ΔI^e. As we see from Models (1), (3), and (4) in Table 13.2, an increment of investment in general by 1 ruble leads to a GDP increment of 2.13 rubles on average for the researched period. At this, investment in certain spheres is more effective, and thus, an additional investment of 1 ruble in machines and equipment can increase the GDP of the current year by 4.5 rubles, and an increase in modernization/reconstruction costs by 1 ruble leads to an increment of GDP by 8.44 rubles on average. Therefore, the effectiveness of technical re-equipment for the Russian economy is undeniable; this path of production reorganization is one of the most promising at a time of restricted financial resources.

To illustrate the multiplicative effect, we have constructed Graphs $\Delta\hat{Y}$ and ΔI^m (Fig. 13.5).

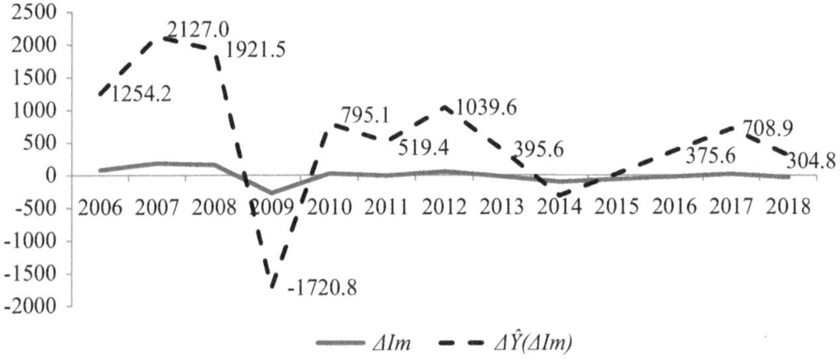

Fig. 13.5 Graph of GDP increment ($\Delta\hat{Y}(\Delta I^m)$) versus increment of investments in modernization/reconstruction (ΔI^m), billion rubles. (Source: Compiled by the authors based on Federal State Statistics Service (2020) and World Bank (2020))

The chart shows that a small reduction or increment of investment in modernization/reconstruction can significantly affect the change in gross output, causing a rise or decline in production with a much larger amplitude.

In this research, using the data of Table 13.1, accelerator models were also built according to Formula (13.2), but the Keynes *b*-effect for the Russian economy in the period 2005–2018 was not revealed. All the received models had determination coefficients not exceeding 0.5, they were insignificant, and their parameters did not pass the 5% confidence barrier. From this, it can be concluded that the volume of investment in general, as well as in various areas under study, has not been directly explained by the dynamics of the gross domestic product of the previous year, nor does it depend on the volume of GDP calculated with lags in two to three years; this does not exclude the existence of a longer-term relationship between these indicators.

Conclusions

Russia's economy today, which has faced a number of macroeconomic challenges, has not completely overcome the technological lag from developed countries; it has an industry structure with the predominance of capital-intensive industries. It must solve several seemingly contradictory tasks at the same time. Firstly, in the industries that are associated with the provision of services of various kinds, it is necessary to actively develop and introduce new digital technologies into production. Secondly, information technologies significantly improve the efficiency of implementing various types of management impact, regardless of the form of ownership of enterprises and the sectoral scope. In the near future, at enterprises of asset-intensive industries, it will be difficult to implement the same digitalization processes in material production for a number of reasons, the most important of which are: (1) consumption of the active part of fixed capital; (2) a shortage of own financial resources; (3) the high cost of borrowing; and (4) the impossibility of complete stoppages in production. Consequently, in addition to the introduction of innovative technological solutions, a phased modernization and reconstruction of existing equipment is necessary.

Investment in production modernization can have a greater effect compared to the full replacement of machinery; this is because it does not impede but only improves the technological processes of production, value chains are not broken, and stable relationships with contractors and other counterparties are maintained. What is more, as a rule, human capital is preserved; indeed, its potential is increased by improving skills and acquiring new competencies. The reconstruction of an enterprise can begin from the most obvious "bottlenecks," the low productivity of which negatively affects production in general. Consequently, moving along the path of technical re-equipment, it is possible to achieve strategic objectives over time.

This work proves that increased investment in modernization/reconstruction has a great positive effect in the form of incrementing gross output in the macro system in general. Moreover, this effect is many times superior to the efficiency of investing resources in the purchase of machinery and equipment (the novelty and productivity of which, compared to the replaced relevant equipment, need to be proved), as well as financing new construction. The multiplier of investment in technical re-equipment of production is 8.44; this means that for each additionally invested ruble we receive an increment of the output by 8.44 rubles.

At the same time, according to research, the volume of investment does not depend on the income of previous years in the short term. This suggests a manual control of investment processes; this will perhaps entail, for example, the "eating into" a high proportion of disposable income, the low effectiveness of existing programs aimed at updating the material base of production, and the low efficiency of the investment management mechanisms in this area. Solving such problems will allow enterprises not only to increase their productivity and thus the volume and quality of their products, but also to reach a new level of competitiveness in material production industries that lag behind global standards.

Acknowledgments The reported study was funded by RFBR, project number 20-310-90008.

References

Antonyan, O., Karpushko, E., & Solovyeva, A. (2017). Problems of Modernization and Technical Re-equipment of Russian Machine-building Enterprises. *MATEC Web of Conferences, 129*, 89–94. https://doi.org/10.1051/matecconf/201712901022.

Biryukov, A. N., Dobryshkin, E., Kravchenko, I. N., & Glinsky, M. A. (2019). Optimization of Management Decisions for Choosing Strategy of Enterprises

Fixed Assets Reproduction. *Engineering for Rural Development, 18*, 1726–1735. https://doi.org/10.22616/ERDev2019.18.N505.

Çalışkan, H. K. (2015). Technological Change and Economic Growth. *Social and Behavioral Sciences, 195*, 649–654. https://doi.org/10.1016/j.sbspro.2015.06.174.

Dementiev, V. E. (2019). Productivity Paradox in Regional Dimension. *Economy of Region, 15*(1), 43–56. https://doi.org/10.17059/2019-1-4.

Federal State Statistics Service. (2020). Retrieved from http://www.gks.ru/.

Goridko, N. P., & Chorovu, A. Y. (2019). Indicators of Knowledge Intensity and Science Output: Theory and Discussion Points. *Economics and Management: Problems and Solutions, 7*(3), 4–9.

Goridko, N. P., & Krasina, E. N. (2018). The Factors of Economic Growth in Germany and the Effectiveness of Their Use. *RISC: Resources, Information, Supply, Competition, 2*, 122–126.

Goridko, N. P., & Nizhegorodtsev, R. M. (2018). The Growth Points of Regional Economy and Regression Estimation for Branch Investment Multipliers. *Economy of Region, 14*(1), 29–42. https://doi.org/10.17059/2018-1-3.

Guseva, N. V., & Shevchenko, N. Y. (2015). Development of Schemes Assess the Economic Efficiency of Investments in the Projects of Modernization of Electric Power Facilities. *International Journal of Applied and Fundamental Research, 9*, 513–516.

Hanushek, E. A., & Woßmann, L. (2010). Education and Economic Growth. In *International Encyclopedia of Education* (Vol. 2, pp. 245–252). Amsterdam: Elsevier.

Kahn, R. F. (1931). The Relation of Home Investment to Unemployment. *The Economic Journal, 41*(162), 173–198. https://doi.org/10.2307/2223697.

Keynes, J. M. (1935). *The General Theory of Employment, Interest and Money*. Cambridge: Harcourt, Brace and Company.

Knoema Enterprise Data Solutions. (2020). Retrieved from http://knoema.ru/

Porter, M. (2011). *The Competitive Strategy. Techniques for Analyzing Industries and Competitors*. Translated from English. 4th ed. Moscow: Alpina Business Books.

Pyrog, O. V., & Stelmakh, K. P. (2016). Operation and Modernisation of Fixed Assets at Machine-building Enterprises. *Economics, Entrepreneurship, Management, 3*(1), 41–49.

Rogatnykh, E. B. (2006). Index of Global Competitiveness: Questions of Methodology of Construction and Evaluation. *Russian Foreign Economic Bulletin, 12*, 13–19.

Rokunova, O. V., & Angelova, O. Y. (2013). Models for the Analysis of Efficiency of Fixed Capital Investments in the Modernization of Enterprises. *Vestnik of Lobachevsky University of Nizhni Novgorod, 4*(1), 275–281.

Romer, P. M. (1990). Endogenous Technological Change. *The Journal of Political Economy, 99*(5, Part 2), 71–102.

Samuelson, P. A., & Nordhaus, W. D. (2009). *Economics*. New York: McGraw-Hill Education.

Schwab, K. (2018). *The Global Competitiveness Report 2018*. World Economic Forum. Geneva. Retrieved from http://www3.weforum.org/docs/GCR2018/05FullReport/TheGlobalCompetitivenessReport2018.pdf.

Shishorin, Y. R., Khokhlov, A. S., Zenkov, V. V., Kozminykh, D. V., & Luneva, E. D. (2014). Analysis of Investment Projects Effectiveness for the Reconstruction, Modernization and New Construction Using the R-INVEST Option of the SKILM-RPMS System. *Oil Processing and Petrochemistry, 6*, 3–9.

Stepnov, I., Kovalchuk, J., & Gorchakova, E. (2019). On Assessing the Efficiency of Intracluster Interaction for Industrial Enterprises. *Studies on Russian Economic Development, 30*(3), 346–354. https://doi.org/10.1134/S107570071903016X.

World Bank. (2020). *Indicators*. The World Bank. Retrieved from https://data.worldbank.org/indicator.

CHAPTER 14

Risks of Modernizing National Economies in the Conditions of the Technological Leap

Zhaklin Sarkisyan

Introduction

The modern economy is undergoing a rapid, inevitable, and overpowering process, being at a point of a new industrial revolution driven by digital technologies and everything connected therewith. Earlier it was possible to pinpoint a clear chronology of changes in the economy occurring due to changes in its main sectors (industrial sectors in this case); now, however, we may speak of multiple revolutions taking place simultaneously around the world:

- The ongoing Third Industrial Revolution (Rifkin 2011) and a turn toward the Fourth Industrial Revolution; this concerns the majority of the developing countries. These countries aim to invest in the purchase of new high-tech equipment and the distribution of communication technology in all fields of the economy and society. At

Z. Sarkisyan (✉)
Moscow State Institute of International Relations (MGIMO University), Moscow, Russia
e-mail: g.sarkisyan@odin.mgimo.ru

I. Stepnov (ed.), *Technology and Business Strategy*,
https://doi.org/10.1007/978-3-030-63974-7_14

the same time, a gradual transition to renewable energy sources is occurring, as well as the development (engineering improvement) of transportation systems as vital physical communication channels.

- The onset of the Fourth Industrial Revolution (Schwab 2017); this is accompanied by active integration of digitally progressive technologies. The main trend is the convergence of industry and digital technologies, which is bound to lead to the emergence of a completely new type of manufacturing based on 3D printing, as the advantages of mass production will be made obsolete by opportunities of production in small amounts or custom-made goods priced by the scale effect. Such a trend is prevalent in developed countries, as it requires not only significant investments into development and integration of new technologies but also the organization and drafting of communications on a digital basis.

The trends described above determine the areas of modernization for countries' economies, taking into account their current level of socioeconomic development, access to capital markets, their political system, and their position on the international arena.

Modernization of the economy is generally considered as an improvement or an upgrade, accompanied by technological and social changes in community development both on a global level and on the level of individual countries, industries, and businesses. Modernization is sure to encompass changes in a country's industrial structure (i.e. some industries are excluded and new industries are formed); it includes innovational activity and the implementation of progressive technologies that will lead to increased labor productivity and economic profits. Modernization of the economy is to be accompanied by the effecting of an adequate state policy and is to facilitate attraction of investment resources.

However, economic modernization is always an individual process, whereby each country chooses its own path of changes: either an original one, or copying the most successful experience elsewhere (Simoniya and Torkunov 2015). This is historically linked to structural and technological economic changes occurring in Western Europe and North America in the seventeenth to nineteenth centuries, which would then spread to other European countries and in the nineteenth to twentieth centuries would go on to spread to the South American, Asian, and African continents. For example, S.N. Eisenstadt, an ideologist of modernization as an area of research, considered modernization as a process of the transformation of a country's social, economic, and political system, having identified four types of modernization: economic, technological, social, and cultural (Eisenstadt 1966).

In effecting economic modernization, society aims to move forward, although there are certain risks on the way toward progressive changes. We do not analyze modernization exclusively in relation to developing countries, even though it is these countries that are in dire need of effective transformations which would allow them to catch up with leading, more developed countries that co-exist with them in the same historical time period, thus all interacting within a single global community.

Methodology

Modernization as a process of changes in society and the economy possesses certain methodological links to the idea of contemporary areas of art, namely modern art. Such a parallel is intriguing, as economic modernization implies bringing the economy up to date in accordance with the relevant and prospective needs of the economic subjects (the population, companies, states, etc.). Modern art rejects the old and traditional, whereas economic modernization is, on the contrary, to take into account past experience, a country's potential, and its resources for securing development. With that in mind, the phenomenon of postmodernism in art, having taken the form of artistic adoption and remakes, is also required for economic modernization. For instance, countries may use development mechanisms that have shown their efficiency with integration and utilizing in other countries as an example.

The author bases her study on the sociological idea of modernization, with modernization being a socio-historical process in the course of which traditional societies become progressive and industrially developed (e.g. the first industrial revolution in the UK, post–World War II restoration and industrialization in the USSR, the economic growth of the Persian gulf states on the basis of using raw resources, the economic development of the "Asian tigers", etc.).

In stating the fact that modernization processes are implemented with different substantive economic aspects in different countries, the author also bases the study on accepted theoretical approaches to dividing market economies into three categories:

- LME countries—liberal market economy aimed at market priorities (Hall and Soskice 2001) and, accordingly, at radical technological and high-tech transformations in order to achieve leadership in the world;
- CME countries—coordinated market economy aimed at non-market collaborative mechanisms in the form of coordinated interaction between economic subjects (Hall and Soskice 2001), albeit with competition based on gradual innovations developing primarily in the manufacturing sector (Hancké et al. 2007);
- DME countries—dependent market economy, defined by low levels of domestic investments and a dependency on foreign capital and transnational corporations (Drahokoupil 2009).

Naturally, this classification of countries is objective, as the liberal market economy may be observed in world leaders (the United States, the UK, Canada, Australia, New Zealand, Ireland), and the coordinated market economy functions efficiently in Germany, Belgium, the Netherlands, Scandinavian countries, Austria—countries defined by stable economic growth rates. Classifying dependent economy countries is subjective (Popov and Jomo 2018), although it has to be noted that westernization processes (i.e. the processes of adopting western values and lifestyles) have also been actively taking place along with globalization, accompanied by increased interdependence and exchange of goods, services, and information (McMillan et al. 2014). This is reflected primarily in the culture, but it also finds its way into politics and the economy.

Catch-up development also exists along with dependent development (Inozemtsev 2004; Landesmann and Stöllinger 2019). It is this notion that will separate countries in terms of integration and the spread of new technologies. Technology transfer from developed countries allows such countries to optimize technological development investments and to minimize venture risks. With that in mind, catch-up development countries are generally sufficiently oriented at using their own resource potential, and it is that potential that secures the larger part of the country's GDP and employment.

However, acknowledging the significance of the determinant effect of various factors such as globalization, the spread of new digital technologies, the need to solve environmental problems around the world, the importance of preserving national culture, language, and other such issues leads to a more complex understanding of economic modernization. This facilitates large-scale country-wide development. As such, an open-ended approach implies that the drafting of economic development strategies is to correspond to the following parameters:

- The country is planning to implement modernization either based on original mechanisms or based on copying the most successful experience of other countries, adopting their institutional decisions;
- Any modernization process taking place today is to hinder the environmental crisis which corresponds to the classic understanding of environmental modernization (Giddens 1991) and remains relevant due to escalating environmental problems around the globe;
- Any changes have inherent risks (Beck 1992), which is why economic modernization carries with it threats to the existing order in society and the economy, and despite the progressive nature of the changes, they may fail to be accepted by society and may fail to be implemented efficiently;
- Individual countries may choose the "super-modernization" strategy for themselves in their quest to achieve superiority over other countries and become the leader (or one of the leaders) of the global economy. Without delving into political motives for such a strategy, it may be acknowledged that such an approach is suitable only for countries with a dominant production, innovational, and economic potential;
- History has shown that economic modernization is to fully correspond to the technological aspects of development, as the spread of new technologies becomes not just the driving force behind economic, industrial, and service development, but also significantly raises the population's quality of life, forming the reserves for ensuring sustainable functioning of the country's economy. With that in mind, the country may not develop its own technologies but simply purchase them; however, the country developing science and technologies a priori has a better chance not only to become a technological leader, but also to become the leader of the global economy, securing its positions or becoming the new leader.

Results

The modern stage of globalization, the global spread of digital technologies, and the prospects of new progressive technology in accordance with the determinants of the Fourth Industrial Revolution force countries to choose a strategy of technological modernization, a decision which unavoidably affects economic development and the country's position on the global arena.

Technology in the modern world is not just a tool for competition between companies. In the course of globalization and the deceleration of economic growth rates around the world, technology has become a tool for economic development and global leadership (and in some cases [e.g. space technology] political leadership as well). All countries, regardless of their level of socio-economic development, strive to support innovational activity not only in the basic industries of economic development (modern manufacturing), but in services, agriculture, and traditional industries. Such an important task is performed by state governments that develop certain economic strategies aimed at the creation of and financial support for innovational companies, national innovational eco-systems, and networks. This approach may also be explained in terms of securing long-term economic growth. According to the research of D. Rodrik, in order to catch up and overtake, one has to not only invest into human resources and create the necessary institutions, but also develop new production industries and adjust the labor market structure, helping workers get new qualifications and switch to more progressive industries (Rodrik 2014).

Some countries have historically concentrated more on technological breakthroughs in modernizing their economies; this is facilitated by large proportions of R&D funding in their GDP. The volume of investments into technological development is one of the main indicators of a country being committed to developing new technologies.

A significant event took place in 2020: Germany became the most innovative economy on the planet according to the Bloomberg Innovation Index 2020, pushing South Korea down from the top spot, with the latter having been the index leader for six years (Jamrisko and Lu 2020). This was thanks to commendable results in the high-tech industry, its patent activity, and a highly competitive value-added production. However, there are risks for Germany as the development of new technologies in services is not as active and more than one-third of R&D expenditures have been allocated to a single industry—the automobile industry—which may seriously threaten the economy, should it become unstable. Bloomberg experts also included the following countries in the top 10 most innovative economies: Singapore, Switzerland, Sweden, Israel, Finland, Denmark, the United States, and France. Also, New Zealand, being a coordinated economy, has been falling from its rating spot for three years in a row.

It should be noted that in 2013 the United States—the country with the biggest GDP in the world—was sitting on the top spot in the Bloomberg Innovation Index rating, and in 2020 it took the ninth place despite the leading global companies developing and utilizing new progressive digital technologies (Amazon.com Inc., Alphabet Inc., Microsoft Corp., etc.) being affiliated with this country. With that in mind, the second biggest economy in the world, China, is in the fifteenth place in the total rating (it has gone up six spots in three years' time), second place in the patent activity rating, and fifth place in higher education efficiency. This is a major result of modernization, as education investments have a positive effect on technological and economic development.

Interestingly enough, the innovative economies rating somewhat reflects the results of global competitiveness rating drafted by the Swiss IMD (Institute of Management Development). In 2019 Singapore took the first spot; Singapore is the leading country of Southeast Asia, it is developing advanced technological infrastructure, and it has a simplified procedure of setting up innovation business and the largest share of developers per capita, as well as a development-oriented STEM (science, technology, engineering, and mathematics) higher education system. The list of the top 10 most competitive countries also included Hong Kong, the United States, Switzerland, the United Arab Emirates, the Netherlands, Ireland, Denmark, Sweden, and Qatar.

China, India, and Russia are at the top in terms of middle-income. These countries have a special goal of economic modernization, as it is particularly challenging to progress from a successfully developing country with middle-income and innovational potential to an innovation center (WIPO 2019). As indicated above, China is making the most efforts here; similarly, steps are taken by India, which is the most innovative country in Central and South Asia, exports IT services, and has a growing number of university graduates with engineering diplomas and natural sciences specialists.

Russia, a country with a rich history of inventions and with a contribution to the global economy, does not occupy high spots in the aforementioned ratings. In the UNESCO rating, Russia is in the top 10 based on

R&D investment volumes (this is a significant portion of all innovation investment); experts estimate its investment to be $40.3 billion in purchasing-power-parity. However, in terms of investment-GDP ratio, Russia is not even in the top 15 countries; UNESCO estimates the percentage to be 1.1% of GDP (the global average is 1.7% and 2.5% for North America and Western Europe) (Belkina 2019).

With that said, as a developing economy, Russia is constantly implementing economic modernization, which can be divided into two main strategies: the innovational strategy and the imitational (adaptive) strategy. This is as, on the one hand, historically speaking Russia has demonstrated its significant scientific and innovational potential, albeit this potential has to be reloaded onto new progressive technologies; on the other hand, time lost during economic restoration after the fall of the Soviet Union necessitated quick decisions for the economy's technological development, which is why importing equipment for traditional industries of the economy is a more economically viable solution than investing into the development of domestic equipment. However, the innovative path to the country's development remains a priority, namely in the development of high-tech production, raising the research intensity of the basic production industries and of services, and increased R&D funding, since in the course of globalization, constant innovational upgrades are a necessary factor for a country's successful economic and socio-political development, and for its integration into the new world order (Glinkina 2012). Innovation-based modernization requires material resources, investment and time, so this does not make it the only solution for developing countries—they can choose imitation, as well as dependent or catch-up development.

Dependent economic development is based on a country's direct dependency on foreign investments, thanks to which transnational companies may purchase certain factories and establish their dominance on a country's domestic market. Due to historic reasons, Eastern European countries (apart from Slovenia) have become the most dependent, as the volume of foreign direct investments per capita in these countries is twice as high as the global average, with trasnational companies providing no less than 20% of jobs for the population (Glinkina and Kulikova 2018). Catch-up development, in turn, is also interesting from a practical point of view: by catching up, a poor, developing country is using rich countries' technologies, and may specialize in a specific economic industry which would secure an inflow of goods and capital.

Regardless of the choice of a liberal, dependent, or catch-up economic modernization, the risks of increased inequality both inside the country and between countries run high, remembering that developing countries are by default in a disadvantaged economic position. Nowadays the issue of the "digital divide" between developed and developing countries is becoming more and more pressing due to the spread of digital technologies: there are countries in the world where the majority of the population still has no access to the internet. The growth of countries' wealth occurs because each country strives for success, yet inequality still remains extremely pronounced. Generally, economic modernization effected by countries is aimed at economic growth, increased production and services volumes, and the growth of the population's personal consumption, yet social equality is not ubiquitous. This is in part due to developing countries focusing on natural resources for their economic development but not focusing enough on human resources. This may be objectively explained through the need to invest in the education system and to create jobs, which is to be strategically outlined and substantiated as jobs are linked to the existing and prospective production and services structure in the country. State governments also have to undertake sustained employment in the course of effecting modernization reforms. A good example of successful modernization is Saudi Arabia, which used to rely on its natural resources for securing budget revenue and transitioned from low-income countries to middle-income countries in less than 20 years. This happened thanks to monetary investments from sales of natural resources into infrastructure, education, and healthcare. It is these indicators that help to grow human capital. It is also important that the opportunity to export resources drives the development of the exchange of various goods and integrational international relations.

However, the resource and export element of a country's economy always runs the risk of damaging the national economy by breaking the balance between the export structure and a country's industrial development as the priorities shift to the extracting industry in relation to manufacturing. It was in 1995 that a negative correlation between natural resource wealth and a country's economic prosperity was proved (Sachs and Warner 1995): by increasing the total production of exported commodities by 25%, a country experiences a slow-down of long-term economic growth per capita by 0.5–1% a year, as well as a decrease in exports share by 6%. That is how the term "the natural resource curse" was coined (Auty 2002). Now research is still being conducted into the economic modernization of Canada, Norway, African countries, and Russia, as these countries have chosen commodities exports, which has had both a positive and a negative effect on the country's economic growth (Godzimirski 2016; Badeeb et al. 2017; Manzano and Gutiérrez 2019). One theory of interest is the decoupling theory (von Weizsäcker 2014) about the strategic basis for moving to an environmentally sustainable economy, which enables, on the one hand, calculating the people's welfare growth rates, and, on the other hand, regulating the consumption of resources and the effect of industrial development (Arsakhanova et al. 2019).

Japan, South Korea, Taiwan, and China have all put a bet on exports as the basis for economic modernization, having implemented the so-called "Asian development model". Goods were exported (and not resources as opposed to the resource development model analyzed above), investments were actively made, and favorable conditions were created for national and foreign businesses. This has led to the exponential growth of the industrial sector; however, unfortunately, it did not allow for a quick transition to the category of countries with high income levels among the population. China, for example, is rapidly developing robotics in production: according to the International Federation of Robotics data, China has 97 robots installed per 10,000 workers (among leader-countries in robotization, South Korea has 710 robots, Germany has 322, and Japan has 308 robots per 10,000 workers). With the advantage of cutting costs, decisions to integrate robotics will allow for lower employment rates as one robot can, on average, substitute three to six workers (Acemoglu and Restrepo 2016). The International Labor Organization (ILO) forecasts that, due to robotization, up 86% of workers in Vietnam and 88% in Bangladesh may lose their jobs, and India will see a significant decline of the largest industrial sector providing employment, namely textiles, clothes, and footwear production, which amounts to 6% of the country's GDP and 13% of its exports.

In light of this it seems obvious that the demand for a highly qualified workforce will grow, which has always been an issue for developing countries. Within the framework of large-scale global competition on the part of China's production and goods imports from certain countries, development opportunities for the exported services sector are also under consideration. The most interesting and relevant options are the IT services exports, as they are in demand all around the world as a symbol of new digital technology; however, problems arise in terms of the availability of highly qualified developers and programmers and the inability to create a large number of jobs. Developing countries also demonstrate high birth rates, which is why securing employment is an extremely relevant task. For example, in India the amount of the working-age population rises annually by 1%, so by 2050 this country will need to create almost 280 million new jobs (Zotin 2018), an extremely large number.

Developed countries, having understood the consequences of the 2008 financial crisis, have begun to effect various economic restoration programs based on moving production back from developing countries. Setting up production in countries with low incomes is known to have been an economically lucrative strategy, as the cost of production decreased significantly due to lower worker labor costs. This policy allowed for the developing countries' economic growth and served to gradually shorten the gap between them and developed countries; however, this can be said only in relation to a number of developing countries, namely China and Eastern European countries.

As such, outsourcing has given way to reshoring over the past ten years, with developing countries having encountered the problem of a decrease in the number of jobs due to international companies having withdrawn their production. However, developed countries have also received a new portion of issues in light of production withdrawal. Modern production has to be as automated as possible, new progressive technologies have to be utilized, and robotics makes production more efficient, which is why developed countries are experiencing the establishment of new industrial businesses and services companies where robots are responsible for the majority of the labor process, so the risk of employment decline is high even in developed countries.

In spite of that, an interesting trend may be observed in terms of the leading countries' high-tech exports indicators. According to the World Bank, in 2018 China became the leader in high-tech exports with a volume of 731 billion dollars; Hong Kong amounts to 322 billion dollars by itself; Germany is in the third place with a high-tech exports volume of 207 billion dollars; the United States is only in the fourth place, with 156 billion dollars (and it must be remembered that this country is home to all the largest high-tech companies of the world using unique new technologies). It seems incredible that China, a developing country, has changed its economic modernization trajectory so fast, having gone from large-scale production to the high-tech industry; however, statistics allow us to see the effect: in 1992 high-tech exports amounted to 6% of the GDP (33% in the United States), in 2000 it was 18% (34% in the United States), and then it increased to 31% in 2005 (33% in the United States), 27% in

2010 (20% in the United States), and 25% in 2016 (20% in the United States) (World Bank 2019). This proves that, despite modernization risks, countries can achieve impressive results and can become stronger economically, even without a prior large technological potential.

Russia, a country with a rich history, having walked down the path of establishing the market economy, having made a unique contribution to modern science and the creation of technologies and inventions, aims to modernize its economy, which will allow the country to become economically successful on the global arena and to reach the position of a global leader. The past 15 years have seen active state support programs for innovational and science and technology development, as well as contributions to high-tech production. For example, these are the main development scenarios for Russia up to 2035:

- The mobilization scenario aimed, at achieving scientific and technological leadership in the world while preserving the economy's traditional specialization;
- The "Independent power center" scenario, aimed at achieving scientific and technological leadership and designed to build a new economy with new progressive technologies able to create new markets;
- The "selective specialization" scenario, in which the country is to gradually transition to high scientific and technological positions internationally by importing the best foreign technology within the framework of global scientific and technological cooperation programs and import phase-out programs for the functioning of the newest industries in the Russian economy.

These scenarios provide the possibility to objectively evaluate the Russian economy's development potential, and to see the risks that may arise in implementing the economic development strategy on the basis of new technologies:

(a) The selection of priority technologies based on foresight research and forecasts. The development of these technologies will receive state support from various state programs, as will the so-called national projects, presidential initiatives for priority scientific, technological, and technical areas, support programs for fundamental and exploratory research including innovational companies, financial support for technological transfer centers;

(b) Commercialization prospects for new goods and developments due to a non-optimal choice of technology defined above. This risk can be minimized by conducting a variative expert evaluation of the efficiency of state research programs and developments, as well as an assessment of scientific grants' recipients;
(c) A "brain drain" due to academic and labor mobility as a result of which inventions, new products, and new technologies may become the property of foreign companies. Talented children, youth, and university science are being actively supported in Russia in order to popularize science and technology among its youth and to make the job of a researcher attractive and competitive;
(d) The risk of a low innovational susceptibility and a need to adjust innovational policy in relation to other types of state policy (industrial, agricultural, social, informational, etc.);
(e) Bigger pressure on Russia in the form of sanctions and the continuing embargo on equipment and technology exports. This may, on the one hand, slow down the development of Russian industry, but has, on the other hand, already created an import phase-out mechanism stimulating Russia's own national production;
(f) Risks of reducing state funding for scientific and technological development programs as a result of the necessity to redirect funds toward solving current economic and social issues;
(g) High loan interest rates for innovational and high-tech production companies aiming to conduct research and development to strengthen their competitive advantages and to bring their products to foreign markets;
(h) Risks of not achieving high labor productivity rates due to technological companies not being interested therein, as the largest industries of the Russian economy belong to the state (military/space industry, the banking sector, transportation, and energy sectors) and their efficiency affects the whole economy;
(i) The risks of a lack of transitioning from progressive technologies such as the atomic, space, and military industries (defined by high performance and innovation rates) to the civil production sector. In order to minimize these risks, it is important to separate special technology and to create a mechanism for increasing the competitiveness of different Russia industries when it comes to dual-use technology.

Conclusions/Recommendations

In the course of global competition and the onset of the Fourth Industrial Revolution, there is no single way for countries to achieve competitiveness. However, it remains indisputable that the source of a country's long-term economic growth are innovations and, therefore, increased production coupled with integrating progressive technology. These tasks can not only be solved by businesses, but are also of prime importance for state governance. This is why a state-business partnership allows for the development of different industries and the services sector, the evidence of which are the positive practices of different countries including developing countries. However, the risks must be remembered of such a partnership linked to the forming of stricter state regulation and bureaucracy systems, the high costs of financial resources, and a lack of access to state or bank funding.

Development of the high-tech industry is becoming the driving force behind economic growth, ensuring the efficient modernization of the economy in modern conditions, which enables a secure transfer of workers from outdated, economically inefficient industries to new and more productive ones, or to the services sector which is currently undergoing an active transformation due to digitalization. The state may support such innovations and projects in different ways, as this will be a contribution to human resources and maintaining employment. Generally, any country's economic modernization, regardless of its market economy type (liberal, dependent, or catch-up), has to be implemented in accordance with the resource component (mainly renewable and alternative energy sources), besides the technological and social aspect, in order to secure long-term economic growth and sustainable or leadership positions in the global economy.

References

Acemoglu, D., & Restrepo, P. (2016). *The Race Between Machine and Man: Implications of Technology for Growth, Factor Shares and Employment.* NBER Working Paper, no. 22252, pp. 1–16.

Arsakhanova, Z. B., Khazhmuradov, Z. D., & Khazhmuradova, S. D. (2019). Decoupling in Economics—Essence, Definition and Types. *Society, Economics, Management, 4*(4), 13–18. (in Russian).

Auty, R. M. (2002). *Resource Abundance and Economic Development*. Oxford: Oxford University Press.

Badeeb, R. A., Lean, H. H., & Clark, J. (2017). The Evolution of the Natural Resource Curse Thesis: A Critical Literature Survey. *Resources Policy, 51*, 123–134. https://doi.org/10.1016/j.resourpol.2016.10.015.

Beck, U. (1992). From Industrial Society to the Risk Society. *Theory, Culture and Society, 9*(1), 97–123.

Belkina, A. (2019, October 9). How Innovations Develop in Russia. *Vedomosti*. Retrieved from https://www.vedomosti.ru/partner/articles/2019/10/09/813027-razvivayutsya-innovatsii.

Drahokoupil, J. (2009). *Globalization and the State in Central and Eastern Europe. The Politics of Foreign Direct Investment*. Abingdon: Routledge.

Eisenstadt, S. N. (1966). *Modernization: Protest and Change*. Englewood Cliffs: Prentice-Hall.

Giddens, A. (1991). *Modernity and Self-Identity*. Stanford: Stanford University Press.

Glinkina, S. P., & Kulikova, N. V. (2018). On the Model of Capitalism in Central-Eastern Europe. *Bulletin of the Institute of Economics Russian Academy of Sciences*, (3), 9–24. https://doi.org/10.24411/2073-6487-2018-00042.

Glinkina, S. P. (Ed.). (2012). *Modernization in the Countries of the Russian Neighborhood Belt: Structural and Technological Aspects*. Moscow, Saint Petersburg: Nestor-Istoriya. (in Russian).

Godzimirski, J. M. (2016). *Russian Energy in a Changing World: What Is the Outlook for the Hydrocarbons Superpower?* Abingdon: Routledge.

Hall, P., & Soskice, D. (2001). *Varieties of Capitalism: The Institutional Foundations of Comparative Advantage*. Oxford: Oxford University Press.

Hancké, B., Rhodes, M., & Thatcher, M. (2007). *Beyond Varieties of Capitalism: Conflict, Contradictions, and Complementarities in the European Economy*. Oxford: Oxford University Press.

Inozemtsev, V. (2004). *Catching Up: The Limits Of Rapid Economic Development*. London: Transaction Publishers.

Jamrisko, M., & Lu, W. (2020, January 18). Bloomberg Innovation Index. Germany Breaks Korea's Six-Year Streak as Most Innovative Nation. *Bloomberg*. Retrieved from https://www.bloomberg.com/news/articles/2020-01-18/germany-breaks-korea-s-six-year-streak-as-most-innovative-nation.

Landesmann, M. A., & Stöllinger, R. (2019). Structural Change, Trade and Global Production Networks: An 'Appropriate Industrial Policy' for Peripheral and Catching-up Economies. *Structural Change and Economic Dynamics, 48*, 7–23. https://doi.org/10.1016/j.strueco.2018.04.001.

Manzano, O., & Gutiérrez, J. D. (2019). The Subnational Resource Curse: Theory and Evidence. *The Extractive Industries and Society, 6*(2), 261–266. https://doi.org/10.1016/j.exis.2019.03.010.

McMillan, M., Rodrik, D., & Verduzco-Gallo, I. (2014). Globalization, Structural Change, and Productivity Growth, with an Update on Africa. *World Development, 63*, 11–32.

Popov, V., & Jomo, K. S. (2018). Are Developing Countries Catching Up? *Cambridge Journal of Economics, 42*(1), 33–46. https://doi.org/10.1093/cje/bex025.

Rifkin, J. (2011). *The Third Industrial Revolution. How Lateral Power Is Transforming Energy, the Economy, and the World.* New York: St. Martin's Publishing Group.

Rodrik, D. (2014). The Past, Present, and Future of Economic Growth. *Challenge, 57*(3), 5–39. https://doi.org/10.2753/0577-5132570301.

Sachs, J. D., & Warner, A. M. (1995). *Natural Resource Abundance and Economic Growth.* NBER Working Paper No. w5398, Retrieved from SSRN: https://ssrn.com/abstract=225459.

Schwab, K. (2017). *The Fourth Industrial Revolution.* New York: Crown Business.

Simoniya, N., & Torkunov, A. (2015). The European Union's Energy Security and Russia. *Social Sciences (Russian Federation), 46*(2), 78–89.

von Weizsäcker, E. U. (2014). Decoupling: Technological Opportunities and Policy Options—Executive Summary. In E. von Weizsäcker (Ed.), *Ernst Ulrich von Weizsäcker. SpringerBriefs on Pioneers in Science and Practice* (Vol. 28). Cham: Springer. https://doi.org/10.1007/978-3-319-03662-5_19.

WIPO. (2019). *Global Innovation Index 2019. Towards a Healthy Lifestyle: The Future of Medical Innovation. Main Conclusion.* Cornell, SC Johnson College of Business (in Russian). Retrieved from https://www.wipo.int/edocs/pubdocs/ru/wipo_pub_gii_2019_keyfindings.pdf.

World Bank. (2019). *High-Technology Exports (% of Manufactured Exports).* Retrieved from https://data.worldbank.org/indicator/TX.VAL.TECH.CD?most_recent_value_desc=true.

Zotin, A., (2018, February 17). Dead-End Branch of Development. How Technological Progress Stopped Economic Growth in Poor Countries. *Kommersant* (in Russian). Retrieved from https://www.kommersant.ru/doc/3533278.

CHAPTER 15

Imperfect Mechanisms for the Use and Protection of Intellectual Property as an Organizational Barrier in the Movement to Global Technological Leadership

Alexander Litvinenko, Julia Lozina, and Lyudmila Chernikova

Introduction

"Technological sovereignty", "technological race", "technological leadership", "sixth technological order"—these are all terms that have entered the vocabularies of politicians and economists. Achieving stable economic growth in modern conditions, based on intellectual innovations, means achieving technological sovereignty, competitiveness, and, in the end, technological leadership. It is intellectual property that has become

A. Litvinenko (✉) • J. Lozina
Saint Petersburg University of MIA of Russia, St. Petersburg, Russia

L. Chernikova
Financial University under the Government of the Russian Federation, Moscow, Russia

I. Stepnov (ed.), *Technology and Business Strategy*,
https://doi.org/10.1007/978-3-030-63974-7_15

the main factor affecting competition, industry efficiency, and resource and energy conservation. This circumstance predetermines the importance of state ventures in the digital technology development field, as well as of state involvement in international competition for intellectual works and for intellectual capital itself. The countries that achieve success in these fields will secure their positions as global technological leaders.

The chapter puts forwards and solves a number of interconnected problems:

- The study of intellectual property use and protection mechanisms in those countries currently leading in the advanced technology field;
- A comparative analysis of how said mechanisms function in Russia with how they operate in foreign countries, identifying flaws and advantages;
- Formulating suggestions on how Russia could overcome organizational barriers in the use of innovations, and developing recommendations on intellectual property protection.

Methodology

The authors utilize general scientific research methods, as well as economic and legal analysis:

- The study of international treaties and analytics let direct comparisons be made between how Russia and other countries (the United States, Germany, China) approach forming key elements of intellectual property management;
- The structural analysis has allowed all the elements in the intellectual property management mechanism to be positioned together, and thus flaws to be identified in intellectual property use and protection, which take the form of organizational barriers to movement to global technological leadership;
- Scientific generalization is utilized for the purposes of clarifying all the categories in the intellectual property field;
- Comparative analysis has provided an opportunity to selectively assess Russian and foreign innovational indicators.
- Content analysis of base legislation has revealed advantages that intellectual property protection possesses.
- An institutional approach helped to highlight national peculiarities of intellectual property use and protection.

Results

In order to achieve the high rates of knowledge accumulation that determines national economies' competitiveness, the role of technology and innovation is to increase. The risks listed in the Russian Scientific and Technological Development Strategy, including the problem of the practical application of developed projects and low research efficiency, create barriers for fortifying the country's technological sovereignty.

The Global Competitiveness Report 2019 results show that the changes in personnel and educational policy made by leading countries have not had the desired effect of technological growth. Statistics indicate that such countries as South Korea, Japan, and France—with high innovation potential—are still experiencing a shortage of personnel, so must continue with transforming their labor markets.

The Russian "inadequacy of the economy's institutional structure proportional to its development opportunities" concept is the main obstacle to implementing the sixth principle of economics due to the existing institutions "being aimed at recreating the existing technological order and not at developing a new one" (Glazyev 2010). Globalization and technology are the main barriers in the way of economic growth. Meanwhile it is technology that influences inequality by decreasing demand for underqualified labor and disproportionately favoring qualified specialists (Global Competitiveness Report 2019).

Advanced Technology Use Experience in the United States

The United States estimates that innovation profits margins make up, at the very least, 300 billion dollars a year. The significance of Intellectual Protection and its protected status are enshrined in the US Constitution, and the Intellectual Property Strategy adopted by the United States features a coherent coordinated structure which includes executive bodies, agencies, and departments. The intellectual property office coordinates and develops general intellectual property policy and strategy aimed at rewarding innovations, as well as ensuring the protection and efficient use of intellectual property both inside the country and overseas.

The strategy of the American approach includes four elements: interaction with trade partners; efficient use of legal instruments, including trade instruments; broad co-operation with law enforcement; dealings and partnerships in the private sector. The country has an intellectual property strategy group, which regularly conducts meetings with representatives of the national economic council, the National Security Council (NSC), the Office of Science and Technology Policy (OSTP), and the Council of Economic Advisers (CEA). Unlike Russia, which favors patent protection, the United States favors all areas of intellectual property; for example, the 2018 Music Modernization Act protects the rights of video and music producers and performers on the internet (Report IPEC 2018).

The 2018 US, Mexico, and Canada Agreement (USMCA) protects from unlawful appropriation of trade secrets (including from government corporations), sets a ten-year data protection period for biological agents, and ensures that border control organizational mechanisms are in place. In recent years, negotiations have been conducted with India, Vietnam, China, and Thailand, mapping out cooperation routes in the intellectual property area. In a number of African countries, special training stations have been opened in the field of technical basics and rights in intellectual property. Interestingly enough, the United States has withdrawn from the Universal Postal Union, with the main claim being the artificial pricing down of postal deliveries between states. A package traveling from China to the United States costs less than a package traveling within the United States. In 2018 the Global Intellectual Property Academy (GIPA) developed potential growth programs in all areas of intellectual property use and protection, including ensuring that intellectual property rights are observed, and that the rules of online-piracy, postal express deliveries, trade secrets, copyright policy, patent, and trademark expertise are observed. As of last year, the programs included around 4000 officials, judges, and prosecutors, out of 83 countries of the world.

The need for intellectual property protection in the United States led to the 2017 assessment of the Chinese sale of counterfeit goods, trade secrets, and technology theft, which had damaged intellectual property rights. Based on the 2018 assessment, the United States decided to increase tariffs on Chinese goods, and the assessment findings were forwarded to the WTO. Despite the damage from the tariffs amounting to over 50 billion dollars, China refused to change this policy.

In order to estimate which transactions could have an effect on national security, the United States employs the Committee on Foreign Investment.

Should such a risk be identified, and should all legal, organizational, and economic means prove ineffective (Inozemtsev 2021), the documents are submitted for review by the President, who has the right to bar the transaction. In 2018, Trump blocked the purchase of the American Qualcomm by its Asian competitor Broadcom, which is the global semiconductor and 5G networks sales leader. The transaction was priced at 117 billion dollars. After this, the Foreign Investment Risk Review Modernization Act of 2018 was adopted in the United States (Report IPEC 2018)

The United States does not only provide legal and economic remedies for intellectual property protection; it also has specialized departments and groups in its Ministry of Justice, in its National Security department, in the Attorney-General's office, and in the FBI, which are all responsible for reviewing and investigating cases infringing on intellectual property holders' rights. The main focus is on export control, consumer rights protection concerning counterfeit goods, food, medicine, cosmetics, software, and computer technology. By the end of 2018, the FBI had 195 ongoing investigations. Those included: trade secrets theft (67 cases), copyright infringement (64 cases), and trademark infringement (64 cases). In 2018, the FBI initiated 54 cases and made 22 arrests, made 12 convictions, and confiscated 3 million dollars' worth of property.

For the purposes of promoting knowledge and technical support in the area of intellectual property, the Ministry of Justice has provided scholarships for the training of workers in review and investigation procedures of intellectual property protection cases. The Intellectual Property Theft Enforcement Program was introduced in order to aid the workers in investigating crimes and other offenses.

Germany's Experience—A University Approach to Promoting Innovation

Innovation research in Germany has its own special procedural features. Universities, industrial companies, and scientific institutions play the role of the organizers. The results of this work have already secured Germany's position in the top ten most scientifically developed countries list. Currently about 650,000 people are employed in the research and development field. The patent applications rate per million of residents is equal to that of Japan and is two times higher than the patent frequency rate in the United States (BMBF 2018)

As of 2017, Germany is fourth in the world in internal research expenditures; the United States and China are first and second respectively, while Russia is ninth. This makes up 2.93% of its GDP, 3.13% in 2018, and plans have been made to increase that to 3.5% by 2025. Only Taiwan and China rank higher than Germany. State expenses number 28.5% (66.2% for Russia). The input of German companies specializing in technological innovations relative to the entirety of German companies is 52.6%, but 7.5% for Russia (Gorodnikova et al. 2019). Out of 105 billion euro allocated to innovation research, 72 billion belongs to private businesses.

As opposed to Russia, intellectual property protection in Germany is regulated by individual acts; there are separate regulations for copyright, patents, and works-for-hire. Germany is yet to adopt an intellectual property protection strategy; however, the High-Tech Strategy is in force up until 2025 (With the High-Tech Strategy, 2025), the main points of which include promoting open market, international knowledge exchange, and free trade. In doing so, the freedom of reproduction must be observed. In order to protect the rights of authors and patent holders, the Patent Court (PatG "Patentgericht") and the Federal Patent Court (BPatG "Bundespatentgericht") have been established.

As per employment contracts, the rights to intellectual property are vested in universities and in associations. The contract contains provisions that limit the employee's additional employment opportunities outside the organization for full-time employees. Employees undertake to disclose any inventions and to produce annual reports on the sources and the volume of any received rewards. Statistically, 50% of developed projects receiving patent status is a good indicator.

A unique feature of intellectual property regulation is the existence of a separately adopted act regulating relations between merchants and their employees who create works-for-hire—the Workers' Inventions Act. The act includes trade secrets provisions, provisions for creating decent conditions for accruing works-for-hire, and provisions for the payment of a reward to the worker. Three main categories of employees are subject to different regulations—civil servants, members of the Bundeswehr, and university professors. University professors are allowed to apply for patents in their own name, unlike private firm workers (Priorität einer nationalen Erstanmeldung [innere Priorität]). The law imposes a duty of patent registration on the employer, which is a positive development. Such a duty is not present in Russian law, which is likely why, in Russia, only 10% of all developments are registered (meaning they are approved by Rospatent) (Fomina 2017).

The level of direct foreign investment by transnational corporations has become the economic indicator of Germany's innovational activity. In the past 20 years Germany has managed to retain the top spots among world leaders, thanks in large to acquiring promising businesses and to proactive innovation policy. According to UNCTAD's data, the transnationality index among German corporations has exceeded 50%; this is through, among other things, a proactive merger policy with foreign companies utilizing the newest technology. For example, the German "SAP" has made over 60 large merger and acquisition transactions over the past 15 years, and in 2016 it acquired the American "Concur" (specializing in the area of travel and expenses management software development) for 8.3 billion dollars (Konina 2018). Currently, the list of countries experiencing the flow of German investment is changing. China, the United States, and Russia are at the top of the list. According to the Russian-German Chamber of Foreign Trade Data, 2018 saw German businesspeople invest more than 3 billion euro, which is the highest figure since 2008 (Deutsch-Russische Auslandshandelskammer 2019). With that being said, the number of German companies in Russia has declined by 8% in 2019 in comparison with 2018, and trade has fallen by 12%. The reasons behind this are economic sanctions, protectionism, and the weakening market conditions (Deutsch-Russische Auslandshandelskammer 2020).

Another area of development is the creation of small- and medium-sized businesses involved in innovations, and at the same time the provision of large corporations with the opportunity to enter into public-private partnerships. The state's task is to create conditions for increasing the flow of German start-ups on the international arena, while simultaneously implementing technology into every aspect of society.

The fulfillment of this task is performed with the help of state bank–funded programs (Deutsche Ausgleichsbank, Kreditanstalt für Wiederaufbau) and non-state companies. In order to increase co-operation among companies and scientific research institutions, project agencies are employed, which are selected on a competitive basis. Project agencies can be both state and private companies. It is them who determine the fate of a particular development project. In this respect, the German approach differs from the EEC; the EEC employs exclusively state organizations for these purposes.

Experts are employed for small businesses consulting; the "innovational vouchers" program, serving to reduce consulting expenses, is in place. Moreover, the government has created a fund for creators of high-tech business ventures—High-Tech Gründerfonds GmbH—the purpose of which is to distribute up to 5 million euros in support of high-tech business (**Kobyshev 2014**).

China's Experience in Intellectual Property Use and Protection

In November 2019, China announced its intention to tighten intellectual property rights protection and to amend its civil and criminal laws. An efficient protection system is planned to be implemented in five years, which will be aimed at increasing compensation sizes in the area of intellectual property, at reducing costs, and at expanding evidence collection opportunities (Harney 2019). The Chinese Ministry of Commerce announced that as consumption increases, foreign trade stabilization and direct foreign investment are to become the main areas of the Chinese economy's development in 2020 (Rambler.ru 2019a).

In 2018, the added value in the Chinese copyright industry amounted to 6.63 trillion yuan (950 billion dollars), which makes up 7.37% of the country's GDP. This indicator has grown by 55% since 2013. The value of the digital economy market has reached 4.6 trillion dollars or 34.8 of China's GDP. E-commerce amounted to 31.63 trillion yuan, and online sales went up to 9 million yuan. High-tech production added value went up by 11.7% as of 2018 (Rambler.ru 2019b).

In terms of legislation, the Chinese Scientific and Technological Development Strategy will be in force until 2020. Copyright, patent, trademark, and scientific progress laws have been enacted; a number of provisions have been added to civil and criminal legislation meant to protect intellectual property. As opposed to Russia, where Rospatent is the main body responsible for intellectual property protection, in China several agencies are responsible for it. The State Intellectual Property Office (SIPO) registers patents, issues certificates for integrated circuit layout designs, and registers rights to genetic resources. Trademark certificates are issued by the Trademark Registration Bureau. The National Copyright Administration is responsible for copyright, and the Ministry of Agriculture and the Forest Office are together responsible for new varieties protection. Only trade secrets are not subject to registration. Trade secrets receive protection from the State Industry and Trade Administration.

The unique features of the Chinese intellectual property protection system include:

- The opportunity to patent inventions abroad, ignoring the principle of national priority, on condition that an expertise certifying the lack of any information constituting a state secret is conducted. The Chinese Penal Code imposes harsh punishments for non-compliance, with the harshest sentence being the death penalty;
- Widespread use of various programs (e.g. “A Thousand Talents”), the main purpose of which is not just to create decent conditions for scientists for the duration of the scholarship and beyond, but also to provide social security for scientists up until retirement. Unfortunately, the short terms of scholars’ employment are limited by the scholarship’s terms, which demonstrates a low level of social security (Kavokin 2017);
- The existence of more than 1500 business incubators designed to provide all manners of assistance to high-tech companies;
- The existence of the small innovation business supporting Investment Fund in the Ministry of Science and Technology;
- The intellectual property protection system, aimed at both internal and external protection of the Chinese right holder (Ostrovsky 2015). Taking into account a lack of protection for trade secrets as a part of intellectual property, a barrier is created for foreign right holders; however, this brings China more profits than losses.

Russia is yet to move from its position in the global countries’ competitiveness rating 2019, having not moved from 43rd place since 2018. The macroeconomic environment (+2.5 points) and the innovation potential (32nd place) have improved thanks to increases in scientific research institutions’ quality, as well as to constant research and development expenses (1.1% of GDP, 34th place). Implementation of Information and Communications Technology (+4.9 points, 22nd place), which thanks in large part to the internet have reached 81% of the population (54th place), also contributes to innovation development. Personnel potential and education levels in which global leaders actively invest have fallen. Workforce qualification level and college graduates’ assessment by the business community have decreased by 0.1 points (54th place and 38th place respectively); this indicates that the quality of education does not correspond to the needs of modern economy.

The second area in which Russia needs to tighten its competitiveness gap is the financial system (95th place). The main challenges include: difficulties in receiving loans (-0.9, 118th place) and the lack of a developed stock market (38.9%, 51st place) relative to the scale of its economy (Global Competitiveness Report 2019).

It was noted during the December 2019 meeting of the Strategic Development and Nationwide Projects Council that five world-class scientific educational facilities have been created with the help of 15.3 billion non-budgetary funds and 1.7 budgetary funds; 32 billion rubles worth of project contracts have been signed. Not counting large players like "Lukoil", "Gazpromneft", "SDS-Ugol", and "Sibur-Holding", 3000 researchers, scientific organizations, and universities are taking part in the project, with 133 educational programs already having been developed (Kudrin 2019). Unfortunately, these results are not yet comparable to world innovation leaders (Abramova and Garanina 2018). One of the reasons for this is the unbalancing of the governing bodies' activity pertaining to the implementation of nation-wide projects; their goals have a 60% achievement rate (Kudrin 2019).

Venture funds and state corporations currently in place across the country, being responsible for end-to-end digital technology development, have encountered a shortage of quality projects; as the participants of the "Global Technological Leadership" forum claim, Russian innovators are stuck in state corporations and are experiencing difficulties entering the global market (Edovina 2019).

In conducting scientific research and experimental constructions, implementing additional financial control, corruption prevention, and corruption risk-monitoring mechanisms are required, with all of these functions being fulfilled by specialized bodies responsible for budget expenditure control (Bastrykin 2019).

Conclusions/Recommendations

As such, the main technological barriers are intrinsically linked with political and social barriers. Technological progress is not a means of achieving technological leadership, but a method with which competition, antitrust regulation, and stable economic growth opportunities are facilitated.

The authors' main conclusions, based on global experience analysis, address the degree to which the existing intellectual property management mechanism in Russia corresponds to the tasks set forth by new state policy, on the path to global technological leadership.

The American experience of using the newest technology shows just how far Russia has fallen behind in terms of intellectual property use, protection, and evaluation. Attributing different intellectual property regulation functions to different systems and agencies reflects inefficiently on its use and protection, including with the assistance of law enforcement. The American external and internal model of intellectual property protection may not be fully realized due to the lack of a unified international rules and regulations; any liability for intellectual property rights infringement takes the form of economic sanctions.

The German experience of utilizing a university-patent-scholarships chain for technological development and short-term manufacturing by small- and medium-sized businesses has secured Germany's place among the international high-tech leaders. Legal protections—provided to intellectual property in the form of mandatory patent publishing, works-for-hire regulations, and authors' guarantees of reward—have a positive effect on the development of innovations. Russia may learn certain lessons from the German experience of employing private project agencies conducting innovational activity evaluation.

China has advanced forward by "borrowing" foreign high-tech. While the United States places trade secrets as one of the most important parts of intellectual property law, China limits itself to enforcing only their protection from outside violations. Special programs collect talented scientists from all around the world, thanks to an individualized approach and authors' long-term social security.

The authors would recommend the following, in order for Russia to overcome its organizational barriers in the use of innovations and intellectual property protection:

- Further development of national legislation in the intellectual property area (patents, copyright, work-for hire, databases, domain names, etc.); this is meant to overcome the disparity between reality and law, which might threaten full-scale technological development;
- A transition to intellectual property strategic management, taking into account the goals and tasks set forward by the economy's innovational development (Rudaya 2019);
- A fair evaluation of intellectual property, since investments into intellectual property are much lower than its real value;

- State assistance and support in subsidizing marketing companies specializing in intellectual property protection;
- Acknowledging worldwide tendencies to reward scientific developments in environmental and social areas by means of providing tax reliefs (Lykova 2019) and ensuring direct state investment;
- Improvements to the mechanism of transforming the results of scientific research into commercialized products, through increasing investments into education and personnel, increasing the number of business incubators, creating partnering agencies, and introducing intellectual property evaluation experts into state governing bodies.

References

Abramova, A., & Garanina, O. (2018). Russian MNEs Under Sanctions: Challenges for Upgrading in GVCs (Cases of Energy and IT Industries). *Journal of East-West Business*. Retrieved from https://www.tandfonline.com/doi/full/10.1080/10669868.2018.1467843.

Bastrykin, A. (2019). Fighting Corruption in the Field of Intellectual Property (Based on the Materials of the Investigative Committee of the Russian Federation). *Pravda I Zakon, 2*(8), 3–9.

BMBF. (2018). *The High-Tech Strategy (2025)*. Berlin: Publikationsversand der Bundesregierung.

Edovina, T. (2019, December 6). Startups are Not Held up to the World Market. *Kommersant* №225. Retrieved from https://www.kommersant.ru/doc/4181831/.

Fomina, M. (2017). *Grigory Ivliev: We Need a National Strategy for Intellectual Property Development*. Retrieved from https://rupto.ru/ru/news/2017-01-27-interviewomsk

Glazyev, S. (2010). *Strategy of Advanced Development of Russia in the Conditions of the Global Crisis*. Retrieved from https://glazev.ru

World Economic Forum. (2019). *Global Competitiveness Report: How to End a Lost Decade of Productivity Growth*. Retrieved from https://www.weforum.org/reports/how-to-end-a-decade-of-lost-productivity-growth/

Gorodnikova, N., et al. (2019). *Science. Technologies. Innovations*. Moscow: Higher School of Economics.

Harney, A. (2019). China Plans Stronger Protections for Intellectual Property Rights. *Reuters*. Retrieved from https://www.reuters.com/article/us-china-ip/china-plans-stronger-protections-for-intellectual-property-rights-idUSKBN1XY0A5/

Inozemtsev, M. I. (2021). Digital Assets in the United States: Legal Aspects. *Lecture Notes in Networks and Systems, 139*, 514–522. https://doi.org/10.1007/978-3-030-53277-2_14.

IPEC. (2018). *Annual Intellectual Property Report to Congress*. Retrieved from https://www.whitehouse.gov/wp-content/uploads/2019/02/IPEC-2018-Annual-Intellectual-Property-Report-to-Congress.pdf/

Kavokin, A. (2017). Thousand Talents. *Izvestia*. Retrieved from https://iz.ru/629593/sinii-dym-kitaia-ili-kak-nam-snova-stat-nauchnoi-sverkhderzhavoi 22/08/2017.

Kobyshev, A. (2014). Innovation in Germany. *Deutsche Gesellschaft für Internationale Zusammenarbeit*. Retrieved from https://www.managerprogramm.de/wp-content/uploads/2014/08/Innovationen-in-Deutschland-RU.pdf/

Konina, N. (2018). Evolution of the Largest Multinational German Companies. *Sovremennaya Evropa, 2*(81), 49–59.

Kudrin, A. (2019). Meeting of the Council for Strategic Development and National Projects. *Kremlin.ru*. Retrieved from http://www.kremlin.ru/events/president/news/62411/

Lykova, L. (2019). Tax Tools for Supporting the Structural Modernization of the Russian Economy. In N. Y. Akhapkin (Ed.), *Priorities and Institutional Factors for the Modernization of the Russian Economy: a Collection* (pp. 186–204). Moscow: IE RAS.

Ostrovsky, A. (2015). The Intellectual Property Strategy of China. *Pravovaya Informatika, 1*, 49–56.

Rambler. (2019a). *The Amount of Digital China's Economy is made up of 31.3 trillion yuan in 2018*. Retrieved from https://finance.rambler.ru/markets/42143267-obem-tsifrovoy-ekonomiki-kitaya-dostig-31-3-trln-yuaney-v-2018-godu/

Rambler. (2019b). *Directions of Development of the Chinese Economy in 2020: Promotion of Consumption, Stabilization of Foreign Trade and Foreign Investment—Ministry of Commerce of the People's Republic of China*. Retrieved from https://finance.rambler.ru/markets/43443917/?utm_content=finance_media&utm_medium=read_more&utm_source=copylink/

Rudaya, I. (2019). Issues of Strategic Management of Russian Innovative Organizations' Intellectual Property. *Upravlenie, 7*(1), 50–59.

Russland.ahk.de. (2019). *German Investment in Russia is Growing*. Retrieved from https://russland.ahk.de/ru/mediacentr/novosti/detail/germanskie-investicii-v-rossiju-rastut/

Russland.ahk.de. (2020). *There are Fewer German Companies in Russia*. Retrieved from https://russland.ahk.de/ru/mediacentr/novosti/detail/v-rossii-stalo-menshe-nemeckikh-kompanii/

CHAPTER 16

Smart Cities' Hyper-Economies as the Reflection of Digital Governance Leadership

Sergey Kamolov and Alexander Blokhin

Introduction

Steady urbanization has a widespread impact on the economic performance of modern states, which can use it to achieve ever greater competitive advantages, increasing their economic performance. Urban territories play a fundamental role in the productivity of economies, being centers of production, accumulation of labor, financial resources, and investments.

Urbanization maintains its growth rate by expanding the infrastructure of urban settlements, as well as increasing the number of urban residents, both megacities and small regional cities, including residents of urban agglomerations. At the same time, there is also a trend toward a decrease in the number of rural residents. According to updated UN forecasts, by 2030 the number of urban residents will be 60.3% of the world's

S. Kamolov (✉) • A. Blokhin
Moscow Institute of International Relations (MGIMO University), Moscow, Russia

I. Stepnov (ed.), *Technology and Business Strategy*,
https://doi.org/10.1007/978-3-030-63974-7_16

population, which, according to forecasts, will be 5.16 billion in absolute terms, which is almost one billion more than in 2018 (UN Data Booklet 2018).

The phenomenon of Smart Cities benefits from the rapid development of technology, the tendency to digitalize all aspects of government and wide urbanization, demonstrates a profound impact on the global economy. The economic power of Smart Cities driven by the Internet of things promises tangible global economic benefits estimated to outreach $20 trillion by 2025 (Bonte 2018).

There are a large number of approaches to the classification of relevant Smart Cities technologies. Gartner distinguishes six main areas of Smart technological developments: Smart Energy, Smart Transportation, Smart Data, Smart Infrastructure, Smart Mobility, and Smart IoT. Gartner also highlights specific technologies that play an important role in the functioning and development of Smart cities, dividing them by the level of relevance and the level of development. The following technologies stand out: Artificial General Intelligence, Circular Economy, Smart Building, Blockchain Business Models, Data Marketplace, Data for Good, Autonomous Driving, City Operations Center, Civic and Community Development, Micromobility, Greenfield Smart City Framework, 5G, Chatbots, Digital Ethics, Digital Security, Energy Water Nexus, Sustainability and COP 21, Smart City Transportation Strategy, Smart City Framework, Connected Home, IoT Platform, Vehicle-to-Vehicle Communications, Blockchain, Microgrids (Velosa and Tratz-Ryan 2019.)

Within the framework of the national projects which are primarily aimed at increasing the standards of living of the citizens and strengthening the competitiveness of the Russian economy, the Russian Federation is striving to introduce the concept of Smart Cities for various settlements of the country. The national projects "Digital Economy" and "Housing and Urban Environment" were specifically designed to support the Russian innovative and high-tech global leadership.

Russian government mainstream ideas are reflected in the main Smart City principles: the orientation to the needs of the population, high-tech urban infrastructure, improving the quality of urban resources management, comfortable and safe environment, emphasis on the economic efficiency of cities, which can be achieved through the widespread introduction of advanced digital and engineering solutions in urban and municipal infrastructure. The goal of the "Smart City" in the Russian Federation is not only the digital transformation and automation of processes, but also a comprehensive increase in the efficiency of urban infrastructure.

Despite the phenomenon of Smart Cities arising relatively recently, there is a serious discussion in the academic field about its elaboration, essence, and prospects. Technology and innovation have entered the discourse of economics and public administration and are currently scrutinized by scholars. A vast array of international experts and researchers analyze the basic conceptual aspects of Smart Cities, as well as the problems of innovative development, creating a viable ecosystem in large cities and many other factors. It is important to emphasize the scientific contribution of B. Cohen, who coined a classification of Smart Cities, dividing them into three generations: Smart Cities 1.0, Smart Cities 2.0, Smart Cities 3.0. Each of these generation of Smart Cities has distinctive features, while each subsequent generation acquires more complex characteristics and features. According to the author's concept, the first generation of Smart City is a hub of innovators and IT product developers who seek to implement their solutions without any specific strategic goals. The second generation of this concept is focused on the targeted implementation of innovations and technological developments in the processes of urban and municipal governance to improve the quality of life of citizens. Smart Cities 3.0. include the same functions as the Generation 2.0; concurrently, its Smart City system interacts with residents. Smart Cities 3.0. is a citizen-oriented territory in which mutually beneficial coexistence and constant development are fruitful for all urban life (Cohen 2015).

We acknowledge the contribution of Rudolf Giffinger and Gudrun Haindlmaier to enrichment of common understanding of the concept. Giffinger and Gudrun classified Smart City technologies into six different groups in order to find an effective approach to compiling global rankings of Smart Cities. The main groups of characteristics for which the analysis was conducted are Economic Competitiveness, Human Capital, Participation and Inclusiveness, Transportation, Environment, and Quality of life (Giffinger and Gudrun 2010).

F.P. Appio, M. Lima, & Paroutis, S. examined in more detail the classification of Smart City technologies by improving the Giffinger's model, on the triangle of which they built an innovative technology model in three key groups: technologies aimed at improving the quality of life in Smart Cities (social sphere), technological innovations for economic activity, and projects for the physical infrastructure of the City (transport, living areas, recreation areas, etc.) (Appio et al. 2019).

D. Amo, M.-L. Medrano, and D. Pérez-Bustamante created the concept of "knowledge-based city". The term comprises the idea of knowledge economy and a knowledge-intensive and high-tech territory. In the chapter the authors point out that the modern concept of Smart Cities is directly related to the knowledge economy, since they are both based on improved living standards (e.g. education, physical, and social infrastructure), high-technology management, business, and so on (Amo et al. 2016).

Methodology

This study aims to consider the existing innovative projects in Russia that are used for the functioning and development of the concept of Smart Cities, published in the Smart City Solutions Bank of the Ministry of Construction Industry, Housing and Utilities Sector of the Russian Federation, and Rostelecom Corporation. This bank of solutions is an open aggregated database of projects implemented in cities across Russia, the purpose of which is to achieve the objectives of the national projects "Housing and Urban Environment" and "Digital Economy".

In this chapter, we conducted a thorough study of the existing urban environment innovative projects in Russia, which have already been implemented and inspected. The studied projects were published in the Smart City Solutions Bank of the Ministry of the Construction Industry, Housing and Communal Services of the Russian Federation and Rostelecom Corporation. The Solutions bank is an open aggregated database of embedded projects of Russian companies. The Bank creators set a task to shape a vision of technological component essential for pursuing goals of national projects "Housing and Urban Environment" and "Digital Economy". The hypothesis of the chapter is that contemporary data-driven governance as a significant part of Smart City concept underpins the formation of the creative economic environment. This research aims to study and analyze projects published in the Solutions Bank. These projects must meet the criteria for "Smart" technologies; in this study they will be examined through the prism of Cohen's Smart City definition and approach to defining this concept in the Russian Federation, adopted by the Ministry of Construction of Russia. We also expected to witness that the projects are coherent to the Smart Cities technologies by the Gartner classification to match current trends in this field.

The main theoretical methods of the present study are the comparative analysis method, expert assessment method and content analysis. In this chapter, we analyzed 364 projects from the open Smart City solutions bank, which were implemented in more than 100 settlements in Russia. The projects' criteria were elaborated on the basis of the key crossing characteristics of the classification of prominent experts, such as B. Cohen, R. Giffinger, and F. Appio as well as the approach of the Ministry of Construction Industry, Housing and Utilities Sector of the Russian Federation. The research used following criteria:

1. Innovativeness. Since the Smart City solutions bank projects have clearly distributed financing, business plans, and so on they can be considered as products. OECD experts define product innovation is a new or significantly improved good or service. This includes improvements in technical specifications, components and materials, software in the product, user friendliness, or other functional characteristics (OECD Oslo Manual 2018).
2. Economic efficiency.
3. Inclusiveness and socially oriented character. Inclusiveness is the participation of citizens in the activities of a Smart City, regardless of personal characteristics. Socially useful technologies encourage creation of a comfortable environment for the population, to fully use the benefits of technological development of Smart Cities and improve living conditions.
4. Flexibility in application.
5. Interoperability. As the most important criterion interoperability is defined as the ability of two or more information systems or their components to exchange information and to use information obtained as a result of the exchange. Since Smart Cities are considered as a citizen data processing system, the collection, analysis, and use of big data become a key feature for any Smart City project. Technologies should be able to be embedded into a homogenous ecosystem to achieve maximal results in its application and prevent failures in data interpretation.

All criteria assigned their values according to the binary system (from 0 to 1). Then, criteria 1–3 were calculated with a multiplier 1, criterion 4 was calculated with a multiplier 2, criterion 5 with a multiplier 3. The multiplier reflects our expert opinion on the criterion role in the overall Smart City governance efficiency and its hyper-economic contribution.

The final score is calculated by the sum of the points received for each of criteria presented.

Results

Based on the methodology, projects were taxonomized into three groups:

1. Stand-alone projects with a low level of flexibility and interoperability (total value from 0 to 3).
2. Industry projects suitable for Smart systems, but with a low level of interoperability (total value from 4 to 6).
3. Projects with high interoperability, developed to analyze big data, forming a separate inclusive integrated ecosystem and creating a demand for data (total value from 7 to 9).

According to the results of the study, we can come to the following conclusions. Firstly, a large number of projects published in the open Smart City Solutions Bank are subsumed under the first group. These projects can be poorly introduced in various environments comparing to other projects. This group is dominated by technology innovation projects (e.g. “Smart bench”, “Trenchless sliplining of the pipeline with a light-curing polymer sleeve”, etc.); however, these projects disaccord with the concept of the ecosystem of a Smart City as a territorial unit for government managers. Secondly, the Type 2 projects, with a high level of universality, flexibility, and greater integration capacity for the ecosystem of a Smart City, are underrepresented compared to the projects of the Type 1. Finally, since Smart Cities are not limited to technology, innovation in production, and anything else, but only accompanied by them, inclusiveness and flexibility of application are their main characteristics. The reason for this factor is the focus of Smart Cities not on the overwhelming implementation of high-tech solutions and digitalization of services and infrastructure, but on creation of a comfortable environment for the population and economic development, attracting investments, and, consequently, boosting the economy. Outstanding performance requires quick, high-quality, and overarching collection, analysis, and transmission of data obtained from various sources. As a result, the functioning of Smart Cities should not be based solely on single projects that increase the economic efficiency of using technology in a certain territory to perform various tasks (Kamolov 2019). The urban population is in the focus of the concept of Smart Cities, which determines the basic characteristics of further components of the concept. Citizens become integral participants of the regional and municipal governmental decision-making systems.

The representative results of the study allow us to provide possible solutions to the problem. Most of the scrutinized projects do not lead directly to the innovative and high-tech environment in Smart Cities of Russia. Undoubtedly, these projects have a positive economic effect and beneficial in short-term for the living conditions of citizens (e.g. the Public Wi-Fi project). However, they have an insignificant impact on the ecosystem from the managerial side of this issue, and do not form a basis for economic development. As previously noted, due to the fact that citizens are the drivers for shaping the direction of the development, we assume that it is the influence of citizens on the goals of the public administration system that determines the scope and architecture of the Smart City software. Since Smart Cities are still high-tech land areas, the creation of a unified system of software and hardware allows to create a responsive and streamlined digital infrastructure required for good governance.

In the modern data-centric era, the introduction of big data enables public managers to address the issues from a different perspective. Indeed, the development of a large industry makes it possible to give an impetus to the development of other related industries (or satellite industries). The volume of satellite markets is often not inferior to the main one, for example, in the case of the development of the mobile device industry. In this case, markets of digital advertising grew in direct proportion to the development and expansion of the mobile device market, the development and implementation of new technologies, and so on. This trend can be applied to the phenomenon of Smart Cities. When creating Smart City technologies, one should rely on integrated data processing systems, which entail individual high-tech solutions.

In fact, such shifts in the introduction of technologies form a separate type of economy, which is based on the movement of data. This trend affects the management system, as data management comes to the fore, as this issue is becoming one of the most sensitive for public administration. In order to be able to respond to emerging challenges, it is necessary to train qualified personnel which has corresponding and adequate knowledge to manage such systems and to have the skills of applied data analysis and forecasting. Being introduced into public administration, big data becomes the strategically important issue. In addition to the classic "digital competencies" of civil servants, there should be profound technical knowledge of public servants in charge of operating specialized software and hardware (Vasilieva et al. 2018).

As a result, as big data management begins to occupy one of the central positions in public administration, the population's demands for a qualified and competent state and municipal government are growing. An extensive analysis of the data is possible on provision that high-quality databases, hardware, and software are implemented and used. There is a need for a decision-making system based on large data flows. Integrated management systems for Smart Cities can solely cope with this task.

We assume that all above-mentioned features constitute a new creative environment. The new creative environment is a region or a city with deployed high-tech and knowledge-intensive governance system designed to generate, process, and inject data for further business use by economic agents, therefore creating next layer of economics (hyper-economy) where the core businesses are created around and on the basis of the marketable data and information.

New creative environment can solve the problems that have arisen as part of the creation of innovation support institutions. The institutional approach has shown its low efficiency due to the unstructured activities of public institutions and the lack of specific key performance indicators (KPIs). In addition, this approach can solve the problem of the program budgeting approach. As a result of its implementation, the aims of Presidential Decree "On National Goals and Strategic Tasks of the Development of the Russian Federation until 2024" to achieve intermediate results of the national project "Digital Economy" were not obtained. This challenge can be addressed by concentrating the innovative activity within the regions—this localizes innovation, effectively allocates budget funds, and finds subsequent application to developments in Smart Cities.

Conclusion

Summing up the results of this study, we can conclude that Smart Cities are becoming a catalyst for the processing of data, their collection, storage, and analysis, becoming the data-driven economy. Autonomous processes of data circulation allow to ascertain the beginning of the formation of a favorable environment for innovation and the development of software and hardware systems. It occurs when governing systems decide to and plan for further business use of the data that Smart City generates. It is by itself high-tech-based governance as it heavily relies on advance IoT solutions. To see where we are in Russia and what direction the concept is evolving, we've studied the Smart City Solutions Bank.

The analytical breakdown shows that the Solutions Bank is composed primarily by basic technologies designed to perform specifically in particular sector (transport, utilities, traffic control). We do not see integrated solutions; thus, we presume that the idea of relating data to the goals of management and, more importantly, using the data for creation of new businesses is not yet in the focus or at least in the priority of the Russian Smart City national project. The creation of technologies existing outside the ecosystem of a Smart City does not allow public managers to achieve synergistic interaction between the City administration services, the urban population, private sector, and the Smart City system itself, through the transit of data from one source to another for its subsequent transformation.

Full implementation and use of the Smart City concept is possible only with its constant development, increased inclusiveness, not only through the creation of a convenient and universal environment for citizens, but also through the systematization of management processes, which is impossible without establishing interoperability within the hardware systems into which the technologies are implemented. Smart Cities, as a new creative environment, should level the problems of inefficient institutions, using geographical localization of all innovative processes in cities, as centers for the development of science and technology using citizens' data.

References

Amo, D., Medrano, M.-L., & Pérez-Bustamante, D. (2016). The Knowledge Economy as a Key Determining Factor to Improve Smart Cities. *Sustainable Smart Cities*, pp. 115–128.

Appio, F., Lima, M., & Paroutis, S. (2019). Understanding Smart Cities: Innovation Ecosystems, Technological Advancements, and Societal Challenges. *Technological Forecasting and Social Change, 142*, 1–14.

Bonte, D. (2018). *Role of Smart Cities for Economic Development.* ABI Research. Retrieved from https://www.chordant.io/white_papers/abi-research-role-of-smart-cities-for-economic-development.

Cohen, B. (2015, October 8) The 3 Generations of Smart Cities. *Fast Company.* Retrieved from https://www.fastcompany.com/3047795/the-3-generations-of-Smart-cities

Giffinger, R., & Gudrun, H. (2010). Smart Cities Ranking: An Effective Instrument for the Positioning of Cities? *ACE: Architecture, City and Environment, 4*(12), 7–25.

Kamolov, S. G. (2019). On Epistemological Nature of the 'Smart Cities'. *Innovatsii i investitsii* (Innovations and Investments), no. 1, pp. 200–205.

OECD Oslo Manual. (2018). *Guidelines for Collecting, Reporting and Using Data on Innovation* (4th ed). The Measurement of Scientific, Technological and Innovation Activities. Retrieved from https://www.oecd.org/science/oslo-manual-2018-9789264304604-en.htm

UN. (2018). *The World's Cities in 2018.* Retrieved from https://www.un.org/en/events/citiesday/assets/pdf/the_worlds_cities_in_2018_data_booklet.pdf

Vasilieva, E. V., Pulyaeva, V. N., & Yudina, V. A. (2018). Development of Digital Competencies of State Civil Servants of the Russian Federation. *Business Informatics*, no. 4 (46). Retrieved from https://cyberleninka.ru/article/n/razvitie-tsifrovyh-kompetentsiy-gosudarstvennyh-grazhdanskih-sluzhaschih-rossiyskoy-federatsii

Velosa, A., & Tratz-Ryan, B. (2019). Hype Cycle for Smart City Technologies and Solutions. *Gartner*. Retrieved from https://www.gartner.com/en/documents/3955915/hype-cycle-for-Smart-City-technologies-and-solutions-201

CHAPTER 17

Smart Contracts and Corporate Governance: Prospects and Risks of Business Digitalization

Alexander Yukhno and Vladimir Osipov

Introduction

The possibilities of blockchain technology have become the basis for the distribution on the market of so-called smart contracts (smart-contracts), which interact with each other in a decentralized and distributed manner (Wright and De Filippi 2015). The concept of smart contracts was proposed in 1994 by American programmer Nick Szabo, who considers the "smart contract" as a computerized transaction protocol that fulfills the terms of the contract. The general objectives of developing such a contract are to satisfy the general contract terms (payment terms, confidentiality, etc.) and minimize exceptions and the need for trusted intermediaries. Relevant economic goals include reducing costs from fraud, arbitration and legal costs, and other transaction costs (Szabo 1994). The author of

A. Yukhno (✉)
Civic Chamber of Russia, Moscow, Russia

V. Osipov
Moscow State Institute of International Relations (MGIMO University), Moscow, Russia
e-mail: vs.ossipov@inno.mgimo.ru

I. Stepnov (ed.), *Technology and Business Strategy*,
https://doi.org/10.1007/978-3-030-63974-7_17

the concept indicates that smart contracts combine protocols with user interfaces to formalize and protect relationships in computer networks. The goals and design principles of these systems stem from legal principles, economic theory, and theories of reliable and secure protocols. The similarities and differences between smart contracts and traditional business procedures based on written contracts, controls, and static forms are discussed. Using cryptographic and other security mechanisms, we can protect many algorithmically determined relationships from violation by principals, from interception or malicious interference of third parties, up to time, the user interface and the completeness of the algorithmic specification (Szabo 1997).

Methodology

From the blockchain perspective, smart contracts are transactions in a distributed journal of records that are not limited to the fact that the goods are transferred from the seller to the buyer. A record in a distributed journal includes any special terms of the transaction that distinguish it from the standard ones. From this point of view, methods of institutional, comparative, and system analysis and synthesis were used in the frame of our research. Institutional analysis let us describe nets and connections between economic actors according to principal and the agent theory. Comparative analysis gave us an understanding of the difference between standard contract in law and smart contract in the system of common law and continental law. System analysis let us describe the architecture of smart contract complex. Synthesis was used in the frame of recommendation part of the chapter, to characterize public administration policy.

Results

We would like to begin from institutional and comparative analysis between smart contract and standard contract from the transaction costs point of view. Thus, time for transaction for standard contract (traditional contract in print version) continues over three to seven days including approval procedures. Time for transaction of smart contract continues over one to three minutes. Also automatic payments are possible in smart contracts compared with standard contracts. Using lawyers always is the most considerable part of transaction costs, and it is very important that there is no need for lawyers in smart contracts. Also there is no need for physical contacts between seller and buyer, and it is possible to make all activity in a virtual area.

Currently, the active development of blockchain technology contributes to a new stage in the development and practical use of smart contracts and allows us to switch from automatic contracts to truly autonomous self-executing and self-enforcing contracts (Lauslahti et al. 2017). A smart contract is not a contractual agreement, but a computer program, which is a piece of code in the implementation of code chains. Upon reaching predetermined conditions, the corresponding clause of the contract is executed automatically. It is important to note that, unlike other codes, it is in the block chain, and not on the server (Raval 2017). This makes impossible even a technical deviation from the terms of the contract. As Nick Szabo notes, the basic idea of smart contracts is that many types of contractual provisions (such as software, property rights, etc.) can be embedded in hardware and software in such a way as to make any violation of them costly for the offender (Szabo 1997). In addition, smart contracts do not need to use artificial intelligence for their work.

Currently, blockchain-based business models are being tested in various sectors of the economy with a predominant number of projects in the financial sector. Technology offers a new way to create, share, and track ownership of financial assets on an equitable basis. Many major players in the financial industry have begun investing in it, and stock exchanges are exploring the possibility of using blockchains to register and trade shares issued by corporations. For example, the Australian Stock Exchange announced in January 2016 its intention to redesign its clearing and settlement systems using blockchain technology. Earlier some researches on how blockchains could be used on stock markets were previously announced by the NASDAQ American Exchange and the Frankfurt German Exchange (Kuo Chuen and Deng 2017). Using the blockchain, debt securities and derivative financial instruments can also be placed, which can be executed autonomously as smart contracts. Using blockchains to register ownership of shares can solve many long-standing problems related to the inability of companies to keep accurate and timely records of owners of their shares. Further development of the technology may allow the use of self-executing smart contracts, such as stock options owned by employees (Yermack 2017; Swan 2015). At the same time, there are a large number of options for using smart contracts in other market segments: healthcare, technology, energy, public administration, and so on (Deloitte 2016).

Smart contracts represent the next step in the development of blockchain technology from simple accounting of financial transaction records to universal use. The fact that, in the legal sense, they are not contracts makes trust an even more important element in the interaction of the actors (Deloitte 2017b). The possibility of concluding and verifying such contracts through the blockchain reduces the costs of the actors (e.g., for preparing documentation) and eliminates the risks of unreliable methods of data transfer (e.g., via email) (Ivanov 2017). The computer network, using protocols agreed by the actors, develops a sequence of actions by which they can agree on the terms of the contract, which will be executed automatically. Thus, a database with a blockchain protocol allows actors to verify the result without the participation of a third-party intermediary (Deloitte 2017b). On this basis develop cities and their agglomerations (Osipov et al. 2018).

Smart contracts allow counterparties to automate tasks that are usually performed manually by a third-party intermediary, significantly accelerating business processes, reducing the possibility of errors in work and increasing cost efficiency (AICPA 2017). In addition, they can be used to perform the operational or administrative functions of the company, consolidate financial statements, including for boards of directors and company's management, which will also have an impact on the internal and external reporting of the company, as well as reduce the time for preparing such reports and avoid delays in their preparation. Targets and budgets can also be translated into smart contracts, which will allow to track the effectiveness of operations in real time. Moreover, non-financial reporting of the company can be simplified, for example, by creating a solution for the transparency of the company's supply chain based on the blockchain (AICPA 2017). The use of such contracts can be explained by the need for reasonable means of control and reduction of information asymmetries between management and other professional users and actors (Szabo 1997). They also ensure coordination of agent relations, excluding the opportunistic behavior of the agent. In this case, information asymmetry between the principal and the agent is completely eliminated (Kaal 2019). Given that at present, in practice, smart contracts are not suitable for all cases, they can be useful in situations where counterparties perform, for example, duplicate tasks for each transaction. In each case, the blockchain acts as a common database to provide a secure single source of information, and smart contracts automate operations (Deloitte 2017b).

Summarizing the above, the main advantages of smart contracts should include:

- Speed and updates in real time;
- Accuracy;
- Security of operations;
- Reducing the risk of contract failure;
- Reduction or complete exclusion of intermediaries;
- Lower cost compared to standard contracts;
- Stimulating the creation of new directions of business or operating models. (Deloitte 2016)

Thus, the automated nature of the execution of smart contracts in accordance with predefined conditions and a clear algorithm contributes to their dissemination in practice.

Despite the obvious advantages of smart contracts, some experts believe that they may not become effective corporate governance tools that cover the risks associated with making certain and irreversible obligations (Piazza 2017). There is no doubt that they require rigorous testing and adequate monitoring to reduce potential risks (Deloitte 2017a). These risks must be considered when using them including:

- Errors in the program code (e.g., due to the human factor);
- Uncertain legal status of such contracts;
- High costs of implementing such contracts;
- The difficulty of amending and terminating such contracts;
- Business and regulatory risks:
- Selection of the applicable law to the relations of the actors and the place of settlement of disputes of the actors;
- Risks of contract's non execution;
- Uncertain status of the legal liability of the actors to the contract;
- Information Security Risk. (Deloitte 2017a; Levi and Lipton 2018)

Actors may not always foresee all possible options for the events development, as well as unforeseen errors or results. Therefore, the continued use of smart contracts can potentially lead to new risks (AICPA 2017). Deloitte identifies the following areas that require close attention in this context. First, the scalability of technology has not yet been explored. Secondly, a deep research of the technology using is necessary when smart contracts are associated with real assets. Thirdly, the immutability of smart contracts based on the blockchain today means that developers must anticipate any possible scenario that requires changes to the contract. Fourth, technology transparency makes it difficult to use confidential information (Deloitte 2016). Thus, it becomes clear that the use of smart contracts in practice is characterized by the presence of both advantages and potential risks that organizations need to consider before deciding whether to use them in their activities.

Any way advantages of smart contract relations for capital markets are the following:

1. Transparency for investments;
2. Decrease of credit risks;
3. Simplifying the identification procedure;
4. Secure election of actor for business in on-line regime;
5. On-line payments;
6. Automatic reporting for stakeholders, including government and its fiscal bodies;
7. Simple and clear control procedure.

All these undoubtedly positive features make smart contracts a very effective instrument of strategic management for companies, who oriented on long-term future in hypercompetition (Silvestrov et al. 2019).

Conclusions and Recommendations

It is imperative that organizations even before making a decision on the implementation of smart contracts take into account their features when creating their development strategy and take appropriate measures to mitigate the risks (Deloitte 2017a). Otherwise, the economic effect of new technologies using may ultimately become negative. It is significant that in practice, organizations are already beginning to take into account these factors in their work. So, EY launched the "Smart Contract Analyzer" service, which allows to monitor smart contracts and tokens for known security threats within the Ethereum platform both before they are released and after they become available within the system (Ernst and Young 2019).

Smart contracts are an example of the concept of Amara's law, which establishes that we tend to overestimate new technologies in the short term and underestimate them in the long term. Recognizing that it will take time for their active use in commercial relations, the fact that they are revolutionizing the incentives of the parties when concluding contracts in the future can't be denied. For this reason, it is important to consider them not only through the prism of current concepts and approaches, but to try to predict the format of their use from positions that are now difficult to even imagine (Levi and Lipton 2018).

Inclusion of smart contacts in their activities implies a clear understanding of the consequences of their use for the organization and adequate measures for their gradual distribution in practice. In strategic development context, it is important to minimize emerging risks, organizations are encouraged:

1. to consider the using of smart contracts in the activity of the board of directors;
2. to develop and approve at the board level the strategy and main directions for the organization to use smart contracts;
3. to determine the value of risk appetite index of the organisation consider to smart contracts;
4. to develop internal documents governing their use within the organization;
5. to analyze the effectiveness of the use of smart contracts by the organization;
6. to increase the level of competence of employees of the organization regarding the use of smart contracts.

Thus, we can conclude that the technology of smart contracts is at an early stage of development, which leads to a large field for its research and practical application. And also we notice the great interest in smart contracts from the side of government, especially fiscal bodies (Osipov 2016). Smart contracts make the fiscal relations between economic actors and government transparent and predictable.

With using the Internet of Things, the introduction of smart contracts is becoming a reality, especially in relations between economic actors and in conditions of absence or weak legal regulation regarding restrictions in concrete jurisdiction. Global financial organizations are actively experimenting with smart contracts and are trying to fit them into their ecosystems. The most interested actors in smart contracts are those companies that turned out to be the most advanced in implementing information technologies based on the Internet of things in their economic activity.

References

AICPA. (2017). *Blockchain Technology and Its Potential Impact on the Audit and Assurance Profession*. Retrieved from https://www.aicpa.org/content/dam/aicpa/interestareas/frc/assuranceadvisoryservices/downloadabledocuments/blockchain-technology-and-its-potential-impact-on-the-audit-and-assurance-profession.pdf.

Deloitte. (2016). *Upgrading Blockchains: Smart Contract Use Cases in Industry*. Retrieved from https://www2.deloitte.com/insights/us/en/focus/signals-for-strategists/using-blockchain-for-smart-contracts.html.

Deloitte. (2017a). *Blockchain Risk Management. Risk Functions Need to Play an Active Role in Shaping Blockchain Strategy*. Retrieved from https://www2.deloitte.com/us/en/pages/advisory/articles/blockchain-risk-management.html.

Deloitte. (2017b). *Tech Trends 2017. The Kinetic Enterprise*. Retrieved from https://www2.deloitte.com/insights/us/en/focus/tech-trends/2017/blockchain-trust-economy.html.

Ernst & Young. (2019). *EY Launches Smart Contract Testing Service for Blockchain Clients*. Retrieved from https://www.ey.com/en_gl/news/2019/04/ey-launches-smart-contract-testing-service-for-blockchain-clients.

Ivanov, A. Y. (2017). *Blockchain at the Peak of Hype: Legal Risks and Opportunities*. Moscow: Publishing House of the Higher School of Economics.

Kaal, W. A. (2019). Blockchain Solutions for Agency Problems in Corporate Governance. Retrieved from https://papers.ssrn.com/sol3/papers.cfm?abstract_id=3373393.

Kuo Chuen, D. L., & Deng, R. (2017). *Handbook of Blockchain, Digital Finance, and Inclusion, Volume 1: Cryptocurrency, FinTech, InsurTech, and Regulation*. Elsevier Academic Press.

Lauslahti, K., Mattila, J., & Seppala, T. (2017). *Smart Contracts—How Will Blockchain Technology Affect Contractual Practices?*. Retrieved from https://ssrn.com/abstract=3154043.

Levi, St. D., & Lipton, A. B. (2018). *Harvard Law School Forum on Corporate Governance and Financial Regulation*. Retrieved from https://corpgov.law.harvard.edu/2018/05/26/an-introduction-to-smart-contracts-and-their-potential-and-inherent-limitations/#3.

Osipov, V. S. (2016). Project-Functional Structure of Management for Public Administration. *Public Administration Issues, 3*, 219–230.

Osipov, V., Zeldner, A., & Skryl, T. (2018). Making the Smart City: Technologies, Experiences, and Future Perspectives. *MATEC Web of Conferences*, Volume 212, ICRE.

Piazza, F. S. (2017). Bitcoin and the Blockchain as Possible Corporate Governance Tools: Strengths and Weaknesses. *Penn State Journal of Law & International Affairs, 5*(2), 262–301.

Raval, S. (2017). *Decentralized Applications. Harnessing Bitcoin's Blockchain Technology*. Translated by Kiselev, A., Piter, St.-Petersburg, Russia.

Silvestrov, S. N., Osipov, V. S., & Zeldner, A. G. (2019). The Role of State Corporations in Redesign of Sectoral Supply Chain Management. *International Journal of Supply Chain Management, 8*(5), 314–324.

Swan, M. (2015). *Blockchain. Blueprint for a New Economy*. O'Reilly.

Szabo, N. (1994). *Smart Contracts*. Retrieved from http://www.fon.hum.uva.nl/rob/Courses/InformationInSpeech/CDROM/Literature/LOTwinterschool2006/szabo.best.vwh.net/smart.contracts.html.

Szabo, N. (1997). *Smart Contracts: Formalizing and Securing Relationships on Public Networks*. Retrieved from https://firstmonday.org/ojs/index.php/fm/article/view/548/469#*.

Wright, A., & De Filippi, P. (2015). *Decentralized Blockchain Technology and the Rise of Lex Cryptographia*. Retrieved from https://papers.ssrn.com/abstract_id=2580664.

Yermack, D. (2017). *Corporate Governance and Blockchains*. Retrieved from https://papers.ssrn.com/sol3/papers.cfm?abstract_id=2700475.

CHAPTER 18

Urban Mobility: From Traditional to Intelligent Forms of Mobility

Tatyana Kreydenko and Julia Kovalchuk

Introduction

Modern socio-economic and technological trends in international development are determined primarily by the nature of urbanization: according to the World Bank, in 2019, 4.2 billion people were living in cities (55.3% of the world's population), and almost half of those were living in cities with a population over 1 million (World Bank 2020). In 1985 there were 273 such large cities in the world; by 2020 that number has reached almost 500.

T. Kreydenko (✉)
Financial University under the Government of the Russian Federation, Moscow, Russia

RUDN University, Moscow, Russia

J. Kovalchuk
Moscow State Institute of International Relations (MGIMO University), Moscow, Russia

Moscow Aviation Institute (National Research University), Moscow, Russia

I. Stepnov (ed.), *Technology and Business Strategy*,
https://doi.org/10.1007/978-3-030-63974-7_18

Cities are the modern drivers of civilization's development: one significant complication of the entire functional-spatial organization of cities is the increase in their size and population growth. The transport system is one of the leading factors in the evolution of a city's functional-spatial structure. Urban transport systems provide communications to more than 4 billion people around the world (54.8% of the total population) and serve many economic processes. In the United States alone, more than 1.1 billion trips are made daily (four trips per day on average per capita, with a length of at least 60 km).

Gradually, cities are losing their well-defined borders, since they are forced to establish closer ties with the surrounding rural areas. A person's vital activity in urban conditions depends on transport, while the choice of residence, work, and leisure is defined by their accessibility (Soloveva et al. 2014). In such a situation, the problem of comfortable living in cities is becoming more acute due to the extremely high load on all of the housing and communal services, urban transport systems, the energy sector of municipalities, and other infrastructural factors. The critical load on urban transport systems and, as a result, the reduction in traffic speed has already provoked the loss of 2–4% of national GDP.

The existing urban management system is no longer able to cope with technological, economic, or social barriers to development, which makes it necessary to change the methods of urban planning and management in both individual areas and the municipal economic system as a whole. This has instigated a fundamental change in the paradigm of urban transport planning, from providing demand to finding effective tools for managing it.

Methodology

The study was based on all existing approaches to understanding urban mobility. Modern urban mobility, which increases the economic and technological efficiency of urban space organization, is most often defined by experts as Sustainable Urban Mobility, Smart Urban Mobility, Integrated Urban Mobility, or Intelligent Mobility.

Intelligent Mobility (IM) is defined by the authors as the use of technology and data to create connections between people, places, and goods in all modes of transport (Kupriyanovsky et al. 2017). Smart mobility is a new way using vehicles, involving not only a wide range of transport, but also new models of ownership, such as the joint use of vehicles (Neckermann 2017).

International organizations view urban mobility primarily in the context of Sustainable Development Goals. For example, the program documents of the United Nations' Human Settlements Programme (UN-Habitat) and the European Commission analyze urban mobility from the perspective of Sustainable Urban Mobility: as a system that meets today's urban mobility needs without draining resources or compromising the ability of future generations to meet their mobility needs (UN-HABITAT 2013; European Commission 2013). Urban transport planners define sustainable urban mobility as providing urban residents with efficient and safe mobility services, and having minimal environmental and social impacts (Lah 2019).

With its foundations in the use of technological solutions within the framework of the Mobility-as-a-Service (MaaS) concept, the technical and economic support for increasing the availability of transport services, in the context of integrating all types of transport into the urban mobility process, is called "Integrated Urban Mobility" (Zhuwaki 2018; Schwedes 2017). The MaaS concept is seen as a tool for integrating various types of urban transport into various types of urban transport systems, to increase the efficiency and inclusiveness of urban logistics (Hietanen 2019).

The study was carried out using general economic and statistical methods of economic analysis. The following mandatory requirements for methods of collecting, processing, consolidating, and graphically presenting analytical information were taken into account, including: the relevance and the reliability of the data; the high reputation status of information sources; professional involvement in a subject of interest, including companies providing analytical materials; study representativeness.

The reports of the largest consulting companies (representatives of the Big Three) were selected as the analytical base of the work: Boston Consulting Group, McKinsey & Company, and Bain & Company were supplemented with information from other agencies. An analysis of the reporting methods revealed the reasons for quite serious discrepancies in assessing the economic characteristics of the Intelligent Mobility (IGM) market, its structure, and key areas of its development.

The analysis of financial stability is based on reports from leading players in the urban mobility market that provide transport mobility services in cities in the most popular segments: short-term rental of vehicles (car sharing); searching for fellow travelers (ride sharing); taxi ordering via mobile apps; and multimodal transportation (Uber, Lyft, Yandex, etc.).

Determining the directions for further development was based on the analysis of national strategic planning documents in the field of urban transport logistics, in part related to the formation of intelligent urban logistics in the United States, China, Singapore, the European Union, New Zealand, and other such countries, as well as the development strategies of the companies.

Results

Urban mobility, as it is today, is the result of several centuries of revolutionary and evolutionary transformations of assorted transport systems. Most of the modern urban transport infrastructure was created during the proactive construction and development of suburban areas, due to return visits to work, as laborers were required to travel to urban business centers in the morning from suburban homes in the evening; in addition, the movement of commercial goods took place at any time of the day.

Experts highlight four global formats of transport mobility (Blinkin 2015; Arthur D. Little 2018)—Mobility 1.0, 2.0, 3.0, 4.0—characterized by significant technological, socio-economic, and behavioral characteristics. Even though Stages of Mobility 1.0 and 2.0 are associated with the events of the eighteenth to nineteenth centuries, they determined the nature of the road network for many modern cities, and created the majority of modern transport problems.

Currently, the transition from Mobility 3.0 to Mobility 4.0 is actively underway, based on changes in the business models of transport service consumption (Stepnov and Kovalchuk 2020), the development of the sharing economy, the closed-loop economy, the digitalization of traditional public transport services based on mobile applications, using mobility as a service (using a combination of various types of services), and the increasing role of public transport as the basis for organizing city life.

There are several groups of factors that form the features, directions, tools, and mechanisms for the development of modern urban mobility. The main groups are described in Table 18.1.

Intelligent urban mobility can significantly increase the efficiency of urban transport, the comfort of the urban environment, and the safety of urban residents. Nonetheless, its development faces serious barriers and

Table 18.1 Groups of factors that determine the development of modern urban mobility

Groups of factors	*Characteristics of factors*
Historical	Differences in the time and intensity of the transition to new urban mobility formats
Financial and economic	The ability to use modern business models, including platform models, financial and economic factors of state support for IGM, etc.
Legal	Legislative development regulation initiatives, ways of organizing urban passenger transport
Technological	The development of intelligent transport systems based on modern technological solutions
Institutional factors (Canitez 2020)	Procedures and mechanisms for cooperation among all parties interested in developing infrastructure: not only an urban transport system but also all elements of the territorial planning system and urban development regulation of land use and development, as well as the opportunities for public-private partnerships in urban mobility

Source: compiled by the authors

limitations. The many barriers highlighted during the study and related to the structure of the cities themselves are presented in Table 18.2.

Attempts to introduce urban mobility in the second decade of the twenty-first century are closely connected with introducing key modern technologies (Industry 4.0) (Smorodinskaya and Katukov 2017).

The technological directions of the Fourth Industrial Revolution are developing based on global industrial networks, which present assorted opportunities: they make it possible to include urban mobility services in global value chains; to use the Internet of Things to digitalize traditional public transport services based on mobile applications, which can form the basis of the sharing economy; or to use blockchain for changing business models of transport services consumption (car sharing, changing the payment system, etc.). The use of advanced analytics and quantum computing expands the possibilities of integrated and accelerated decision-making in the management of the urban economy, based on the data received from all elements of an intelligent urban transport system. The development of immersive technologies promotes the use of interactive platforms in the management of urban transport systems, increasing efficiency in modeling traffic flows. Within the framework of creating a "Smart Space", intelligent transport systems are included in integrated territorial

Table 18.2 The manifestation of barriers and restrictions on the development of modern urban mobility

Barrier	*The nature of the manifestation*
Socio-psychological (Moody et al. 2020)	The predominance of the auto-centric culture, unwillingness of urban residents to actively use modern technologies (e.g. autonomous driving) urban mobility in real life, etc.
Organizational barriers	Disinterest in cooperation within the organization of the "Mobility as a Service" system by established operators, including in the development of joint planning approaches and new effective ways of providing transport services
Legislative	Existing legislation mainly concerns only certain elements or segments of urban mobility, is mainly prohibitive (e.g., it restricts Uber's work in several countries), and does not stimulate legislative initiatives
MaaS solutions and business model scalability	There is a need for better understanding what motivates customers in various segments to use urban mobility technologies and creates incentives for their sustainable use
Infrastructure and technological barriers	Poor quality of roads, the poor general condition of road infrastructure, poor 4G network coverage (5G in the future), low density of the electric vehicle charging stations, etc.

Source: compiled by the authors

planning, improving the reliability of public space, as well as that of the smart distribution of scarce urban space (Herrera-Quintero 2019).

The success of introducing urban mobility projects into the urban economy is determined by the nature of urban transport systems: the role played by certain types of transport, the impact of certain types of factors and development barriers, the role of municipal authorities in implementing projects, and so on (Canitez 2019). Experts of the MIT Energy Initiative have created scenarios for urban mobility development across twelve types of cities, identified according to various combinations of the nine leading factors of urban mobility development: a metro, rapid bus service, bike sharing, their development, their population, indicators of sustainability, congestion, road and transport network density, and the nature of urban transport infrastructure expansion (MIT Energy Initiative 2019; Oke et al. 2019).

According to experts of the American consulting company Arthur D. Little, there are four definitions of cities according to the nature of the development of modern urban mobility (Arthur D. Little 2018):

- city with incipient mobility systems (a city with an undeveloped mobility system that forms its sustainable core through investments in sustainable urban mobility infrastructure);
- personal city (a mature city with a large share of personal transport and a break in modality, while pursuing the transition to openness and sustainability, including new approaches to urban and transport policies);
- public city (a mature city with a high share of public transport, walking, and cycling, with active integration between various market players and citizens);
- integrated mobility (integration of all modes of transportation to reduce the share of personal vehicles, characterized by an innovative approach, transparent integration with the digital "assistant" for multimodal mobility, high convenience, and positive feedback).

Some countries have created an entire transport policy within their own cities, taking into account their type. For example, the Chinese authorities have formed the directions of state transport policy in cities based on their definition, taking into account the trends of urbanization and motorization (Moody et al. 2019).

Urban mobility platforms are gradually becoming a global phenomenon, but the nature and directions of their development are regional. For example, analysts of the Boston Consulting Group estimate the urban mobility market, based on the use of mobile platforms, to amount to \$25 billion in 2035, of which half will be accounted for in Europe (\$12.4 billion, 35 billion trips per year), the United States (\$5.2 billion, 11 billion trips), and China (\$3.9 billion, 35 billion trips). The average number of trips made in these countries per user will be 400 trips annually by 2035 (Boston Consulting Group 2019).

In the United States, major urban service providers, such as transport network companies and travel companies, are leaders in the urban mobility market. The key direction of development for these companies is to expand the functions of their intermodal platforms, introduce high service standards, and open up the possibility for other companies to join these platforms. Urban mobility projects in the United States are connected both with intelligent vehicles (the ChargePoint project, an open network of car chargers, the NEXT Future Transportation project for developing and producing modern electric vehicles), and the public transport market based on platform solutions (UrbanFootprint—software development mobility decision support, the Swifly project to improve the efficiency of the transport system based on improving the quality of passenger service).

In Europe, municipalities themselves determine the development of urban mobility, taking a leading role in organizing services as a single and interconnected ecosystem. The success of European commercial projects depends primarily on how they fit into solutions for priority urban mobility problems. A significant part of these projects is related either to platform-based public transport (Unifly in Antwerp, GoodVision in London, Cabture in Amsterdam, the Whim project in Helsinki) or to the organization and management of urban mobility (AppyParking in London, Worldsensing in Barcelona, etc.).

The most successful projects in East and Southeast Asia have been implemented in the format of public-private partnerships (China, South Korea) and are aimed at stimulating the market for new energy-efficient vehicles and the shared market. Micromobility is becoming one of the priority areas of development (China accounts for more than 85% of the nearly $6 billion of global investments in this segment) (Heineke et al. 2019).

The Russian practice of implementing Intelligent Urban Mobility (IUM) projects is only just beginning to take shape. It is most often associated with a small number of start-ups (mainly in the field of transport technologies, rather than platform solutions) and investment projects, particularly government IUM initiatives dedicated to major events (e.g., urban transport logistics in the metropolitan area of Greater Sochi for the Winter Olympics 2014, in cities hosting matches of the 2018 World Cup, etc.).

Analysis of the current situation in the urban mobility market allowed us to identify several segments that are extremely dynamic and closely interconnected. There are sufficient conventions in the allocation of market segments (the user can receive various services using the same mobile platform, and companies trying to take a more stable position in the market can diversify the entire package of services provided) which determine the significant differences in the analysis.

The ***Ride Hailing*** segment has the widest boundaries: most companies define it as the market for mobile taxi services, but several analysts (e.g., Statista) see it more broadly as the market for all online platforms and applications that unite passengers and drivers (apart from car sharing). According to Statista, revenue in this segment amounted to $184.7 billion in 2019 (Statista 2019). Active development will continue in the next four to five years: CAGR of 14.8% is expected to lead to an almost twofold increase in market volume by 2023, with an increase in user penetration to 20%. The average revenue per user (ARPU) will grow by 13% by 2023 (to $208.14).

Analysis of the statistical data in Table 18.3 shows that Asia is the most significant region in terms of key indicators (number of users, market size). These indicators are associated with a significant population living in the region and high urbanization rates, as well as rapid social and economic development, the growth of the purchasing power, and the active formation of the middle class (primarily in China and India) with the corresponding consumption standard at this stage.

The main factors in the segment's development include reduced taxi fares and ease of booking using mobile apps. Promising areas for the segment's development are its integration with public transport, the use of electric and autonomous vehicles given modern requirements for a stable environment, and the work of network transport companies and taxi

Table 18.3 Regional ride hailing market differences

Region	*Users (million people)*		*Segment revenue ($ million)*	
	2019	*2023*	*2019*	*2023*
Global market	996.7	1531.5	183,677	318,765
Europe	94.42	135.81	19,534	31,808
Asia	730.7	1128.41	99,919	183,464
Africa	24.5	40,706	1487.9	3057.5
North America	73.1	107.4	51,303	78,167
Latin America	76.6	122.4	12,040.6	22,732.1
Australia and Oceania	5.54	8.46	2002	3408
Region	**ARPU**[a]	**CAGR**[b]	**Penetration rate (%)**	
	2019	**2019**	**2019**	**2023**
Global market	184.28	14.8	13.5	20
Europe	178.12	14.04	8.85	12.83
Asia	155.30	18.36	10.82	15.27
Africa	42.75	2023	1.92	2.92
North America	496.4	11.9	19.45	27.45
Latin America	85.24	17.8	7.8	11.8
Australia and Oceania	221.6	16.3	10.4	15.3

Source: calculated by the authors based on data from Statista

[a]**ARPU**—average revenue per user ($ per person)

[b]**CAGR**—compound annual growth rate (%)

companies. The competitive advantages of such companies are related to regional market characteristics (in terms of legislative norms, forms of state support for individual players, etc.), as well as the use of various pricing models (e.g., the Lyft heat map pricing model).

The economic situation ***of the short-term car rental market*** is characterized by the greatest discrepancies: the volume of segment valuation ran from $1.5 to more than $60 billion, at a more comparable average annual growth rate (17–20%) (GlobalMarketInsights 2017; Prescient & Strategic Intelligence 2019). Prospects for the development of car sharing are associated with its economic efficiency: if the mileage of a personal car does not exceed 16,000 km, it is more profitable to stop using it in favor of car sharing.

The car sharing market is in Asia is not only the largest such market (40% of users), but is also the most dynamic (along with the Russian market). The market of European countries is the second largest (37%). One distinctive feature of this segment is its localization; almost all companies (even world leaders) tend to operate in solely one country, except for SHARE NOW, which operates in the United States, Canada, and Europe (although it closed car2go services in China).

The volume of the ***travel sharing market (carpooling search market)*** varies, according to estimates of consulting companies, from $7 to $50 billion, with an emerging aggregate average annual growth rate of 19–20%. The increase in travel sharing is due to the benefits of a private vehicle without the costs and responsibilities of being a car owner. Rising vehicle prices along with rising fuel prices are the main factors driving growth in the global travel exchange market. However, the priorities in the state policy of some countries, including economic restrictions, significantly reduce market growth.

Factors hindering the development of this market segment include resistance to its development from users who trust traditional transport services (due to concerns about personal safety and the security of users' personal information), and comprehensive national transport policy.

The main areas for developing carpooling may include the following (Bresciani et al. 2018):

- The growth in daily average distance travelled in the carpooling system.
- Improving efficiency by implementing door-to-door travel opportunities.

- Expansion of BlaBlaLines (daily trips over medium distances).
- Integration with buses.

The highest average annual growth rates are forecasted to take place in the segment of ***multimodal and intermodal transportation***: up to 50.3% by 2030, with current market volume at about $11 billion and 11% of CAGR (Arthur D. Little 2018). Most of this growth is expected to come from Europe and China. Multimodality of urban mobility exists within four dimensions: information integration, service integration, fare integration, and physical integration (MIT Energy Initiative 2019). The development of the segment is related to the main technical element of organizing multimodal trips—contactless payment (transport smart cards and mobile payments for transport services, which significantly increase the efficiency of the seamless principle).

The fastest-growing region in the multimodal transportation market is Asia (primarily due to South Korea, India, China, Malaysia, and Thailand [government initiatives being the main factor]). Electronic transport cards are most actively used in economically developed countries like Northern Europe, Germany, the United States, or Singapore.

Micromobility is actively developing as a segment of the IGM market: it is formed when traveling at distances of 5 miles (8 km) or solving the "first mile" and "last mile" problems, which constitutes about 50–60% of the total number of trips. However, it is also affected by weather conditions, age restrictions, the low penetration of micromobility in suburban areas and rural areas, and various pricing models. This is why only 8–15% of the market for such transportation can be satisfied by micromobility. As a result, the US market potential in 2030 is estimated to be from $200 to $300 billion, while that of the EU will be $100–150 billion, and in China it equals $30–50 billion (Bouton et al. 2015).

The formation of all segments of the urban mobility market is accompanied by active mergers and acquisitions of companies, both horizontally (combining companies in one segment—the market for short-term rental vehicles), and according to the expansion-geographical principle (the absorption of regional players by world leaders in the mobile services market of taxi services). Compared to the giants of the mobile taxi service market, the weaker competitiveness of car sharing players has led to active mergers and acquisitions by segment companies: Getaround (the United States) acquired Drivy (France) in 2019 and Communauto (Canada) bought Vrtucar, Atlantic Carshare in 2018. SHARE NOW is the segment leader that emerged after Daimler and BMW integrated car2go and DriveNow services.

Financial analysis of the leading companies in the car sharing, carpooling, and mobile taxi markets shows their loss ratio. At the same time, companies dealing with multimodal and intermodal transportation are more financially stable. This is primarily since the latter conduct more diversified economic activities and are focused on a wider range of consumers.

Conclusions

Modern urban mobility forms one of the most dynamic intersectoral markets, which includes not only the direct organization of mobility in the city but also the formation of all infrastructural elements. This market has a high multiplier effect; the development of all segments is impossible without the integration of all industries involved in its formation (in the automotive industry, the production of all technical elements of an intelligent road network to the development of business models of all forms of mobility need not be integrated). In 2019, analysts of CB Insights identified 33 industries that can significantly transform under the influence of modern urban mobility, the key areas of which are related to developing and implementing those technologies related primarily to autonomous driving, as well as new forms of urban mobility (including air taxis), technologies that contribute to road transport infrastructure, and mechanisms for the interaction of all interested parties (CB Insights 2019). States that invest heavily in their technological solutions based on existing technologies become leaders in modern urban mobility.

The key areas of market development at the present stage are increasing its energy efficiency, reducing its environmental impact, developing joint forms of mobility assisting in planning the entire door-to-door route, and expanding the functions and capabilities of applications that provide services within the framework of modern urban mobility and create conditions for integrating several types of transport, both public and personal, into a seamless route, minimizing passenger costs. The key players and market regulators are state authorities, developing both a regulatory framework and stimulating the development of urban mobility in general and its segments.

As a result of the study, several of the most successful areas of development were identified:

- projects aimed at the widespread deployment and full integration of all joint, connected, and personalized next-generation mobility services: creating a single market for Mobility-as-a-Service (MaaS), and developing unified plug-and-play smart city tools with active cooperation of both municipal authorities and large transport and automobile companies (projects in Northern and Western Europe);
- integrated solutions for implementing an integrated approach in meeting and balancing the social, environmental, and economic needs of consumers (e.g., projects in Austrian cities);
- system-oriented innovations in the field of passenger and freight transportation, taking into account the users' needs (the cities of North America, Europe).

An analysis of the current situation in the market of urban mobility services, and a forecast of its development, shows significant expansion of investment projects occurred in the last three to four years alongside the active financing of such projects in Asian countries, while the recognized leaders in the field of integrated urban mobility are the cities of Europe, North America, and East and Southeast Asia. A significant part of investments is focused not on products, but on technologies that underlie mobility changes, including those in the field of organizing public transport based on platform solutions. Projects dealing with autonomous driving technologies (almost half of the volume) and solutions for vehicle sharing (around a third) received the best funding.

From a technological point of view, in the field of intellectual urban mobility, four of the most attractive areas and routes for successful investment projects can be distinguished: communication (telematics, cybersecurity, user interface construction technologies, parking and mobility optimization technologies, voice and gesture recognition technologies), automatic driving (sensors/semiconductors, technologies of autonomous solutions), smart mobility (sharing technologies, vehicle leasing, fleet management), and electric mobility.

References

Arthur D. Little. (2018). *The Future of Mobility 3.0. Reinventing Mobility in the Era of Disruption and Creativity.* Retrieved from https://www.adlittle.com/sites/default/files/viewpoints/adl_uitp_future_of_mobility_3.0_1.pdf

Blinkin, M. (2015). The Quality of Urban Transport Network Planning: In the Mirror of Classical Models of Traffic Flow Theory. *Urban Research and Practice, 2015*, 55–66.

Bouton, M., Knupfer, S. M., Mihov, I., & Swartz, S. (2015). Urban Mobility at a Tipping Point. *McKinsey & Company*. Retrieved from https://www.mckinsey.com/business-functions/sustainability/our-insights/urban-mobility-at-a-tipping-point

Bresciani, C., Colorni, A., Costa, F., Lué, A., & Studer, L. (2018). Carpooling: Facts and New Trends. *2018 International Conference of Electrical and Electronic Technologies for Automotive, Milan, 2018*, pp. 1–4.

Canitez, F. (2019). Pathways to Sustainable Urban Mobility in Developing Megacities: A Sociotechnical Transition Perspective. *Technological Forecasting & Social Change, 141*, 319–329.

Canitez, F. (2020). Transferring Sustainable Urban Mobility Policies: An Institutional Perspective. *Transport Policy, 90*, 1–12.

CB Insights. (2019). *33 Industries Other than Auto That Driverless Cars Could Turn Upside Down*. Retrieved from https://www.cbinsights.com/research/13-industries-disrupted-driverless-cars/

European Commission. (2013). *Urban Mobility Package*. Retrieved from https://ec.europa.eu/transport/themes/clean-transport-urban-transport/urban-mobility/urban-mobility-package_en

GlobalMarketInsights. (2017). *Car Sharing Market*. Retrieved from https://www.gminsights.com/industry-analysis/carsharing-market

Heineke, K., Kloss, B., Scurtu, D., & Weig, F. (2019). Micromobility's 15,000-Mile Checkup. *Mckinsey Insights*. Retrieved from https://www.mckinsey.com/industries/automotive-and-assembly/our-insights/micromobilitys-15000-mile-checkup

Herrera-Quintero, L. (2019). Disruptive Technologies in Intelligent Transportation Systems. *2019 2nd Latin American Conference on Intelligent Transportation Systems (ITS LATAM)*.

Hietanen, S. (2019). Why Cities Should Call the Shots in the Mobility Revolution. *Whim*. Retrieved from https://whimapp.com/sampos-blog-why-cities-should-call-the-shots-in-the-mobility-revolution/

Kupriyanovsky, V. P., Akimov, A. V., Pokusaev, O. N., Alenkov, V. V., Namiot, D. E., & Sinyagov, S. A. (2017). Intelligent Mobility and Mobility as a Service in Smart Cities. *International Journal of Open Information Technologies*, 12.

Lah, O. (Ed.). (2019). *Sustainable Urban Mobility Pathways*. Amsterdam: Elsevier.

Lang, N., Hagenmaier, M., Egloff, C., Collie, B., & Keupp, D. (2019). The Leaders in Urban Mobility Will Be Regional, Not Global. *Boston Consulting Group*. Retrieved from https://www.bcg.com/publications/2019/leaders-urban-mobility-will-be-regional-not-global.aspx

MIT Energy Initiative. (2019). *Insights into Future Mobility. A Report from the Mobility of the Future Study*. Cambridge, MA: MIT Energy Initiative.

Moody, J., Bailey, N., & Zhao, J. (2020). Public Perceptions of Autonomous Vehicle Safety: An International Comparison. *Safety Science, 121*, 634–650.

Moody, J., Wang, S., Chun, J., Ni, X., & Zhao, J. (2019). Transportation Policy Profiles of Chinese City Clusters: A Mixed Methods Approach. *Transportation Research Interdisciplinary Perspectives*, 2.

Neckermann, L. (2017). *Smart Cities, Smart Mobility: Transforming the Way We Live and Work*. Leicester: Troubadour.

Oke, J. B., et al. (2019). A Novel Global Urban Typology Framework for Sustainable Mobility Futures. *Environmental Research Letters, 14*, 095006.

Prescient & Strategic Intelligence. (2019). *Car Sharing Market by Car*. Retrieved from https://www.psmarketresearch.com/market-analysis/car-sharing-market

Schwedes, O. (2017). *Urban Mobility in a Global Perspective. An International Comparison of the Possibilities and Limits of Integrated Transport Policy and Planning*. Zurich: Lit Verlag.

Smorodinskaya, N. V., & Katukov, D. D. (2017). Key Features and Consequences of the Industrial Revolution 4.0. *Innovations*, 10(228).

Soloveva, M. V., Krivtsova, M. K., & Podzorova, M. A. (2014). The Main Problems of Development of Modern Cities and Ways of Their Solving. *ISJ Theoretical & Applied Science, 9*(17), 120–125.

Statista. (2019). *Ride Hailing*. Retrieved from https://www.statista.com/outlook/368/100/ride-hailing/worldwide#market-revenue

Stepnov, I. M., & Kovalchuk, Yu. A. (2020). Measuring Value Created by Business Models in the Sharing Economy. *Upravlenets – The Manager, 11*(5), 58-69 (in Russian). http://doi.org/10.29141/2218-5003-2020-11-5-5.

UN-Habitat. (2013). *Planning and Ensuring Sustainable Urban Traffic: Installation Recommendations. Global Human Settlements Report 2013*. Abingdon: Routledge.

World Bank. (2020). Official Site. Retrieved from www.worldbank.org

Zhuwaki, N. (2018). Towards an Ecosystem of Integrated Urban Mobility Services. *NewCities*. Retrieved from https://newcities.org/the-big-picture-towards-ecosystem-integrated-urban-mobility-services/

CHAPTER 19

Banking Business Strategies in the Paradigm of Digital Solutions and Sustainable Development Goals

Galina Panova

Introduction

The United Nations Sustainable Development Goals (SDGs) were formulated in the "Sustainable Development Agenda to 2030", and adopted at the conference in New York in 2015. The SDGs aim to achieve environmentally friendly economic growth, combat climate change, and improve the quality of life and prospects for people around the world. The SDGs help to open up new market opportunities, offer new business models, and build new win-win relationships among economic actors, thus giving credibility to the ability to meet the challenges of our time which require concerted and coordinated action (UN 2015).

Major investments are needed to achieve sustainable development goals. The financial resources needed to close the infrastructure gap in such areas as water, sanitation, transport, energy, irrigation, and flood

G. Panova (✉)
Moscow State Institute of International Relations (MGIMO University), Moscow, Russia

I. Stepnov (ed.), *Technology and Business Strategy*,
https://doi.org/10.1007/978-3-030-63974-7_19

protection may vary between 2% and 8% of GDP annually by 2030, depending on the strategic choices of countries. Currently, according to the UN Secretary General, there is some progress in many areas, but in general, actions to achieve the Goals have not yet reached the necessary pace and scale (UN 2019a).

At the national level, steps should be taken to align financing with national sustainable development strategies and priorities; these include the development of integrated national financing systems, public and private strategies, and financing instruments, as well as greater alignment of public expenditure with national sustainable development strategies. In addition, it is important to strengthen the capacity to mobilize domestic resources and enhance fiscal space, prevent and disrupt illicit financial flows, and provide access to available financial resources. Governments, as noted in the Report, should promote an enabling environment for investment through, inter alia, predictable and coherent policies and transparency and disclosure requirements on sustainable development impacts. Measures to improve access to financial services, combined with the adoption of financial technology, proper risk management, and consumer protection, can make credit more affordable for millions of people.

Digitalization of the financial sector can also dramatically increase transparency and encourage new types of investment flows.

However, the negative impact of objective and subjective factors on the global economy (the COVID-19 pandemic, the curtailment of entire industries and sectors, the oil crisis, climate change, the technological revolution, the digitalization of the economy, urbanization, etc.) requires an active response from states, governments, and society at large to address global and national challenges.

At the SSD Summit in September 2019, world leaders proposed a decade of action and progress for sustainable development, and committed themselves to mobilizing financial resources, improving national processes, and strengthening institutions, in order to achieve this goal by 2030.

According to the PWC, 71% of the world's companies are already working to integrate the SDGs into their work systems (PwC 2017), which UNCTAD believes opens up new opportunities for the global economy (UNCTAD 2015). The UN estimates that achieving the SDG by 2030 will create new markets worth a total of $12 trillion, and offer 380 million new jobs (UN 2019b).

However, the coronavirus outbreak has made adjustments to these plans. Experts predict a sharp decline in global economic growth and, consequently, an economic crisis. It was planned that the world's largest economy (the USA) should have shown growth rates of 2–2.5% in 2020; however, in April this year, the US investment bank JP MorganChase gave a forecast of economic decline in the USA in 2020 by 15–25%. Furthermore, there had already been expectations for a prolonged period of recession around the world, comparable to the period of the Great Depression of the 1930s, called by JP MorganChase "the Super Crisis".[1]

At present, the process of reformatting the global economy is underway—the question is only how and at what "cost" countries will be able to overcome the global economic (including financial) crisis triggered by the pandemic. Under these circumstances, the role banks play in stimulating both economic growth and more general development socially and economically in individual countries, regions, and the world as a whole becomes particularly important.

Meeting the challenges of sustainable development requires the mobilization of huge financial resources. The main sources of raising funds to stimulate the achievement of sustainable development goals are budget funds, bank credit, and security issues. As for budget allocations, in the context of the coronavirus pandemic (both in the world and in Russia), it is difficult to consider such allocations as the main source of funding for sustainable development.

In 2018, in accordance with the Presidential Decree "On national development goals and strategic objectives of the Russian Federation until 2024", the Government of the Russian Federation approved national projects (programs) in 12 areas, including the environment. The national project "Environment" includes 11 federal projects for a total of 4041 billion rubles, including 701.2 billion rubles for the federal budget, 133.8 billion rubles for budgets of the subjects of the Russian Federation, and 3206.1 billion rubles for non-budgetary sources.[2]

In Russia, assets of financial and credit institutions can hold significant potential for credit organizations, investment funds, pension funds, and insurance companies. As of 01.10.2019, the volume of funds attracted by banks (in rubles and currency) exceeded 50 trillion rubles; of these, the

[1] https://www.mirprognozov.ru/prognosis/economics/jp-morgan-chase-predskazal-«superkrizic»-v-2020-godu/.

[2] http://www.mnr.gov.ru/activity/directions/natsionalnyy_proekt_ekologiya.

total volume of relatively long-term financial resources (for a period of more than three years) is rb 7.7 trillion. The Bank of Russia, having systematically reduced its key rate over the past five years, has outlined the general trend of reducing the profitability of financial market credit instruments. This factor determines the reduction of interest rates on loans for final borrowers, which contributes to the expansion of credit use, including for sustainable development purposes. The use of bank loans in this situation is possible for environmental protection purposes, technologies that allow reducing or absorbing greenhouse gas emissions, and other such projects. There are instruments for stimulating business efforts in this area: one significant instrument is developing and consolidating international standards for accounting for so-called ESG risks (environmental, social, and governance risks) when banks lend to projects and programs; another is encouraging private businesses to participate in the implementation of the SDG. Banks thus, on the one hand, finance economic development (such as through lending) and, on the other hand, attract private capital to address global development challenges, environmental protection, overcoming social inequality, and similar incentives.

Such activities are currently carried out by classical commercial and special-purpose banks (e.g. development banks and so-called green banks). This is mainly the case for banks' activities aimed at meeting the objectives of the SDG. In 2015, in Brazil and China, approximately 10% of bank loans were classified as "green" according to national classifications. The OECD defines a "green" bank as a public or quasi-governmental institution established specifically to stimulate the development of so-called green industries (OECD 2016).

Methodology

The genesis of the development of banking activities in implementing the SDG took place through a similar set of earlier principles: firstly, standards of responsible business conduct (which are usually regarded as instruments for achieving sustainable development goals) and rules of conduct (aimed at the favorable development of society, the environment, and risk reduction) were adopted by the OECD in 1976, within the framework of the OECD Declaration for International Investment and Multinational Enterprises (48 states are parties to the Declaration). These standards apply to trade relations between companies, financial institutions, and their clients.

Studies show that about 90% of the SDGs are based on the concept of responsible investment, which implies the integration of environmental, social, and governance factors (ESG factors) into the investment decision-making process, in order to improve the quality of risk management and ensure sustainable return on investment on a long-term basis.

In 2001, the Institutional Investors Group on Climate Change (IIGCC) was established, which by 2019 had managed to attract over 190 participants with management assets in excess of €28 trillion to address the issue of carbon reduction.

In 2005, UN Secretary General Kofi Annan appealed to the heads of the G20 states—the world's largest investors—to develop the principles of "responsible" investment, which were published in 2006; in 2019, according to the PRI organization, these principles were followed by more than 2.3 thousand investors with total assets under management of more than $89 trillion (UN 2019c). The Basic Principles for Responsible Investment require companies to: include environmental, social, and corporate governance factors in investment analysis and decision-making processes; be active managers and use ESG factors in asset management; ensure investment recipients properly disclose information; promote the adoption of responsible investment principles in global practice; and cooperate to improve implementation of the principles of responsible investment.

Instruments to stimulate business efforts in this area include, in particular, the development and consolidation of international standards for accounting for ESG risks in bank lending to projects and programs, as well as encouraging banks to encourage private business to participate in the implementation of the SDG. Banks thus, on the one hand, finance (by crediting) economic development and, on the other, attract private capital to address global development challenges, preserve the environment, overcome social inequality, and more tasks.

Results

International standards for responsible business conduct have been adopted at different times by IFC, UNEP, UN PRI, IDFC, and OECD. These standards provide guidance for companies in various industries and areas in assessing risk, and are used by regulators to verify the responsible conduct of companies. In these circumstances, banks independently develop internal risk management policies (including financial risk management and ESG risk management, which they voluntarily adopt to reduce the risks of funded [credited] projects).

The Global Sustainable Investment Alliance, which has brought together the largest responsible investment organizations since 2012 (Association for Sustainable & Responsible Investment [Asia]; European Sustainable Investment Forum [EU]; Responsible Investment Association Australasia [Australia]; Responsible Investment Association [Canada]; UK Sustainable Investment and Finance Association [UK]; US Forum for Sustainable and Responsible Investment [the USA]; and Vereniging van Beleggers voor Duurzame Ontwikkeling [the Netherlands]), publishes reports on implementation of "responsible" investment principles in the world (GSI 2018).

The introduction of responsible investment principles is of great importance for banks, influencing, firstly, the definition of criteria for long-term profitability and sustainability of borrowers and issuers of securities, and secondly, the approaches to assessing their own creditworthiness.

The main documents influencing the further development of investment activities are: Directive 2014/95/EU of the European Parliament and of the Council of the European Union (2014); UN Paris Agreement (2015); UN Practical Guide to incorporating ESG into investment (2016); European Commission Guidelines for Non-Financial Reporting (2017); recommendations of the G-20 Task Force on Climate-related Financial Disclosures (TCFD) (2017); WFE Sustainability Principles (2018); and London Stock Exchange Guidelines for ESG reporting.

In 2012, the **Sustainable Banking Network (SBN)**, an association of financial sector regulators and banking associations from developing countries, committed to promoting sustainable investment in line with international best practice, became operational. The SBN promotes collective learning among its members and supports them in developing policies aimed at achieving SDGs in their countries. The idea for the SBN originated during the First International Forum on Environmental Credit, which was held by the International Finance Corporation (IFC—International Finance Corporation, member of the World Bank Group) and China Banking Regulatory Commission (CBA) in Beijing in May 2012, when banking regulators and associations from ten countries approached the IFC for assistance in building a global knowledge network on sustainable banking.

In December 2017, at the One Planet Summit in Paris, representatives of eight central banks and supervisors established the **Network of Central**

Banks and Supervisors for Greening the Financial System (NGFS), which currently unites almost 40 central banks, supervisors, and international organizations. The purpose of the organization is to contribute to the development of the global measures needed to achieve the objectives of the Paris Agreement, therefore to enhance the role of the financial system in risk management and capital-raising for green and low-carbon investments within the broader context of sustainable development. The organization's main areas of work are supervisory, macrofinance, and green finance (NGFS 2019).

The Network Steering Committee brings together regulators from Europe, Asia, and Latin America. An observer of the Network is the Bank for International Settlements in Basel.

Governments can use so-called green banks to mobilize private capital, as demonstrated by a number of examples in developed countries. For example, the English Green Investment Bank, established in 2012, is the most active investor in the renewable energy and energy efficiency sector, and provides a 1:3 ratio of investment: every dollar of public investment provides an inflow of three private dollars.

The world has created a network of so-called green banks—**the Green Bank Network**, a special platform through which green banks exchange information, experience, and so on. The founders of the network were "green" banks in Australia, Japan, Malaysia, the UK, and the USA (GBN 2016).

In 2012, a network of banks was created called **Sustainable Banking Network** (SBN), the purpose of which was to introduce ESG investment standards across the world through consultations and training programs with banking regulators. The members of the organization are mainly developing countries (in particular Indonesia, Kenya, Vietnam).

The objectives of the above networks are almost similar, differing only in membership. Different countries introduce special conditions for lending for environmental purposes. For example, in China, such requirements for banks regarding the allocation of a certain part of loans for environmental projects, regular reporting, and so on were introduced in 2007 (Zhang 2014).

The International Organization Loan Market Association (LMA) and the **Asia Pacific Loan Market Association (APLMA)**, with the support of **the International Capital Markets Association (ICMA)**, prepared a framework of standards for green loans, called the Green Loan Principles. However, the so-called green banking business is not yet widely used in Russia, for example. As for companies in traditional industries, adapting their operations to modern so-called green standards requires large investments.

In March 2018, the LMA and the APLMA, with the support of the International Capital Markets Association (ICMA), adopted **The "Green" Loan Principles (GLP & SLLP)**. The purpose of this document is to create a high-level structure of market standards, ensuring a consistent methodology for the use of so-called green loans in the wholesale market. In March 2019, the LMA, together with the APLMA and the LSTA (Loan Syndications and Trading Association) and with the support of the ICMA, **adopted "Long-term Lending Principles"** (SLLP). Long-term lending is a product that allows lenders to stimulate the improvement of the borrower's sustainability profile by matching loan terms (e.g. margins) with the borrower's performance against predetermined sustainability targets.

The transformation of investment approaches cannot but affect Russia. The introduction of responsible investment principles certainly affects investors' attitude toward Russian assets. First of all, the risks of noncompliance with ESG criteria fall under the risks of mining companies, which account for about 11.5% of the country's GDP (Analytical Centre 2019).

Studies of scientists confirm the connection between compliance with ESG principles and their financial results. For example, in 2015, Gunnar Friede, Timo Bush, and Alexander Bassen aggregated data from more than 1.8 thousand scientific papers on the correlation of ESG and financial indicators, and concluded that most studies confirm the positive correlation of these parameters (Friede et al. 2015).

In 2019, S&P Global Ratings published a report on the results of an analysis of the impact of ESG factors on the company's financial performance, its profitability, and its long-term financial stability. ESG factors are currently considered by Fitch Ratings, S&P Global Ratings, and Moody's in various components of the rating analysis. For example, in 2017, ESG factors were considered by Fitch Ratings, S&P Global Ratings, and Moody's. S&P Global Ratings has revised its outlook on Banco Agropecuario S.A. to "negative" due to a change in its assessment of asset quality and business stability, due to the worsening climate in Peru, and in 2018 and 2019 it is expected that the outlook will remain negative. S&P has negative outlook on the ratings of Danske Bank and Mulhacen Pte. Ltd. after the release of materials confirming Danske Bank's involvement in money laundering operations and the growing number of complaints from customers of Mulhacen Pte. Ltd. on the overvaluation of interest rates, which resulted in reputational problems and pressure on the bank's capital.

The use of ESG factors by Russian rating agencies in their work is largely due to the interest of investors.

Analysis of international and Russian banking practice reveals that banks employ established mechanisms to manage ESG risks. Nonetheless, internationally, different banks use different approaches to risk management.

In the process of discussing this issue within the framework of the Expert Group for the Development of Principles for Responsible Investment of BRICS Development Institutions, which operates on the basis of Vnesheconombank, it was noted that the approaches of BRICS development institutions are not always synchronized with each other. For example, the Brazilian Development Bank had adopted a Social and Environmental Responsibility Policy as well as a Socioenvironmental Policy. The bank has established a system for ranking environmental and social risks they financed, as well as mechanisms for interaction and the impact of non-financial risks on the borrower. As a result of a project risk analysis, the bank can make recommendations for project changes and offer additional measures and resources to mitigate non-financial risks. The project may also be denied credit resources if non-financial risks that cannot be mitigated under the project are identified. They also uses a social clause that allows them to terminate a contract with a borrower if discrimination or forced labor is identified. Vnesheconombank of the Russian Federation uses measures aimed at managing social and environmental risks, having adopted them in 2013: the Policy on Responsible Finance. The Export-Import Bank of India (Eximbank of India) has adopted: (a) the Environmental, Social and Governance Policy (and is reviewing projects for compliance with this policy); and (b) the Declaration on Modern Slavery aimed at preventing the use of forced labor. The State Development Bank of China (China Development Bank) is implementing an active green economy development agenda by assessing the social and environmental risks of projects. The Development Bank of Southern Africa uses a risk management system that identifies non-financial risks of projects and their management mechanisms, and has formulated standards to which companies with which the Bank cooperates must comply. These standards establish mechanisms for identifying and mitigating ESG risks, interaction with stakeholders, and other systems (Panova and Kishmariya 2020).

In general, it can be argued that, against the backdrop of a number of global problems and the development of financial markets, there is a significant transformation in investment approaches. Investors are paying more attention to how companies care about the environment, their working conditions, and the level of corporate culture—in other words, investors are becoming more "responsible". The reasons for this transformation include not only generational change, altruism, and environmental care, but also the increasingly obvious relationship between the level of responsibility of a company in doing business and how successful it is. Usually, the amounts invested by credit institutions in environmentally risky projects are insignificant, but a significant risk may arise in case of a high concentration of loans in a certain sector or specific projects. The quality of management largely determines a bank's appetite for risk, and thus directly affects the quality of its assets.

Regulatory measures related to environmental protection (e.g. regulatory relaxation for a bank's participation in environmental projects or, conversely, increasing risk weights for investments in environmentally unsafe projects) may affect the level of capital adequacy of a bank. Regulators may also consider the resilience of banks to climate change as part of stress testing.

ESG factors may have a direct impact on banks' profitability, which is particularly important, for example, for banks with a high concentration of their loan portfolios in the agricultural sector (such an example in Russia is Rosselkhozbank). Poor quality of bank management can lead to substantial fines, while shortcomings in the implementation of responsible investment principles can lead to the loss of clients. Conversely, the positive influence of factors, such as the social importance of a region, can have a positive impact on the profitability of banks that need to increase their capital to ensure optimal growth and development (Panova 2020).

The use of responsible investment instruments (e.g. green bonds) leads to a diversification of funding sources. The first "green" bonds appeared on the Russian market in December 2018, when the company RSB KHMAO LLC completed an issue of bonds on the Moscow Stock Exchange for a total amount of 1.1 billion rubles to finance a concession project for the construction and operation of a landfill for the placement, neutralization, and treatment of solid municipal waste, having received confirmation of an independent assessment of the leveling of environmental, social, and management risks by the company (the second opinion) from Rating-Agentur Expert RA GmbH. Then, in February 2019,

Swedish fund Alfred Berg Ryssland announced that it was the first Russian equity fund in the world to use an ESG filter to make decisions about investing in Russian companies' securities.

In April 2019, the Moscow Exchange joined the global initiative "Sustainable Stock Exchanges" (SSE), which unites 85 exchanges around the world. Within the framework of the SSE initiative, stock exchanges work out the solutions necessary to achieve the UN goals on sustainable development and growth of investments in creating a sustainable future. In May 2019, the International Capital Markets Association (ICMA) included Rating-Agentur Expert RA GmbH in the international register of External Review Service Mapping, which contains information on verifiers of "green", social, and sustainable bonds issues. In addition, as part of the development of a responsible investment infrastructure, the introduction of requirements for companies to disclose information on ESG factors, as well as the inclusion of this information for project justification, lending, and portfolio valuation of banks and funds (including pension funds), is being considered.

At the same time, there are currently barriers to the active implementation of responsible investment principles in Russian banking practice. These are: insufficient awareness of ESG issues on the market; weak demand for green finance products; the lack of a system of comparable indicators published by companies; and undeveloped incentives for companies to achieve high ESG indicators. In this regard, it can be argued that the demand for information on ESG risks is only formed on the Russian market. However, most of the aforementioned problems can be solved if regulators, companies, and society as a whole are interested.

In this regard, efforts should continue to support governments in mobilizing domestic resources, combating tax evasion and illicit financial flows, aligning global economic policies and financial systems with the 2030 Agenda, and helping reduce the perceived risk to private investment in developing countries.

However, building resilience to shocks remains a challenge for many countries, as it requires a systemic approach based on the understanding that many adverse events occur at the global, regional, national, subnational, and local levels, and indirectly affect the interrelated social, governance, economic, environmental, and physical systems. In the current global environment, all policies and investments must be planned and implemented bearing such risks in mind.

Conclusions/Recommendations

Progress toward sustainable development goals in a rapidly changing world depends on the ability to anticipate, prepare for, and cope with sudden changes in health, economic, and socio-political systems. In addition to disasters, many sustainable development goals are affected by climate change, which requires an integrated response through adaptation and mitigation measures. In general, building resilience to shocks could be a powerful tool to combat poverty and social exclusion, and a reliable way to prevent crises and risk escalation. In turn, such sustainable development goals are vital to achieve so as to increase resilience to shocks.

In modern banking practice, the use of ESG metrics in the process of lending and investment is not yet widespread; ESG factors are not considered when assessing the level of troubled assets. However, it is obvious that such metrics should be used in banks: firstly, because they should improve modern approaches to assessing the creditworthiness of borrowers, and, secondly, because investors will also assess banks in terms of ESG risks.

The dynamics of implementing responsible investment principles, the number of existing initiatives, and the efforts of international organizations will certainly lead to a wide and uniform use of ESG indicators by analogy alongside companies' financial information (such as IFRS reporting).

Russia is actively participating in the process of implementing the principles of "responsible" investment in financial market institutions. However, the use of ESG metrics in lending and investing has not yet become widespread among Russian banks. Under these circumstances, it is proposed to intensify the work of banks and regulators, so as to form uniform standards of responsible business conduct in the process of servicing bank customers.

References

Analytical Centre of the Russian Government. (2019). *Bulletin on Current Trends in Russian Economy, Dynamics and Structure of Russian GDP*. Retrieved from http://ac.gov.ru/files/publication/a/21979.pdf

Friede, G., Busch, T., & Bassen, A. (2015). ESG and Financial Performance: Aggregated Evidence from More than 2000 Empirical Studies. *Journal of Sustainable Finance & Investment*, 5(4), 210–233.

GBN. (2016). *The Green Bank Network: Connecting Leaders in Green Finance to Share Best Practices and Increase Green Investment, Yale Centre for Business and the Environment*. Retrieved from http://cbey.yale.edu/events/the-green-bank-network-connecting-leaders-in-green-finance-toshare-best-practices-and.

GSI. (2018). *Global Sustainable Investment Review*. Retrieved from http://www.gsi-alliance.org/wp-content/uploads/2019/06/GSIR_Review2018F.pdf

NGFS. (2019). *The Central Banks and Supervisors Network for Greening the Financial System (NGFS): About Us*. Retrieved from https://www.banque-france.fr/en/financial-stability/international-role/network-greening-financial-system/about-us.

OECD. (2016). OECD Declaration and Decisions on International Investment and Multinational Enterprises. Retrieved from https://www.oecd.org/investment/investment-policy/oecddeclarationanddecisions.htm

Panova, G. S. (2020). *Banks and Banking Business in the Global Economy*. Moscow: MGIMO.

Panova, G. S., & Kishmariya, I. L. (2020). Principles of Responsible Investment in Russian Banks. *Banking Services*, № 4, pp. 2–10.

PwC. (2017). *Delivering the Sustainable Development Goals*. Retrieved from https://www.pwc.com/m1/en/publications/documents/delivering-sustainable-development-goals.pdf

UN. (2015). *Sustainable Development Goals*. Retrieved from https://www.un.org/sustainabledevelopment/ru/sustainable-development-goals

UN. (2019a). *General Sustainable Development Goals Report*. New York: United Nations Publications.

UN. (2019b). Principles for Responsible Investment: An Investor Initiative in Partnership with UNEP Finance Initiative and the UN Global Compact. Retrieved from https://www.unpri.org/download?ac=6303

UN. (2019c). *Roadmap for Financing the 2030 Agenda for Sustainable Development*. Retrieved from https://www.un.org/sustainabledevelopment/wp-content/uploads/2019/07/EXEC.SUM_SG-Roadmap-Financing-SDGs-July-2019.pdf

UNCTAD. (2015). *General Assembly Resolution 17/08/2015*. Retrieved from https://unctad.org/meetings/en/SessionalDocuments/ares69d313_ru.pdf

Zhang, Q. (2014). *The State of Chinese Climate Finance, Green Credit Policy and Main Challenges*. Retrieved from https://www.academia.edu/29709232/The_State_of_Chinese_Climate_Finance_Green_Credit_Policy_and_Main_Challenges

CHAPTER 20

The Role of the Directors' and Officers' Insurance Contracts in Corporate Governance

Akhmed Esendirov and Maxim Inozemtsev

Introduction

The aim of the chapter is to determine the correlating factors between corporate governance and its officers' liability insurance. A distinctive feature of this chapter is its comparative analysis of the insider corporate governance model (prevalent in the Russian Federation) and the outsider model (mainly employed in England and the USA).

Methodology

This research was conducted with the use of analysis, deduction, induction, and modeling. Special methods were used, including comparative analysis to compare corporate governance and corporate liability insurance

A. Esendirov (✉) • M. Inozemtsev
Moscow State Institute of International Relations (MGIMO University), Moscow, Russia
e-mail: inozemtsev@inno.mgimo.ru

I. Stepnov (ed.), *Technology and Business Strategy*,
https://doi.org/10.1007/978-3-030-63974-7_20

in Russia and in other states, as well as grammatical, systematic, and teleological interpretation of norms, legal formalization, and a historical and systematic analysis.

Results

The conducted study showcases the extreme methodological novelty in comparing existing works on the topic of such liability insurance in the Russian legal doctrine. This work is a great contribution to worldwide research into the problem of directors' and officers' (D&O) insurance, as it is one of the few studies on the effect corporate governance has on D&O insurance contracts in both the continental legal and corporate governance system. The conclusions reached in the course of this study have a wide-reaching practical application. Demonstrating the stimuli of the insured and the insurers presents itself as a fully realized recommendation for making relevant contracts and for the building of corporate governance.

Corporate Governance in Modern Corporations

Corporate governance is a system of relationships between the members of a corporation's governance bodies, its employees, its shareholders, and its other investors, in connection with the corporation's activity. A corporation is normally understood as an entity created by its members for the purpose of consolidating their capital on a membership basis (Suhanov 2014). For the sake of simplicity, we will be using the term "corporation" in a wider sense alongside remarks concerning the use of the term "company" (England), and "business association" (the Russian Federation); a separate entity is "corporation in the narrow sense", as is used in the US legal system.

Corporate governance has existed for exactly the same amount of time as the concept of a legal entity in the form of a corporation. It can be said that corporate governance is an indispensable part of any corporation (oglu Huseynov and Inozemtsev 2018). However, the systematic conceptualization of corporate governance as a focused management entity—used to define the respective rights and obligations of governance bodies, investors, and employees, and to find the balance of interests thereof—emerged only at the end of the twentieth and the beginning of the twenty-first centuries. Those corporate scandals that still echo around the world (Barings Bank case [1995], Enron case [2001], Parmalat case [2003],

Satyam case [2008], etc.) demonstrated that the corporate regulations that were in force back then lacked efficiency and were insufficient as the only means of regulation, as they did not take into account the specific nature of individual corporations (Mallin 2019). Hoping to increase companies' investment appeal, to increase transparency, to improve accounting statistics, to make it possible to take the companies' individual features into account, and to prevent crises on the scale of the aforementioned ones, newer rules of corporate governance were developed (which later took on the form of Corporate Governance Codes), which became a "softer" and more flexible corporate regulation tool than a system of corporate law, and which were meant to fulfill their special tasks.

The "progenitor" of the corporate governance rules system is thought to be the United Kingdom of Great Britain and Northern Ireland. It was there that the main approaches to corporate governance, and a compliance mechanism, were developed, due to many years of hard work starting from 1992 (Cadbury Report 1992); this work would then go on to take the form of the Corporate Governance Code (UK Corporate Governance Code, 2010). The rules of corporate governance, having shown their effectiveness, were applied globally: the European Union adopted them (Directive 2006/46 EC of the EU Parliament and of the European Counsel [June 4, 2006]), the Organization for Economic Co-operation and Development adopted its own version in the form of principles (OECD Principles of Corporate Governance 1999 [revised 2004, 2015]), the USA passed the Sarbanes-Oxley Act 2002 and later the NYSE Corporate Governance Rules (2003), and the corporate laws of the state of Delaware were revised (Mallin 2019).

The existence of Corporate Governance Codes is not exclusive to jurisdictions with a shareholder capital distribution system (such as England or the USA). Also called the "outsider corporate governance system", as the codes can also be found in jurisdictions with a concentrated shareholder capital or an insider corporate governance system (such as Germany), alternative codes exist (Kraakman et al. 2009). The Russian Federation, with its concentrated shareholder capital system, insider corporate governance model, and the preponderance of state involvement in corporate finance, is no exception. The year 2002 saw the development and the adoption of the Corporate Behavior Code, which in 2014 was superseded by the Code of Corporate Governance (hereinafter CCG).

Modeled after the European corporate governance system, page 139 of the CCG 2014 contains guidelines for joint stock companies on insuring the Board of Directors members in case of damage to the company or to other persons arising from their misconduct. The D&O insurance contract (the conclusion of a corporate governance member's liability insurance contract) traces its roots back to England and, having been extensively developed in the USA, is now common practice for foreign insurance corporations as well as for insurance companies. Despite insurance companies in the Russian Federation having started to offer such services, the liability insurance contract itself is still to be properly studied. The main causes for the necessity of D&O liability insurance in Russia are the appearance of a new shareholder remedy in the form of a class action suit (article 65.2 of the Russian Civil Code [hereinafter CC]), and the tightening of corporate governance member liability, by way of amendments to the Federal Act №14 FA "Limited Liability Corporations Act" from February 8, 1998, later amended on November 4, 2019 (hereinafter LLC Act), and to the Federal Act №208 FA "Joint Stock Corporations Act" from December 28, 1995, later amended on November 4, 2019 (hereinafter JSC ACT). It should be noted that the first act (preliminary Federal Act N 394587-5 "Amending certain legislative acts of the Russian Federation concerning the liability of the members of corporate governance") failed to receive approval in 2010, and the second preliminary act (preliminary Federal Act N 394587-5 "Amending certain legislative acts of the Russian Federation concerning the liability of the members of corporate governance") met the same fate. Currently, as a result, the conclusion of a D&O insurance contract is but a recommendation, as per the CCG 2014.

The General Link Between Corporate Governance and the D&O Liability Insurance Contract

Consecutive attempts at D&O insurance contract regulation on a federal level, as well as recommendations provided for in the CCG 2014 and the real number of such contracts in the market, require extensive research into their nature; this is not just in the context of the law of obligations, but also in the context of its potential influence on the insider corporate governance model that business associations in Russia favor.

The effect that D&O liability insurance contracts have on corporate governance can be divided into direct and indirect. "Direct effect" is defined as the influence on the behavioral stimuli of the insured corporate governance members. "Indirect effect" correlates to the influence on the behavioral stimuli of the shareholders in corporate governance.

Depending on who is subject to such insurance and which risks are covered by the according insurance policy, several types of D&O insurance can be singled out. Type "A" insurance policies cover the liability risk of individual members of corporate governance. By entering into a type "B" insurance policy, the corporation is the end beneficiary: should the corporation pay on a warranty that a company has provided for a member of its governing body, the insurer undertakes to cover this risk. Upon entering into a type "C" insurance contract, the corporation that has incurred liability becomes the beneficiary. In each case, the type of insurance contract entered into by the parties must be acknowledged in order to determine its effect on corporate governance. (Baker and Griffith 2009)

Moreover, it is necessary to take into account that the insurance company seldom (at least in the USA and in England) fully covers D&O liability claims. Normally, D&O liability claim coverage is delegated to a number of insurance companies, with each of those diversifying the claims within the scope of its insurance coverage limits. This results in the buildup of "insurance towers", with each insurance company having provided its own insurance policy (Ghalleb 2008). Furthermore, the key role in monitoring the corporation and in interacting with the corporation is played either by the insurance company at the top of a list of insurers, or by the insurance company that has provided wide insurance coverage limits (Baker and Griffith 2009).

The first and crucial positive aspect in D&O insurance is the monitoring performed by the insurer upon the insured party's claim assessment. This form of the contract's effect on corporate governance is called "indirect effect". The insured shall disclose all relevant information in a special survey list drawn up by the insurer (art. 944 CC). Information that is usually subject to disclosure in this form consists of financial accounting and other important circumstances, the full list of which is not exhaustive. The insured shall disclose the information to the insurer in a complete manner in accordance with the uberrima fides doctrine (Arkhipova 2015), so that the insurer has no basis for future claims of fraud by means of concealing certain material facts and, as a result, no basis for denying the insured their insurance payment. This measure is often employed in the USA by the insurer in order to downsize the insurance payment sum in D&O liability insurance contracts (Baker and Griffith 2009). Some researchers, upon analyzing the application practices of D&O insurance contracts in England, presuppose that the insurer reduces agency expenses for shareholders by exercising this form of control over the company's activity, with the shareholders normally being the ones to exercise control over the members of corporate governance in JSCs (O'Sullivan 1997).

From our point of view, this statement is too far-fetched. The point is that the shareholders of a business association are not denied basic monitoring methods, such as hearing the annual report during the general assembly, the right to vote either "for" or "against" on any question in the agenda, and suchlike. The monitoring conducted by the insurer can truly have positive effects in this case, while only slightly reducing the shareholders' expenses on monitoring the activity of the corporation's executive bodies. Moreover, the specific nature of the Russian insider corporate governance model must be taken into account, since in such a model the main conflict of interests arises between majority and minority shareholders. Majority shareholders are thought to be able to control the activity of the corporation's executive bodies, due to representing a large concentration of shareholder capital, by essentially bringing decisions the majority shareholders deem necessary into life. Having taken this into account, we can assume that, within the framework of the corporate governance model currently in action in Russia, the insurance company's exercise of monitoring cuts control expenses, not merely for the entirety of the shareholders. and not in relation to the executive body, but also for minority shareholders in relation to both executive bodies and majority shareholders.

The fact that the Russian system of corporate governance employs a two-layer corporate governance system in JSCs must also be taken into account. According to subs. 4 art. 65.3 CC, should the Civil Code, other acts, or the corporation's articles so provide, a collegial governing body can be established (supervisory or another council), the aim of which shall be the exercise of monitoring and control. The monitoring conducted by the insurance company is thought to be unsuccessful in reducing control expenses, since this function is delegated to the supervisory council; in the outsider corporate governance model, in cases of delegating, this function falls to a group of minority shareholders. The control over the activity of the supervisory council is meant to protect the corporate interests of minority shareholders and employees, and the interests of the company as a whole, on a permanent, professional basis. However, the insurance company must assess the risk pertaining to the company as a whole based on information provided to it. Regardless, upon the insurer's analysis of the executive bodies' activity, the degree of efficiency with which the supervisory council exercises its control can be observed.

Another positive effect of the D&O liability insurance contract is that they urge governing bodies to demonstrate improvements in corporate governance (Boyer and Tennyson 2015). This is a direct effect. The insurance company indirectly urges the corporation to reform its own governing system: to hire independent directors into the supervisory council, to create an efficient system of committees in control and accounting, and to improve the standings of minority shareholders. The point being that the premium paid by the insured to the insurer for the insured's risk coverage is directly dependent on whether the corporation's activity is "risky" or not. The bigger the risk discovered by the insurance company—of the CEO failing to fulfill their obligations, of the shareholders filing a class action suit, of a deadlock during decision-making procedures—the bigger the premium the insurer will require. A big degree of risk is generally associated with a company lacking a proper corporate governance system (Gelter 2013). As a result, in its quest to purchase an insurance policy at a reasonable price, a company, with the potentiality to be insured, will seek to improve its corporate governance system, which will serve to increase its efficiency and optimize its position on the market.

Nevertheless, many researchers believe that a D&O insurance contract may negatively have a direct effect on the behavioral stimuli of the insured persons (Boyer and Tennyson 2015). Knowing that infringement on the rights of some minority shareholders (or the rights of the corporation) will not result in the director being liable under a class action suit (or a derivative suit)—and not having to compensate should the suit succeed due to such liability having already been covered by insurance and the insurance payment covering all the damages potentially awarded to the shareholders (or the corporation)—the director is thought to act opportunistically in the worst sense of the word. However, some researchers disregard this by saying that D&O liability insurance would allow the CEO to act with more discretion without fear of making risky—but by their virtue also profitable—decisions, and would also allow the supervisory council to act without fear of approving certain risky steps taken by the executive bodies of a corporation. Weighing up these conflicting modes of analysis, it can be seen that they balance each other out. Both viewpoints and interpretations of D&O insurance assessment are possible, but in order to determine what is currently more vital for the legal order—to allow D&O insurance contracts with expectations of positive effects from risk diversification, or to ban such contracts—depends on several external factors. We consider the alternative means of control and the prevention of decision making that could damage the corporation, imposed by corporate laws, to be a good argument in favor of increasing the business activity of governing bodies by means of allowing for the conclusion of D&O insurance contracts. Examples of such corporate laws include the regulation of large transaction approval (art. 46, LLC Act; art. 79 JSC Act) and the regulation of transaction approval carrying personal interest (art. 45 LLC Act; art. 83 JSC act); the powers of the general assembly on decision-making provided for in statute (art. 48 JSC Act, art 33 LLC Act); the control powers vested in the collegial managing body (the supervisory council) (art. 64 CC); and the existence of independent directors in corporate structures. The second, no less important, argument is the current degree of rigidity in regulating D&O liability. The specified provision is especially unfavorable for the development of a business without a risk diversification mechanism, as in such cases there is often a lack of clarity regarding the regulation of those obligations by which their corporate governance members incur liability. Unfortunately, the empirical study of case law, as conducted by Russian researchers, shows that this is indeed the case (Stepanov and Mikhalchuk 2018). Thus, as of this moment, as well as of it being economically sound, the balance has tilted in favor of diversifying the risk of both the corporation and its corporate governance members by means of entering into D&O liability insurance contracts.

Conclusions

We have demonstrated in this study that D&O liability insurance is a generally accepted recommendation on the part of corporate governance codes, and an efficient way of diversifying the risks of incurring such a liability. Moreover, we have pinpointed a correlation between corporate governance making of such a contract and the existence of a valid insurance policy, as well as a correlation between negotiation leverage in the process of making such a contract and the system of corporate governance in effect at a particular corporation.

Two forms of how a D&O insurance contract affects the balance of member interests in corporate governance have been identified. "Direct effect" is linked with how a D&O insurance contract affects the behavior of the insured. "Indirect effect" is linked with how a D&O insurance contract affects the general structure of corporate governance, which in large part is defined by the degree of control other members of the corporation have over the activity of members of corporate governance.

The following consequences of entering into a D&O contract have been identified: (1) the reduction of agency expenses on control over governing bodies; (2) a motivational effect, manifested in the form of improvement to the entire system of corporate governance for the purposes of downsizing the insurance premium as per the D&O insurance contract; (3) the development of a more effective approach to decision-making by the corporations' governing bodies, oriented at business risk.

This study shows the need to take into account the difference between the outsider and the insider corporate governance models, as well as the differences between corporate laws in common law and continental law countries, which arise upon implementation of a D&O insurance contract (especially on a legislative level). It is especially imperative that the differences in building the system of corporate governance and in shareholder capital concentration be taken into account.

References

Arkhipova, A. G. (2015). Doctrina uberrima fides v strahovanii i ee voplshenie v rossiiskom prave. *Vestnik grazdanskogo prava*, №4, pp. 7–35.

Baker, T., & Griffith, S. J. (2009). How the Merits Matter: Directors' and Officers' Insurance and Securities Settlements. *University of Pennsylvania Law Review, 157*(3), 755–832.

Boyer, M. M., & Tennyson, S. (2015). Directors' and Officers' Liability Insurance, Corporate Risk and Risk Taking: New Panel. Data Evidence on the Role of Directors' and Officers' Liability Insurance. *The Journal of Risk and Insurance, 82*(4), 753–791.

Gelter, M. (2013). Risk-shifting Through Issuer Liability and Corporate Monitoring. *European Business Organization Law Review, 14*, 497–533.

Ghalleb, N. (2008). *Managerial Opportunism and Directors' and Officers' Liability Insurance.* Retrieved from http://biblos.hec.ca/biblio/theses/002147.PDF

Kraakman, R. H., et al. (2009). *The Anatomy of Corporate Law: A Comparative and Functional Approach.* Oxford: Oxford University Press.

Mallin, C. A. (2019). *Corporate Governance* (6th ed.). Oxford: Oxford University Press.

oglu Huseynov, S. R., & Inozemtsev, M. I. (2018). Contradiction between the Modern Corporate Governance Theory and Practice of Business and Companies within Digital Transformation. *MGIMO Review of International Relations, 6*(63), 294–316 (in Russian).

O'Sullivan, N. (1997). Insuring the Agents: The Role of Directors' and Officers' Insurance in Corporate Governance. *The Journal of Risk and Insurance, 64*(3), 545–556.

Stepanov, D. I., & Mikhalchuk, U. S. (2018). *Liability of a Corporation Director for Damages Caused in Court Practice [Ответственность директора перед корпорацией за причиненные ей убытки в судебной практике].* Moscow: Publishing House «Статут».

Suhanov, E. A. (2014). *Comparative Corporate Governance [Сравнительное корпоративное].* Moscow: Publishing House «Статут».

CHAPTER 21

On the Constitutional Court's Position about Freedom and Privacy as Business Strategy in the Banking Sector

Anna Shashkova and Michel Verlaine

Introduction

State authorities and agents responsible for the supervisory function, and subsequently the courts, including the Constitutional Court of the Russian Federation, are faced with the problem of secrecy in different aspects. This problem must be solved at the highest level with the direct application of the constitutional norms.

Attempts by the banks to "over-implement" anti-money laundering law under the threat of severe sanctions of the regulators actually lead to failures in the execution of the normal economic activity. Therefore

A. Shashkova (✉)
Moscow State Institute of International Relations (MGIMO University), Moscow, Russia
e-mail: a.shashkova@inno.mgimo.ru

M. Verlaine
ICN Business School, Metz Technopôle, France
e-mail: Michel.verlaine@icn-artem.com

I. Stepnov (ed.), *Technology and Business Strategy*,
https://doi.org/10.1007/978-3-030-63974-7_21

individuals got huge problems with payments on a clearing basis in addition to problems with cash withdrawals.

The Bank of Russia sets requirements for the banks to execute Federal Law No. 115-FZ[1] too high. Under the threat of revocation of the license for banking activity such requirements simply drive banks into the corner. The political establishment thus has to act. Recent changes in Russian legislation, for example, allowing banks to refuse opening of accounts unilaterally, simplified banking activities in Russia.

Methodology

Banking secrecy actually refers to a particular type of information that becomes known to a credit institution during the execution of banking activities. Certain other persons are acquainted with such information as well. Such persons receive the information from credit institutions in the course of its examination and its application.

The banking secrecy is a specific type of commercial secrecy. It consists, first of all, of the secrecy of a bank as an independent subject of economic relations and, secondly, of all commercial secrets of the clients, which the bank is aware of because of contractual relations with the clients.

Results

Considering the nature of the legal relationships concerning banking secrecy the author distinguishes three kinds of relations:

- relations between the bank and the client,
- relations between the client and the government, and
- relations between the government and the bank.

Such relations are governed by a set of rules of the Constitution, legal norms, and regulations.

On the one hand, the banking secrecy protects the interests of the client and prohibits third party access to the confidential information of the bank. Such third parties include the state represented by the state agencies.

[1] Federal Law No. 115-FZ—Federal Law of August 7, 2001 «On Combating Legalisation (Laundering) of Proceeds from Crime and Financing of Terrorism».

On the other hand, legal acts and regulations reinforce the interests of the state, establishing the order of access to the banking secrecy (Galbraith, 2007). The author agrees with the opinion of a Russian judge and professor Sarbash that the legislative regulations of the access of the state to confidential information of individuals need to be improved. The state bodies carrying out public functions represent the state in a particular case.

Therefore, one of the sharpest current issues is the problem of compliance by credit institutions with banking secrecy rules while implementing anti-money laundering measures. These problems are of current importance not only in the Russian Federation, but also in the whole world.

Currently in Russia there is quite a number of cases where courts clearly recognize violations of constitutional rights of citizens. It is not a single case of judicial practice. The burden of proofs and excuses falls on banks. Banks are forced to introduce some ridiculous limits, as the banks have to follow the law. And one law contradicts the other. No one knows how to implement all these contradictory provisions.

According to the decision of the Central District Court of Volgograd passed on 4 February 2012 on the claim of citizen O. I. Petrova to the Volgograd branch of Promsvyazbank, the court declared illegal the refusal of the Bank to pay cash in the amount of 1.35 million rubles from the account of such natural person. The reason for such refusal of paying money was non-presentation by the client of documents proving the origin of funds upon the bank's request.

The present example is an evidence of multiple cases of a direct violation of the constitutional rights of individuals while trying to comply with the anti-money laundering legislation.

The above example of refusal of cash withdrawal from a bank is a common way to attempt to comply with the Federal Law № 115-FZ. Since direct banking services to cash funds became more expensive, banks are faced with the fact that for money laundering purposes money is used extensively on deposits and current accounts as well. The method recommended by the Bank of Russia to deal with protective tariffs frightens away "good" customers. At the same time banks face the revocation of the license and the serious reputational risk while working with "bad" customers, even if they timely notify the Rosfinmonitoring[2] on suspicious transactions.

[2] The Federal Financial Monitoring Service of the Russian Federation (Rosfinmonitoring) is a Federal Service that was created 1 November 2001. It is aimed to collect and analyze

What about banking secrecy if the law "On Banks and Banking Activity"[3] is almost entirely devoted to the duties of banks to disclose banking secrets to the public authorities? The subsequent Order of the Rosfinmonitoring[4] with 2014 year amendments does not clear up the situation. Hence, the institute of banking secrecy has not yet received a clear legal regulation in Russia. Such institute is required to build a legal state and a developed economy in the country.

Very many persons illegally receive and disclose banking secrecy. The access to the banking secrecy and its preservation is almost impossible to track. Law enforcement agencies from time to time establish the facts of dissemination of confidential information about clients of banks in the public domain, for example, on DVDs, which are available for sale in computer markets, for example, at "Gorbushka" (Shashkova, 2018). "Each of them contains confidential information gathered by law enforcement and other government agencies of the Russian Federation. Here you can find everything from a dossier of detention, personal addresses, passport details, statistics, telephone calls and address book data to bank accounts, contact lists, tax data and database of air travels" (Clover 2009).

Due to the bank secrecy information leakage the value of the banking secrecy is decreasing. This leads to irreparable damage to banks and their customers (Gololobov, 2014). Another problem arises at this point: crimes aimed at illegal data accessing are not considered crimes itself (Tutikhtin, 2019). The Russian Civil Code does not consider information as property. To make a person answer for banking secrecy disclosure, a broad interpretation of Article 158 of the Criminal Code is required.

Meanwhile, the institute of banking secrecy is necessary for the effective functioning of the Russian economy. Adverse acquisition risks in the provision of information are still very high in Russia. Adverse acquisition main risks lay neither in the legal vulnerabilities of the assets (which gives skilled aggressors legitimate opportunities on buying controlling stakes) nor in the possibility of the abuse of rights (e.g., suing a "victim" with formally legal, but in fact groundless claims). On the contrary, the main risks are:

information about financial transactions in order to combat domestic and international money laundering, terrorist financing, and other financial crimes.

[3] Article 26 of the Federal Law "On Banks and Banking Activity" No. 395-1, dated 2 December 1990.

[4] The Order of the Rosfinmonitoring No. 103, dated 8 May 2009, which approved "The Recommendations for Developing Criteria for Detecting and Identifying Signs of Unusual Transactions".

- illegal seizure of property (e.g., using fake documents) with the support of corrupt employees of all involved in deals with state bodies and courts, which have legal access to banking secrecy;
- a compulsion to convey the property title by personal pressure on the owner (usually under the threat of criminal prosecution).

According to Russian experts, the loss of 20% of the information consisting of commercial secret leads to the bankruptcy of the company in 60 cases out of one hundred. Losses from the actions of unscrupulous competitors using espionage in the financial sector amount to 30% of all damage, which is incurred by banks.

Considering all the above one has to acquit the justification to protect the property from the potential effect of such claims. Does banking secrecy induce problems for the state if it seeks to protect the interests of the citizens of this state? Why, once again, we have to oppose the interests of the individual and the system, which consists of such individuals? The answers to such questions are crucial for understanding the development of the constitutional system of the country at issue.

The submission of information constituting banking secrecy to the bodies combating corruption, money laundering, and other crimes is, of course, not considered as violation of banking secrecy (Chiltom and Versteeg, 2018). Such practice is used not only in Russia but also on the international practice basis. At the same time it is necessary to outline the strict framework of the submission of information, access to this information, its storage, use, and non-disclosure agreements. Currently, all officials ranging from minor officials to directly interested persons are ready to fight with banking secrecy. What about such important legal institutions as the presumption of innocence, privacy, and ownership? The answer to that question is of the same importance as to the previous ones.

The right of an individual to the confidentiality of client's information about their banking accounts and banking deposits and other information is derived from the constitutional guarantees of inviolability of private life, personal secrets, and the inadmissibility of the dissemination of information about a person's private life without their consent. The law shall establish the types and amount of such information (Dressel, 2018). The appropriate duty of the banks and other credit organizations is to keep the banking secrecy.[5] The duty of the state is to guarantee such right in the legislation and by legal enforcement. Thus, the Constitution of the Russian Federation defines the basis of legal regime and legal regulation of the banking secrecy as a condition of freedom of the economic activity, arising from the nature of market relations, and guarantees the right of citizens to freely use their property from entrepreneurial and not prohibited by law economic activities, as well as a way to protect information on private life of citizens, including their financial situation, and protect their personal secrets.

Repeatedly filed complaints to the Constitutional Court of the Russian Federation concern the constitutionality of various articles of the Federal Law No. 115-FZ. For example, Subparagraph 1 of Paragraph 1 of Article 7 requires the organizations carrying out operations with monetary funds or other assets to identify natural persons with the surname, name, and patronymic (if the law or national custom does not provide for otherwise), citizenship, details of the identity document, data migration card, document confirming the right of a foreign citizen or persons without citizenship for stay (residence) in the Russian Federation, address of residence (registration) or place of stay, and taxpayer identification number (if any). One of the applicants to the Constitutional Court claims that such provision of the Federal Law No. 115-FZ restricts the right of ownership disproportionately in light of protected constitutional purposes. Therefore Subparagraph 1 of Paragraph 1 of Article 7 of the Federal Law No. 115-FZ shall be recognized as contrary to Articles 2, 17 (Part 1), 18, 34 (Part 1), 35 (Parts 1 and 2) and 55 (Part 3) of the Constitution of the Russian Federation.[6]

According to the legal position of the Constitutional Court of the Russian Federation the right to private property does not belong to those rights that in accordance with Article 56 (Part 3) of the Constitution of

[5] *The Resolution of the Constitutional Court of the Russian Federation* No. 8-P, dated 1 May 2003 «On the Verification of Constitutionality of Paragraph 2 Article 14 of the Federal Law "On Court Bailiffs" under the inquiry of the Langepas city court of Hanty-Mansijsk" autonomy district", at http://www.garant.ru/products/ipo/prime/doc/12030881/.

[6] *The Resolution of the Constitutional Court of the Russian Federation* No. 519-O "On Refusal in Acceptance to Consideration of the Complaint of Citizen Golubkov Sergei Alexandrovich on Violation of the Constitutional Rights by Subparagraph 1 of Paragraph 1 of Article 7 of the Federal Law No. 115-FZ "On Countering The Legalisation Of Earnings Received In An Illegal Way (Money Laundering)", dated 1 December 2005, at http://base.consultant.ru/cons/cgi/online.cgi?req=doc;base=ARB;n=23738.

the Russian Federation shall not be restricted under any circumstances.[7] At the same time the Constitutional Court of the Russian Federation states that restrictions and their character should be determined by the legislator in accordance with the Constitution of the Russian Federation but not arbitrarily. Article 55 (Part 3) the Constitution of the Russian Federation shall be used in the particular case. It provides that the rights and freedoms of citizens may be limited by a federal law only to the extent that it is necessary in order to protect the foundations of the constitutional system, morality, health, rights and lawful interests of other persons, national defense, and state security.

The Constitutional Court of the Russian Federation pointed out that the provisions of Article 55 (Part 3) of the Constitution of the Russian Federation correspond to the international law and international treaties of the Russian Federation. According to such international treaties while exercising their rights and freedoms a person can be subjected only to those limitations provided by law and necessary to ensure due recognition and respect for the rights and freedoms of other persons, for the protection of the state (national) security, territorial integrity, public order, prevention of crime, protection of health or morals (good morals), satisfaction of fair requirements of morals, and the general welfare in a democratic society.

International law prevails to domestic federal laws under Article 15.4 of the Constitution of the Russian Federation. Based on the above the Constitutional Court has concluded that the federal legislation when establishing the legal mechanism for combating money laundering and preventing terrorism financing may provide for the measures to prevent such acts and to identify natural and legal persons acting in this way, as well as to oblige financial institutions and other organizations effecting operations with monetary funds to identify their customers.

Thus, the Constitutional Court states that the challenged Subparagraph 1 of Paragraph 1 of Article 7 of the Federal Law No. 115-FZ serves the public interest and is aimed at the realization of participants of civil turnover of their mutual rights and duties. Such provision, under the Resolution of the Constitutional Court of the Russian Federation, cannot be regarded

[7] *The Resolution of the Constitutional Court* No. 20-R, dated 17 December 1996, The Resolution of the Constitutional Court No. 14-R, dated 12 May 1998, The Resolution of the Constitutional Court No. 8-R, dated 14 May 1999, The Resolution of the Constitutional Court No. 3-R, dated 24 February 2004. At https://rg.ru/2004/03/02/ks-dok.html.

as violating the constitutional right of ownership, civil law principle of freedom of contract, and autonomy of will of the parties to such agreement, and thus as contrary to the Constitution of the Russian Federation, its Articles 17 (Parts 1 and 3), 34 (Part 1), 35 (Parts 1 and 2), and 55 (Part 3). Under the Resolution of the Constitutional Court of the Russian Federation the provision is in conformity with the Constitution of the Russian Federation.

This conclusion of the Constitutional Court of the Russian Federation took off the responsibility for a highly controversial interpretation of the legislation of the Russian Federation concerning anti-money laundering. The Constitutional Court of the Russian Federation refused to review the above complaint. In the opinion of the Constitutional Court of the Russian Federation there exists certainty in the matter of compliance of Subparagraph 1 of Paragraph 1 of Article 7 of the Federal Law No. 115-FZ to the Constitution of the Russian Federation.

Summarizing the practice of the Constitutional Court of the Russian Federation on this issue, the author notes that keeping secrecy, including banking and professional, is considered by the Constitutional Court as a necessary constitutional guarantee of the principle of adversarial proceedings laid down in Paragraph 3 of Article 123 of the Constitution.

Judicial proceedings shall be held on the basis of controversy and equality of the parties.

The Resolution of the Constitutional Court of the Russian Federation No. 33-P, dated 17 December 2015; the Resolution of the Constitutional Court of the Russian Federation No. 8-P, dated 14 May 2003; the Resolution of the Constitutional Court of the Russian Federation No. 439-O, dated 8 November 2005; and the Resolution of the Constitutional Court of the Russian Federation No. 10-O, dated 19 January 2005, appeal for a balance of the constitutional values protected to prevent distortion of the substantive law guaranteeing privacy. While analyzing the concept of attorney-client privilege, the Constitutional Court of the Russian Federation comes to the conclusion that not all of the information that the attorney and their principal would be willing to give a confidential character is in fact within the attorney-client privilege secrecy. A similar provision applies to the banking and other types of secrecy.

The Constitutional Court of the Russian Federation does not support broad interpretation of the concept of secrecy. The Constitution does not protect the regime of secrecy of information indicating the committing of an offence or a crime. Consequently, the constitutional regime of secrecy applies only to those objects and documents obtained by legitimate means. The presence of signs of a crime provides a reasonable basis for the removal of information from a regime of professional secrecy. Instruments, documents, and information received by a criminal way do not fall under the regime of protection of professional information. This is reasonable both from the perspective of the legal interpretation of the Russian legislation and from the point of view of common sense. The European Court of Human Rights gives a similar interpretation. It says that a search warrant should, whenever possible, ensure the limitation of its consequences within reasonable limits.[8]

The Resolution of the Constitutional Court of the Russian Federation, dated 14 May 2003, follows such European practice. The subsequent practice of the Constitutional Court of the Russian Federation also unified the court practice on the issue of the professional, banking, and other secrets.

From one point of view the author concludes that the legislation on banking secrecy contains more questions than answers. Certain questions arise automatically. Where is the guarantee, what are the components of the guarantee, what conditions must be fulfilled? The protection of information is the problem of primary importance. Such issue requires political solution and legislative settlement. The higher is the level of information protection, the higher is the preservation of banking secrecy—the stronger is the authority of the credit institution and its potential customers, the greater is the benefit of the bank to the economy of the state. At the same time the bank will not violate the legislation on anti-money laundering. Swiss banks (even despite the occasional scandals) are famous for the absolute safety of the information about the deposits and transactions of their clients. Such safety of the information creates an important condition for ensuring the stability of their work, a guarantee of observance of constitutional principles, and one of the conditions of the European welfare state.

The author concludes that the meaning of the Constitution of the Russian Federation poses the institute of banking secrecy in its nature and purpose in public-private nature. Such institute aims at ensuring conditions for effective functioning of the banking system and civil turnover, based on the freedom of its members. At the same time the institute of

[8] Resolution CM/ResDH, 2008, 37 Execution of the judgment of the European Court of Human Rights Van Rossem against Belgium (Application No. 41872/98, judgment of 9 December 2004, final on 9 March 2005).

banking secrecy guarantees the basic rights of citizens protected by the Constitution of the Russian Federation, the interests of individuals and legal entities (Shashkova et al., 2017). Powers of public authorities shall follow from such institute in carrying out public functions, in their relations with the banks, other credit organizations, and their clients. The scope and content of the rights and responsibilities of clients in their relations with the banks and other credit organizations that are the carriers of financial information and with the public authorities and their officials shall also base on the above institute. Such institute can be used only to implement these functions to use banking secrecy, thus not affecting the private lives and privacy of citizens.

All the above make the author conclude on the necessity of the political establishment to improve the Russian legislation with the aim of compliance with the provisions of the Constitution. It is also necessary to establish a clear balance between the constitutional rights of the individual and the limit of these rights when carrying out various control activities by public authorities.

References

Chiltom, A., & Versteeg, M. (2018). Courts' Limited Ability to Protect Constitutional Rights. *University of Chicago Law Review, 85*(2), 293–335.

Clover, C. (2009, November 25). The Golden Bottom for the Russian Black Data Market. *The Financial Times.*

Dressel, B. (2018). Tonsakulrungruang, Khemthong, «Coloured Judgements? The Work of the Thai Constitutional Court, 1998–2016». *Journal of Contemporary Asia*, 1–23.

Galbraith, J. (2007). *The New Industrial State* (p. 576). Princeton University Press.

Gololobov, D. (2014). Businessmen v. Investigators: Who is Responsible for the Poor Russian Investment Climate? *Russian Law Journal, 2*(2), 114–144.

Shashkova, A. V. (2018). Corruption Is a Problem of Political Theory and Practice. *Montenegrin Journal of Economics, 14*(3), 143–154.

Shashkova, A., Rakitskaya, I., & Pavlov, E. (2017). Emergence and Activity of Legal Entities in Russia in the Pre-Revolutionary Period (Comparative Analysis). *Bylye Gody, 46*(4), 1333–1344.

Tutikhtin, V. (2019). *The Defence from Russian Adverse Acquisition Risks.* Retrieved from www.vvtlaw.com.

CHAPTER 22

Advantages and Challenges of Digital Technology

Igor Stepnov

This book presents a variety of works covering various aspects of digital solutions to gain experience and generate a new methodology for the commercialization of technologies in the digital environment. The importance of such research today is reflected in the scientific foundations of practical solutions and the development of a new field of knowledge: the digital economy. If the superiority and advantages of specific new solutions were disclosed in different chapters of this book, then, in conclusion, we consider it appropriate to summarize and to systematize the problems and pitfalls of the digital path of development.

Despite the general digital optimism (despite the upcoming unemployment of laid-off workers and the disappearance of several professions), digital euphoria is still extremely rare, but, with the discussion already

I. Stepnov (✉)
Moscow State Institute of International Relations (MGIMO University), Moscow, Russia

Financial University under the Government of the Russian Federation, Moscow, Russia

I. Stepnov (ed.), *Technology and Business Strategy*,
https://doi.org/10.1007/978-3-030-63974-7_22

becoming more and more reasoned, is being replaced by a discussion about the effectiveness of digital strategies based on technological innovations.

The need for such a discussion was justified at the beginning of 2018 in the McKinsey review “Why digital strategies fail”. Pointing to five reasons for failure, McKinsey experts identified two of the most significant: the duality of the modern world and the need to form an ecosystem (Bughin et al. 2018). In our opinion, the main reason is that the digital economy is still a concept first and foremost. There are some examples of how digitalization has been able to increase a company’s operating income; there are other known cases of how digitalization helped to reduce costs. But there are also known cases of digital failures.

The present situation is characterized by the fact that, at present, both at the level of global research and at the level of Russian research, the problems and achievements of the digital economy are considered in the example of five to seven large digital corporations, and private solutions are developed within the framework of individual companies that do not have a unified research methodology.

Developing the topic raised, we also touched upon the effectiveness of technological superiority, observing that the financial results of technology leaders do not fit into the dominant paradigm of the industrial age, allowing, for example, successful shares placement by an entity being in the red (Kochetkov 2019). Besides, H. Gebauer and his colleagues (Gebauer et al. 2020) have confirmed that the digital paradox makes the return on digital investments fall short of expectations for large companies. In their opinion, with small aggregate investments, revenue growth is in line with expectations, but as aggregate investments increase, companies do not receive the expected increase in revenue. This proven hypothesis points toward the conclusion that the tools used for the commercialization of digital technologies are not perfect.

According to M. Attaran, the industrial twentieth century was marked by massive increases in industrial productivity, including a 50-fold increase in manual productivity (Attaran 2019), which was undoubtedly related to automation. The digital age can finally succeed only if productivity increases, while the source of such growth in modern organizations is information.

A change in euphoric perception is characteristic of most radical innovations, which at the initial stage aroused great interest across the entirety of society. Already at the subsequent stages, the rationality of the ongoing processes is understood, including both economic efficiency and utility. Efficiency is related more to the commercial sphere of activity, while utility is a measure widely accepted for assessing the importance of technology for the entire society. The exclusive character of digital technology means that we can observe a combination of utility and efficiency through the social approval of technological innovation. Technological excellence, at its core, is not only the possession of the best, most advanced technology, nor the technology with the best prospects and the best ways to commercialize and create value for the consumer. Digital technologies are implemented based on digital business models, using the information as a means of increasing efficiency.

Despite the popularity of the information format, the citizen-centered model of societal development still remains in play (Torkunov 2019), while more and more solutions are transferred to the sphere of artificial intelligence.

We believe that the most radical manifestation of digitalization is the use of artificial intelligence, which is irreversibly transforming many social relations today. The transition to data and data processing systems is not an end in itself but becomes a transformative factor which provides the basis for introducing artificial intelligence. This approach allows us to eliminate a significant number of individual digital solutions while integrating the manifestations of digitalization on the way to the top of digital progress—artificial intelligence.

Today, weak artificial intelligence does not enable many IT developers to see this trend in digital transformations accumulating structured data and technologies for their transformation.

We believe that the highest point of digitalization should involve the introduction of technologies integrated with artificial intelligence, after which the S-curve of digital technologies will be able to enter a gentle segment.

However, until artificial intelligence reaches maturity, there will be a large sequence of digital solutions that are diverse, contradictory, and seek to gain superiority over similar ones.

In our opinion, the ongoing transformation of industrial enterprises and entire industries represents a significant advantage of new technological solutions, not only based on other methods of data processing, and not only created due to new information and communication capabilities, but rather based on the classical invention of fundamentally new approaches with digital design. In the latter case, the novelty of technological solutions has turned out to be "disguised" as "digitalization", since digital representation becomes the predominant feature of the new, and technological solutions are initially "formatted" to meet new requirements. This is an essential point that should be noted: that new technologies no longer imply digital transformation, but are already being created in their digital form.

In this case, systems of standards play a significant role, which sometimes becomes a problem—how can one create standards for a long period for something that has not yet been invented? The current popularity of a particular standard does not guarantee its long-term advantage. Nevertheless, the existing standards reduce barriers to new technologies in commercialization.

Digitalization creates another format for creating superiority: based on digital platforms and abandoning the use of a product in favor of using a service (and in this case, the market), acceptance of the digital platform leads to the fact that digital platforms users, in technological terms, become imitators of the developed technology. At the same time, the profits of imitators of platform innovations are not guaranteed, and are even limited, by platform owners.

To summarize with clarity, modern technology leaders can be divided into four major groups:

- well-known industrial technologies that have gained competitive advantages due to digital transformation;
- technologies specially designed for the digital environment;
- transformational technologies developed in the "format" of digital solutions; and
- technologies that replace the consumption of goods with the consumption of services.

Each technology has specific advantages, but their implementation and the problems associated with their implementation are of a general nature.

Therefore, we further systematize the known problems and threats to individual strategies for technology commercialization and their implementation within the business model (Stepnov and Kovalchuk 2020). To improve the efficiency of technology, organizations must determine their strategic position in accordance with their competitive environment, since studies have shown that the effectiveness of strategic orientation (including innovation) depends on environmental factors (Chiua and Yang 2019).

Accordingly, we distinguish two groups of problems and threats: external and internal.

External problems affect the ability of the business model (and if the business model is implemented within the organization, then the organization itself) to adapt to the external environment and/or to reduce or cope with uncertainty.

Internal problems are solved by the ability to find solutions within the business model using internal sources.

Perhaps the new content of the external and internal environment is the biggest difference between the digital age and the industrial one. The internal environment is expanded through the business model to the ecosystem, and the external environment is reduced to participants who are not involved in the business model, the system of state regulation, or public recognition.

Internal Problems and Threats (A)

A1. Dependence on the Chosen Strategies

Most companies achieve digital success when implementing growth strategies. There is no credible evidence that digital technologies and platforms, in particular, have made a significant contribution to implementing growth strategy. There is still no clear answer to the question of who creates value: whether it is the need and this value was monetized using digital technologies, or the value was created using digital technologies and monetized in the context of growing demand. Most likely, the success of the current strategies is associated with the euphoria after digitalization and its monetization. This conclusion is a warning that, so far, the effectiveness of digitalization has been achieved by generating additional income only with the growth of the market segment and an increase in the number of consumers. Other conclusions are more dangerous and unpredictable. In general, it is not recommended to apply digitalization solutions in those business models that differ from growth strategies. In other words, there are still no universal solutions known for bringing digital success in any strategy.

A2. A Small Number of Consumers at the Start

There is a well-known thesis that, for companies in the digital environment, network interaction does not lead to the formation of decreasing marginal utility, but to the spread of network effects and, consequently, increasing marginal utility. Nonetheless a potential threat is posed by a small number of consumers during early use the technology, whose total revenues are insufficient to cover the costs of technology development. As a rule, a small volume at the start of commercialization is replaced by promises that it will be significantly larger in the future. However, high competition in small segments leads to the fact that initially uninvolved users are hijacked by other entrepreneurs and embedded in other business models. Accordingly, the segment value should be enough for the perceived customer value to be sufficient to generate a return on investment. Therefore, for example, the attractiveness of application stores—such as App Store and Google Play, which provide a developer with access to a significant segment of consumers—is high.

A3. "Winner Takes All"

The threat that a large company will eventually remain the only player in a market segment, or even integrate several market segments, exists. The digital winner can get the whole segment. The profitability of followers in this segment should theoretically approach zero. Apart from concentrating business in the hands of individual companies and creating a barrier for followers, however, there is a threat to these large companies. Adherence to selected technologies, no requirement for radical change, and no requirement for renewal can lead to the emergence of an "unexpected" leader, with its prevailing technologies. Such technologies can be hidden during development at the initial stage, since they will be mostly intangible. Today this issue is being resolved through the acquisition of growing companies by market leaders, but it remains highly relevant. Therefore, there is a need to fight for "leadership", but there is also an understanding that one of the well-known industrial approaches—"catch-up development"—contains the threat of zero profitability in the digital age.

A4. The Art of Replacing a Product with a Service

The famous slogan that a product is replaced by a service is being fulfilled. But for some companies, there is a threat that such an action will be misunderstood by customers, and there will be no significant revenue growth. For each company, it is necessary to create a business model to provide a service that creates a competitive advantage over various types of intermediaries. Otherwise, the service would be provided, but due to the redistribution of income, the bulk of the profit will go to other participants in the value chain. Also, one should pay attention to the complexity of solutions: the consumer is more focused on the so-called package offer, and not on the search for highly specialized services.

A5. Ineffective Pricing Model

Choosing a pricing model and its correct application is very important. A poor pricing model can cause consumers to resist the offer (including a lower price). Besides, the idea of a fixed or zero price for the basic acquisition and a higher payment for additional options (including those for telecommunications companies, car sales, etc.) is starting to develop. It should also be noted that pricing in digital markets is losing its cost base, focusing (for the most part) on a comparative approach (as a rule, which initially relies on a comparison with pre-digital solutions, and, then, on the prices of competitors), and, to a lesser extent, on profitability. New companies that focus on classic pricing models are largely doomed to failure, as they cannot expect to be compensated proportionally for their sales costs after incurring the cost of overcoming entry barriers.

A6. Incomplete Accounting of Savings

Quite often, for the sake of transparency, in detailing the costs of implementing digital solutions, companies only include those costs that are directly related to such solutions. This is not due to a deliberate mistake, but rather to a desire to allocate only the costs associated with this technology. However, economists often forget about indirect and additional costs, which can change significantly during digital transformation. Therefore, full cost accounting can show that there are no actual savings from going digital.

A7. Exit from the Business Model

A situation often arises whereby it is most advisable for a newly created digital company not to invest in infrastructure development. This solution shifts focus to implementing the digital strategy as a priority, renting the space of platforms provided with the necessary service. However, in this case, with the initial investment savings, the amount of infrastructure investment may be a barrier to exit from the platforms. Therefore, this threat is a warning for small- and medium-sized companies about the exit barriers.

A8. Distribution of Profits in the Business Model

The profits generated by digital assets can be concentrated within a limited number of individuals—"digital rentiers" (Stepnov and Kovalchuk 2018)—who have created and own digital platforms and ecosystems. Therefore, it is possible that innovators with new digital technologies will not receive sufficient remuneration for two reasons: (a) high rent for a new area or platform area, (b) a lack of funds to create their infrastructure. In this case, it is necessary to search for a business model in which the new technological innovation will receive the maximum rating. Given the transience of technology obsolescence, though, there is a high likelihood of zero rewards for an innovator.

A9. Insufficient Diversity of Digital Technologies

Existing digital solutions strive for greater uniformity. This situation can lead to systemic instability. Maintaining sustainability will require additional costs to strengthen controls or build stocks. Such reserves, for example, can include analogue duplication, which ensures the safety of information in case of problems with a single digital technology. Besides, the predetermination of artificial intelligence solutions and the replacement of predictive calculations with modeling and optimization can provoke the situation when the formed balance of forces will be destroyed by unexpected factors. Therefore, it is necessary to develop competition among digital technologies within even one single company.

A10. Priority of Technical Capabilities

Due to how engineers think, almost all digital technologies are still focused on prioritizing technical capabilities, and only then taking into account consumer expectations. On the one hand, this is true—and even justified—if engineers manage to surprise the consumer (exceed expectations), but it should be kept in mind that value is formed specifically on the consumer side, and today not even by an individual consumer but social groups—therefore, such thinking must be overcome. If expectations are not confirmed or maintained at the same level, a significant portion of consumers may be lost.

External Problems and Threats (B)

B1. Accuracy of Solutions

The current fascination with digital marketing does not unambiguously confirm the effectiveness of digital analysis (including deep learning). The speed of computing and the volumes of data used do not guarantee the uniqueness of solutions. This is partly due to the peculiarities of human thinking. The decision-maker does not have the opportunity to verify the accuracy of the recommendations received, which raises doubts about their reliability. This problem is also related to the oversaturation of the information and the data the company collects and processes, which requires disposal, archiving, and so on. In fact, this leads to additional costs of information technology and information obesity (Content Obesity (Parapadakis 2012)). Unfortunately, the old intuitive way of making a decision remains, but now it can be reduced not to a new vision, but to deciding on the reliability of assumptions.

B2. Replication

In the industrial economy, project scaling has always served as the basis for efficiency gains. The digital economy, largely informational, is characterized by the fact that replication of pilot projects is very difficult and in many respects impossible, even within the company. This leads to an important conclusion that pilot projects can be ineffective if the prospect of their replication is not determined or not accepted by the market. This view shows that increased usage (as savings on fixed costs) is not always applicable in the digital environment. Besides, one should take into account the fact that scaling and decentralization (as one of the possible models for developing the digital economy) conflict with each other, which can further exacerbate this problem.

B3. Additional Products and Services

The digital economy seeks to shape ecosystems. In addition to the advantages of coordination, the "ecosystem" implies creating an opportunity to meet the needs of the consumer comprehensively. This ignores the possibility that creating additional services can lead to losses either of the main product or of service in connection with the consumer's outflow to those ecosystems where more complex services will be offered. Moreover, the success of the main service raises the expectation that additional services will also be successful. On the one hand, the development of additional services creates a monopoly, but, on the other hand, it also ensures the growth of income from the main service. The role of the technology community should also be considered. The digital world has made tangible contribution: professional associations have begun to significantly influence the development of new technologies, while the communication capabilities of such communities are only expanding. Taking this factor into account is important from the point of view that the emergence of new technology can occur at any point in the technology community, not just in a new leader company. However, additional products and services should not be confused with the options of the main product, as they are part of the pricing and in-house solution. Additional products and services are an external solution, while the failure to use it will lead to significant losses of customers.

B4. Digital Taxes

The inequity of digital taxation raises a lot of criticism from both government agencies and industrial companies. The extraterritorial nature of many digital companies, inherent in the digital economy, leads to a significant reduction in the tax burden. The resulting savings from paying taxes expose some states to rather high risks to adopt the concept of paying taxes at the location of the consumer and the location of the remote employee. This approach will restore justice from the point of view of sovereign states, but will create additional difficulties for digital companies.

B5. Legal Protection of Digital Solutions

The AI and Machine Learning Department of the World Economic Forum[1] believes that granting patent rights to inventions created by artificial intelligence can accelerate innovation, allowing progress that would have been impossible only through human ingenuity (Firth and Chae 2018). Today, though, there is a fairly large number of digital assets and solutions that require legal status. Therefore, changes in legislation may lead to significant costs for a company.

B6. Leadership Ethics

Research can be of any nature, showing a variety of technological perspectives. It is very important to understand the usefulness of newly selected technological innovations that will affect the competitiveness of the firm and its professional and ethical concerns in the use of new technologies (Lin et al. 2020). Companies that lead their industries within the framework of social responsibility and other ethical standards adopted in society must comply with them. Therefore, leading companies must bear the burden of responsibility for both using and opening access to technologies that could violate ethical standards. Digital technologies significantly expand the range of ethical issues: from protecting personal information to violating property rights, from manipulating individuals to negative impacts at the genetic level. G. Leonghard, in his book, insists on the idea of digital ethics, arguing that "technology has no ethics, but humanity depends on it"; in his opinion (which we cannot but agree with), human ethics develops linearly, in contrast to technologies which develop exponentially, and a society with unlimited technological progress without ethics is doomed (Leonghard 2018).

B7. Standards and Future Consumption

Changing standards lead to the rapid obsolescence of technology. Due to the exponential growth of various digital solutions, companies must integrate their business models with standard-setting bodies. There are two solutions regarding standards: monitoring changes, or the ability to reconfigure (tune) them to another standard. Today, there is a trend toward

[1] https://www.weforum.org/agenda/authors/kay-firth-butterfield

convergence of standards around the world (which is due to the problem of each solutions being unique); nevertheless, companies should take this problem into account, since its consequences are usually disastrous.

B8. Partners' Trust

Failure to build trust among digital partners will prevent them from building business models or an ecosystem. As a rule, digital value chains provide a high level of flexibility, which requires mutually agreed solutions between all participants. A similar problem arises when creating an ecosystem—the ecosystem must describe a more trusting relationship than previous strategic concepts, which can play a similar function in strategic management. A distinctive feature of a successful ecosystem is that it does not support a deterministic concept of the environment and provides maximum opportunities.

B9. State Regulation

Another important point includes the principles of regulating the use of digital technologies and everything connected with them—digital assets, digital platforms, digital ecosystems, and so on. The state provides one of the three following options: a laissez-faire strategy, a preventive impact strategy, and a strategy for coordinating and "active" control of forming digital business models. Public digitalization covers all countries with different levels of their socio-economic development. Efforts to create a state digital infrastructure with appropriate state policy and state regulation of universal digitalization bring both tangible benefits to business and impose significant restrictions on them. Government-trusted digital operators are supposed to have special responsibilities for maintaining the integrity and social order as the caretaker of this modern public square (Marique and Marique 2020). Compliance with government decisions is an unconditional rule for business since the implementation of various government decisions (sanctions) in the digital environment through telecom operators is more efficient.

B10. Living in a Digital Environment

A person is still a person, not a digital consumer of digital services. Businesses have to take this into account. There are still no answers to the following questions: Will a person be able to obey digital solutions? Is a person able to perceive the manifestations and consequences of digitalization? Is he or she able to perceive the results obtained by artificial intelligence? Is he or she able to correctly interpret digital solutions?

Human-digital interaction can be very costly for many activities, such as education and healthcare. Undoubtedly, a lot of effort will be spent on educating a person to live in a digital environment and developing the necessary skills. However, digital technologies must maintain the tendency of a citizen-centered attitude; otherwise, any digital technologies and strategies will not be in demand. Therefore, we conclude this book with the firm conviction that, through all that is provided by digital technologies, the future of humanity will be the best period of its whole history.

References

Attaran, M. (2019). Increasing Productivity in the Information Age. *Industrial Management, 61*(1), 16–21.

Bughin, J., Catlin, T., Hirt, M., & Willmott, P. (2018, January 26). Why Digital Strategies Fail. *McKinsey Quarterly*. Retrieved from https://www.mckinsey.com/business-functions/mckinsey-digital/our-insights/why-digital-strategies-fail.

Chiua, C.-N., & Yang, C.-L. (2019). Competitive Advantage and Simultaneous Mutual Influences Between Information Technology Adoption and Service Innovation: Moderating effects of environmental factors. *Structural Change and Economic Dynamics, 49*, 192–205. https://doi.org/10.1016/j.strueco.2018.09.005.

Firth, K., & Chae, Y. (2018). Robot Inventors are on the Rise. But are They Welcomed by the Patent System? *World Economic Forum*. Retrieved from https://www.weforum.org/agenda/2018/04/robot-inventors-on-rise-patent-system-US/.

Gebauer, H., Fleisch, E., Lamprecht, C., & Wortmann, F. (2020). Growth Paths for Overcoming the Digitalization Paradox. *Business Horizons, 63*, 313–323. https://doi.org/10.1016/j.bushor.2020.01.005.

Kochetkov, E. P. (2019). Digital Transformation of Economy and Technological Revolutions: Challenges for the Current Paradigm of Management and Crisis Management. *Strategic Decisions and Risk Management, 10*(4), 330–341 (in Russian). https://doi.org/10.17747/2618-947X-2019-4-330-341.

Leonghard, G. (2018). *Technology vs. Humanity: The Coming Clash between Man and Machine*. Moscow: Publishing House AST (in Russian).

Lin, W. L., Yip, N., Ho, J. A., & Sambasivan, M. (2020). The Adoption of Technological Innovations in a B2B Context and its Impact on Firm Performance: An Ethical Leadership Perspective. *Industrial Marketing Management*. https://doi.org/10.1016/j.indmarman.2019.12.009.

Marique, E., & Marique, Y. (2020). Sanctions on Digital Platforms: Balancing Proportionality in a Modern Public Square. *Computer Law & Security Review, 36*, 105372. https://doi.org/10.1016/j.clsr.2019.105372.

Parapadakis, G. (2012). *Content Obesity—Part 1: Diagnosis*. Retrieved from https://4most.wordpress.com/2012/06/22/content-obesity-diagnosis/.

Stepnov, I. M., & Kovalchuk, J. A. (2018). Platform Capitalism as the Source of Digital Rentier's Superprofit. *MGIMO Review of International Relations, 4*(61), 107–124 (in Russian). https://doi.org/10.24833/2071-8160-2018-4-61-107-124.

Stepnov, I., & Kovalchuk, Y. (2020). The Economic Pitfalls of Artificial Intelligence Introduction. *Ekonomika. Nalogi. Pravo [Economics, Taxes & Law], 13*(2), 92–102 (in Russian). https://doi.org/10.26794/1999-849X-2020-13-2-92-102.

Torkunov, A. V. (2019). University as a Part of National Economy. *Voprosy Ekonomiki, 12*, 111–122 (in Russian). https://doi.org/10.32609/0042-8736-2019-12-111-122.

Index

I. Stepnov (ed.), *Technology and Business Strategy*,
https://doi.org/10.1007/978-3-030-63974-7

D

The manufacturer's authorised representative in the EU is Springer
Nature Customer Service Centre GmbH, Europaplatz 3, 69115 Heidelberg,
Germany. If you have any concerns regarding our products, please
contact ProductSafety@springernature.com

Printed and bound by CPI Group (UK) Ltd, Croydon, CR0 4YY
30/09/2026
02225702-0018